Jacks on Tax

Your Do-It-Yourself Guide to Filing Taxes Online

2014 Edition for 2013 Returns

Evelyn Jacks

KNOWLEDGE BUREAU
NEWSBOOKS

WINNIPEG, MANITOBA, CANADA

Evelyn Jacks

JACKS ON TAX
Your Do-It-Yourself Guide to Filing Taxes Online
2014 Edition for 2013 Returns

©2014 Evelyn Jacks Productions.

Knowledge Bureau Report: A free subscription to this national electronic publication will help readers stay up-to-date with news at Canada Revenue Agency, Finance Canada and the consequences of financial and economic developments in Canada and around the world. To subscribe and participate in opinion polls, go to www.knowledgebureau.com.

Printed and bound in Canada

ISBN No. 978-1-927495-20-9

Library and Archives Canada Cataloguing in Publication

Jacks, Evelyn, 1955-, author
    Jacks on tax : your do-it-yourself guide to filing taxes online / Evelyn Jacks. — 2014 edition for 2013 returns.

Previously published: 2012.
Includes index.
ISBN 978-1-927495-20-9 (pbk.)

    1. Income tax—Canada—Popular works. 2. Tax planning—Canada—Popular works. I. Title.

HJ4661.J33 2013   343.7105'2   C2013-907140-7

Published by:
Knowledge Bureau, Inc. www.knowledgebureau.com
187 St. Mary's Road, Winnipeg, Manitoba R2H 1J2
204-953-4769
Email: reception@knowledgebureau.com

MIX
Paper from
responsible sources
FSC® C016245

Research and Editorial Assistance: Walter Harder and Associates, Deanne Gage
Cover Design: Evelyn Jacks, Carly Thompson and Walter Harder and Associates
Page Design: Typeworks

Acknowledgements

This book is a labor of love. It takes a team of dedicated professionals who research tax and economic changes all year long to meticulously translate them into what we hope will be an understandable, yet comprehensive book for average Canadian taxpayers who want to know more about their complex tax system at tax filing time. There are many thousands of pages of complicated tax law behind these words; the topics have been chosen to help the broadest base of tax filers. Many of you may find however, that you may need extra help from the pros.

An empowered, educated taxpayer will get better financial results over time. Doing your own tax return is a great first step in understanding and managing your family's wealth. Knowing when to seek professional advice is an important follow-up to this self-empowerment. This is one of the key messages in this book: you are not alone.

In completing this year's edition, I am again very fortunate to be supported by the best: our management, instructional and editorial team at Knowledge Bureau. Special thanks are also in order to my research assistant, Walter Harder and to Sharon Jones, who does such a wonderful job of presenting the layout of this book for you. When I founded this national post-secondary educational institute ten years ago, it was to help raise the standards in professional wealth management services provided to taxpayers from coast-to-coast. The academic achievements of our graduates can be recognized in the certification marks: MFA™ (Master Financial Advisor) and DFA-Tax or Bookkeeping Services Specialist.

These students bring purpose to our work as financial educators and you, the taxpayer who may need help along the way as you deal with changes in your life events—bring purpose to the work we all do.

Thank you for the privilege of sharing tax knowledge with you.

As always, I am grateful for the loving support of my husband, Al, and my sons, Cordell and Don. There are really no words that adequately express how brightly you light up my life.

Sincerely,
Evelyn

Table of Contents

Introduction

This book is about filing a better tax return in an electronic world. It has a twin mission for you: first, learn how to file a more accurate tax return. Then leap ahead in your financial life by learning how to do some tax planning, so you can build lasting wealth.

That's important these days, because governments need more tax dollars, and they expect you to take more responsibility for your financial future. The successful do-it-yourself, online tax filer, understands that the tax filing exercise is really about taking control of your money—before and after taxes. Yet, despite the ease of electronic filing with sophisticated software, it's still a very complicated tax system and you may have a complicated personal, career and financial life, too. There may be many ways to file a tax return that is mathematically correct. The opportunity, however, is to file the *best returns for your family unit*—the ones with the least taxes owing and the biggest possible tax benefits.

Here's another issue; a bit more frightening: if you don't file, or your filings cross a legal line, you could be subject to substantial penalties... and yes, in severe cases of tax fraud, delinquent filers can go to jail. Almost as bad: failure to file often means you have cheated yourself out of thousands of dollars in missed tax refunds, refundable or non-refundable tax credits, and the contribution room you need to maximize your tax deferred retirement plans or balance out capital gains and losses over your lifetime.

So the value proposition in this book is quite simple: it is full of tips to help you get more of your hard-earned money back. Consider it to be your online tax filing companion and keep it right next to you as you navigate this year's tax filing requirements.

There are several features to help make the read easier, too:

- **What's New?** An update of recent tax law and policies.
- **Case Studies.** Examples of true-to-life situations to help you understand your rights.
- **Audit Defence.** What you need to keep for potential review by CRA.
- **Tax Sleuthing.** Little known tax tips and traps.
- **Tax Pro Alert.** When you should see a pro and why.
- **Check it Out.** Quick tips about completing your forms.
- **The Bottom Line.** Straight advice for a bigger refund.

This year, learn how to:

- **Accumulate** more money in the right savings accounts—registered and non-registered —because you have *created more cash flow* by filing a more accurate tax return.
- **Grow** more "real" wealth—after taxes—to ensure as much of your hard-earned money as possible is working for you now and with *purchasing power* in the future.
- **Preserve** more of your money from the ravages of tax erosion by saving in tax-advantaged accounts like the Tax-Free Savings Account (TFSA). *If you do, you'll never have to worry about taxes in retirement.* That's really powerful… and yet so few people take advantage of the opportunities.
- **Transition** more wealth into the future. When you file a more accurate tax return, and save in the right accounts, you may even *have more money than you ever dreamed possible*, to transition into retirement. You'll forget about the question… "will I have enough?" and think more about "what's next on my bucket list?"

Those are the four stages of Real Wealth Management.™[1] It all begins with making sure you pay only the correct amount of tax—not one cent more.

Let's do that together now, because in an electronic world, it's important to slow down long enough to make sure you have filed your family's tax returns to your very best benefit.

Yours in tax savings,
Evelyn Jacks

---

[1] Real Wealth Management is a framework for building tax efficient wealth, taught exclusively by Knowledge Bureau.

PART 1

Getting Started

According to Statistics Canada[2], 95% of Canadians age 15 years and older have some form of income. Collectively, 27.3 million of us earned $1.1 trillion. Two thirds of us pay income taxes and, on average, we fork over 16.4% of total income. Fully 70% that income came from employment income.

Because tax is over-deducted at source by employers—which means the government gets a good share of the first dollars you earn—the vast majority of us must file a tax return to get a refund.

Just as important: 70% of Canadians receive government transfers, which represent 12.5% of their total income. And for just under 13% of Canadians, government transfers are their only source of income. These include the Canada/Quebec Pension Plan (CPP/QPP), Old Age Security (OAS), Guaranteed Income Supplement (GIS), Employment Insurance (EI), Child Benefit Programs and various forms of social assistance, workers' compensation and numerous refundable tax credits from both federal and provincial governments.

The amounts owing to you can be large—the average refund last year was just under $1,700. To apply to receive all that money, you must file the Income Tax and Benefits Return: also known as the T1. Accurate tax filing begins with this reality: in most cases, the CRA already knows what your income is, because they have a copy of your information slips.

What they don't know about is the legitimate deductions and credits you may be eligible for. That's why, making sure you file the best tax returns for your family begins with hard copy—the various receipts for expenses you have throughout the year that can be

---

[2] 2011 National Household Survey: Income of Canadians, released September 11, 2013, based on 2010 tax filing statistics.

legitimately claimed on your tax return to reduce income. For many people that's the hardest part of the tax filing ritual, but it's also the most lucrative....

What's New

This year more people will file tax returns electronically rather than in paper. The personal online environment you will use to communicate with CRA, "My Account" has been greatly improved, allowing you to see your Notice of Assessment or Reassessment, carry-over amounts, tax slips, account balances, payments made to CRA, benefits receivable and RRSP information.

You'll be able to make changes to your return online, submit receipts to verify your claims electronically, and change your marital status... your entire relationship with CRA can be an electronic one. So if you haven't already done so, set up your access to "My Account" with the CRA. Check it early and often to see the figures on your T-slips posted there: the T4, which reports employment income; T4A which reports pension, retirement, annuity and other income; T4A(P) which reports Canada Pension Plan Benefits; T4A(OAS) which reports Old Age Security Benefits and T4E which reports Employment Insurance Benefits.

Hard Copy

You'll still need to manage hard copy—receipts for everything but the slips mentioned above. This is where all the extra tax refunds lie: you need a filing system to collect medical expenses and charitable donations, RRSP contributions, receipts for moving expenses and child care among others. It's a good idea to be really organized—to save time entering the data on the right returns for your family, but also to be audit-proof... you'll enjoy the summer more that way!

Software Tips

If you are a first-time do-it-yourselfer, finding the right tax software package is important. It's also your ticket to filing your return without a stamp and to optimizing all your tax deductions and credits. Sign up or get your copy early, so you can enter data from your hard copy as it arrives. Do make sure there are planning options in the software to help you create "what if" scenarios to make tax-efficient investment decisions throughout the year.

Tax Sleuthing

In getting ready for tax filing, you need to nail a couple of moving targets: annual changes in tax forms and rules, plus changes in your family's life events and financial milestones. Taking the time to update yourself on the tax changes that could apply to you will save you time and money. Write down all the life events from the past year—births, deaths, marriages, divorces, illness, job loss—and any significant financial events—like starting to receive your Canada Pension Plan. Then update yourself to the changes within your tax software as a final primer.

Tax Pro Alert

Your relationship with a tax professional is important even if you file your own tax return. Throughout various life events, the services of a trusted financial educator, advocate and steward will pay off. If you don't have one, do take the time to interview at least three, asking your top three most pressing tax questions.

1

Start With Hard Copy

Despite paperless filing, it all begins with the hard copy: gathering and sorting your tax receipts and slips. Not always fun, especially if you are a hoarder or just disorganized, but here are three reasons why it's important that you take the time to do it with precision:

- Data entry will be easier, and more importantly, faster.
- You'll be surprised how much more you can deduct and save.
- As important: a future tax audit, ever a reality, will be a breeze.

In this chapter you'll learn about:

- What to keep and "My Account";
- Tips for entering data—and when;
- How long you have to keep the hard copy;
- Tips for that hard-to-keep auto log;
- What to keep in your permanent data file and your working copy file;
- How to avoid the fear and be ready for a CRA audit;
- The seven basic elements of the tax return;
- Some new reporting requirements if you have offshore assets; and
- How to avoid penalties if you've made a mistake on a prior filed return.

What Should You Keep? Not sure what to keep? Keep everything! This includes all investment statements, and purchase, sale or maintenance details regarding your non-financial assets like cars and real estate. Personal expenses, like medical expenses, transit passes and children's extracurricular activities count, too.

And, if you are required to work from a home office, use your car for work, or pay your own expenses, your "mixed-use expenses," that is, the expenses for your car, home office and entertainment, may be deductible, as long as you subtract the personal use component in them. Keep a log of your business-related travel and an appointment log if you see clients or employees in your home office.

When it comes to the various T-slips you get in the mail, file them as they come in with your charitable donations and RRSP slips. Or print them from your CRA "My Account" page.

✓ **CHECK IT OUT** | **How do I access "My Account"?** Setting up your My Account access with CRA is a four-step process:

Step 1: Provide the following information to CRA after clicking on the "Register" button at http://www.cra-arc.gc.ca/esrvc-srvce/tx/ndvdls/myccnt/menu-eng.html

- Your social insurance number
- Your date of birth
- Your current postal code
- The amount requested from your current or prior year tax return (the amount requested varies randomly)

Step 2: Create a User ID and Password

Step 3: Set up your security questions and answers

Step 4: Wait for your CRA security code—which will be sent to you in the mail. If you've moved since you filed your last tax return, you'll have to contact CRA by telephone to correct your address information before applying for your My Account access.

Once you have you CRA security code, you can log in to My Account at http://www.cra-arc.gc.ca/esrvc-srvce/tx/ndvdls/myccnt/menu-eng.html by clicking on the "CRA Login" button.

Or, if you have a login with your bank for internet banking you can access My Account using your internet banking login (BMO, CHOICE REWARDS MasterCard, Scotia Bank, and TD Bank).

Using My Account, you can view your assessments from previously filed returns, make changes to previously filed returns, find about your RRSP/PRPP and TFSA contribution limits, see your loss carryover information as well as view all of the information slips that CRA has already received for you for the current tax year.

How Long Do You Keep Records? When it comes to staying on the tax man's good books, tax filing is about doing it all on time and ultimately, on a tax audit, it's all about retrieval!

CRA won't want most of your receipts now, but be prepared to send supporting documents if required. That's true even if you have a scanning system.

The required record retention period is six years after the end of the year in which you file your tax return. Storing, sorting and filing hard copy properly, therefore, is an important part of the job, because when it comes to pleasing a tax auditor down the road, retention is everything!

How do you keep track during the year? I carry a wallet designed for receipt saving. I sort the chits once a week and store them in ever-ready tax files in a nearby file cabinet. It's pretty foolproof—it's a rare receipt that goes missing. My personal electronic devices help me keep an exact calendar of activities and appointments, including driving to and from appointments.

 Any tips for keeping auto logs? To claim auto expenses you must keep track of personal and business driving. Use Google Maps to calculate distance for business/personal travel logs.

It also pays to start three working files:

1. The Permanent Data File
2. The Working Copy File
3. The Audit Defence File

1. The Permanent Data File

This file carries information you'll use from one year to the next:

- Documents to verify changes in names, address, marital status, date of immigration/ emigration or date of death
- Employment contracts or severance package details
- Information about employer-sponsored pension plans, group benefits or stock options, private savings like RRSP or TFSA deposits
- Purchase price and/or proceeds of disposition of business assets, or non-registered investments
- Capital and non-capital loss carry-forwards
- Capital gains deductions or elections previously claimed
- Unclaimed moving, charitable, medical or tuition expenses
- Adjustments made to prior filed returns

While some of these tax terms may be foreign to you now, don't worry, you'll get to know them better throughout this book. Start this file now and have it handy so you can add some notes, definitions and questions as you learn more. This is also the place for questions for your tax, legal and financial advisors.

Carry Forward Summaries. Because this Permanent Data File is carried forward for use every year, enclose a copy of the carry forward statements printed from your software or your "My Account" page with CRA.

Some tax software packages also have a multi-year summary of your prior filed returns. Drop a copy of this into your permanent file for quick review. If you have switched software vendors or are using software for the first time, check to be sure that all the prior year information required to reduce your taxes this year has been carried forward.

Having a hard copy of prior filed tax returns and their significant schedules and forms is a good plan B, in case you lose a laptop, or suffer a loss of your internet access.

2. The Working Copy File

Create one file per taxpayer and label it prominently with the current tax year and the taxpayer's name; then place copies of last year's Notice of Assessment or Reassessment from CRA at the front, all carry forward information, followed by all T-slips. Check the data entry framework in your tax software for the order it requires and sort slips accordingly— T4A, T4A(P), T4A(OAS), T3, T5, etc.

Behind this, keep a hard copy of the summary of the final return and all significant supporting schedules and working papers you may wish to refer to. This file may also contain additional notes and calculations that explain how you prepared the return, and why, in case of audit.

 CHECK IT OUT | **What's the date on your N of A?** The date on your Notice of Assessment or Reassessment will determine deadlines for your appeal rights. Circle it and keep this Notice on top of your file copies.

Print Out the Tax Return. This is a great checklist for all receipts you may need to file your return. A great roadmap, it will act as your "anchor document" if you get lost in your tax software. This exercise is also good way to test out the print functions as you set up your software. (If your software doesn't allow you to print out a certain blank form, you may want to download the forms in PDF format from CRA's website.)

Basic Elements of the T1 Income Tax and Benefit Return. When you know the basic elements of this tax return—the framework you'll be working in—you'll be better able to "drive" your tax software. You'll find many tax filer profiles discussed in this book will refer to the following elements.

- **Identification Area:** The information here must be precise. From birthdate to marital status to address and dependant information, it determines the size of income-tested social benefits and tax refunds/balances due, when the return is finished and how to deposit them (by cheque or direct deposit).
- **Line 150: Total income**.
- **Line 236: Net income** (your tax credits are based on this number).
- **Line 260: Taxable income** (used to compute your taxes payable, if any).
- **Line 350 on Schedule 1:** (Total Non-Refundable Tax credits).
- **Line 435 Total Payable:** (federal, provincial or territorial taxes before total credits on Line 482, CPP contributions on self-employment, EI and OAS repayments and Yukon First Nations Taxes).
- **Line 484/485: Refund or balance owing**.

Provincial Returns. While all Canadian resident filers complete a federal tax return, in every province, except Quebec where a separate tax return is filed, all provincial tax calculations are conjoined with the federal results. You'll look for Line 428 for provincial taxes payable and Line 479 for provincial tax credits on page 4 of the T1 tax return.

Auxiliary Tax Forms. This is also a good time to print out some of the additional forms CRA provides. This can include statements for Rental Income (T776), Income from Self-Employment (T2125) or Moving Expenses (T1-M). Often your software will ask you to select these as you set up your tax files. Printing them can help you to chase down the information you need to complete the return and attach the audit-required calculations and notes. The first such form to address on the return is Form T1135.

 Form T1135 | This year, CRA is looking for more information about your off-shore holdings.

Form T1135 Foreign Income Verification Statement. Canadian residents who own assets abroad must submit this form to CRA to disclose whether they had "specified foreign assets" held during the year, if the total cost at any time exceeded $100,000 Canadian. This includes funds held outside Canada; shares of non-resident corporations (other than foreign affiliates); certain real property situated outside Canada and other types of foreign property such as intangible property not used in a business and certain rights under contract.

Excluded from the foreign disclosure requirements are personal-use properties like a vacation home used exclusively for personal use, property used exclusively in an active business, property in an RRSP, RRIF and a registered pension plan, mutual funds that include foreign investments, property of immigrants (those who file a return for the first time in Canada) and shares in a foreign affiliate.

The new Form T1135 is more detailed, and at the time of writing, it could not be filed electronically; although CRA has indicated it soon will accept electronic records. Taxpayers must report the following information about their property on the new 2013 return:

- the name of the specific foreign institution or other entity holding funds outside Canada;
- the specific country to which the foreign property relates; and
- the income generated from the foreign property.

Also note that the reassessment period has increased from three to six years effective for 2013 and subsequent years if foreign income is not reported and Form T1135 is not filed on time or included incorrect or incomplete information concerning a foreign property. Significant penalties could result: Fines as high as $12,000, $500 a month for up to 24 months, plus an additional penalty of 5% of the total cost of the foreign holdings, can be charged.

3. The Audit Defence File

This is the audit copy of all your back-up documents, which you may have to forward to the CRA if they request it. This might include medical expenses, babysitting, charitable donations, business expenses, utilities, etc. Always keep a copy of all information sent to CRA when they do ask for it.

Taxpayer Relief Provisions. This is also the file in which you keep copies of adjustments to your prior filed returns.

 CHECK IT OUT | **Do you know about Taxpayer Relief Provisions?** You can reach back and correct errors and omissions on most federal tax provisions for 10 years under the Taxpayer Relief Provisions. If you missed something, file an adjustment to your prior-filed returns.

A taxpayer has 10 years from the end of a relevant tax year to request relief from penalties, request a refund or payment reduction, or to ask the Minister to accept late filed, amended or revoked elections. This includes elections to have assets transferred to a spouse at fair market value for tax purposes (an important planning tool) and certain elections to roll assets over to family members when a taxpayer dies. There are also rules that allow a business owner to defer a capital gain when a replacement property is acquired.

This 10-year adjustment period rolls forward every January 1, so for the 2013 tax-filing year, for example, you have until December 31, 2023 to request taxpayer relief for most federal provisions.

CRA will be able to cancel penalties or interest when there are factors beyond your control: illness, death, disaster, civil disturbances and so on. When interest or penalties result from errors or omissions in public documents or delays in providing information to the taxpayer, it is possible to apply for relief.

When you request taxpayer relief for refunds, do know that "permissive deductions" are not included. You will not be allowed to request adjustments to Capital Cost Allowances (CCA) where less than the maximum claims were made, for example. In this case, you must make adjustments within 90 days on the date of the Notice of Assessment or Reassessment. Other permissive deductions include deductions that reduce business or rental income.

 Turn in International Tax Cheats | You'll get 15% of the taxes collected over $100,000 if you provide information to the CRA about major international tax fraud. This does not include penalties, interest and provincial taxes collected and, wouldn't you know it, your reward is taxable in the year you get the money from CRA.

Provincial Tax Adjustments. Provinces usually offer a Statute of Limitations of three years. You need to keep track of this too. Always adjust your returns for any errors or omissions, bearing in mind that CRA will want to see back-up documentation and that such a request can initiate a review of your returns as a whole.

Voluntary Compliance. If you think you may have understated your income or overstated deductions or credits, it's important to adjust your returns (or file missed returns) before you are asked by CRA to do so. That way, you can avoid gross negligence and tax evasion penalties.

Formal Appeals. Taxpayers who cannot get relief as described above may appeal formally to the Chief of Appeals at CRA or through the court system, by filing a Notice of Objection within 90 days of the mailing date of your Notice of Assessment or Reassessment.

 The Bottom Line | Address the seven major sections of the tax return in order, for a consistent tax preparation experience. If you do tax returns for your whole family, this will save you time and money as you transfer provisions from one to another or split income between spouses.

2

Forget the Math:
Use Software

Good news! Tax software can help your family benefit from your tax filing rights in many ways… and you can largely forget about the difficult tax computations.

In fact, because the federal and provincial tax calculations are automatically working in the background, recalculating your results with every new number you enter, you'll be amazed to see the end game change with every keystroke. Your tax refund can change instantly, depending on what data is entered and how it is manipulated to give you the best results. That can be a lot of fun—especially when you see how much each deduction can increase your tax refund!

Your goal is to take advantage of all the tax provisions available to reduce the income taxes you pay, or to get the most from social benefits available through the tax system. Using tax software can help with this. It can also help you be more compliant with the tax department.

In this chapter you'll learn how to:

- Choose the right software, especially, a package to help optimize your tax filing results;
- Set up to carry forward important tax filing information from last year and check that against your records from CRA;
- Set up basic identifying information for yourself and your dependants; and
- Think about taking a certificate tax course if you are preparing returns for others.

Remember, you are only required to pay the correct amount of tax. It is your legal right and duty to arrange your affairs within the framework of the law to pay the least taxes legally possible. So it's important to "optimize" the results on your family's tax returns to get the best benefits for the household.

CHECK IT OUT | **What is optimization?** Optimization is the process of taking advantage of every available income tax provision to report income so it attracts less tax and to claim each deduction and credit so that they save the most in taxes.

Tax software can assist with the optimization of provisions that help you invest the right amounts into your RRSP, split income between family members, maximize transfers of tax credits between family members and carry forwards of historical information. These are the little tricks that can make you much richer!

 Case Study | **Optimization of Medical Expenses**

Les and Rachael's total medical expenses for 2013 were $1,800. Les's net income was $45,000 and Rachael's was $22,000. The medical expenses could be claimed by either spouse but the claim must be reduced by 3% of the claimant's income. If Les makes the claim, his claim will be $1,800 – $45,000 x 3% = $300 which results in a federal tax saving of $45.

If Rachael makes the claim, her claim would be $1,800 – $22,000 x 3% = $1,140 which results in a federal tax saving of $171. By claiming the medical expenses on Rachael's return, the family's federal taxes are $126 less. There is also a provincial tax saving which varies from $33 to $92 depending on where the couple lives.

Choosing the Right Software

 CHECK IT OUT | **How do you choose the right tax software?** You can buy tax software at the store or download it from the internet, but which is the right one for you? Here are some tips:

- What tax filer profiles can the software do? (Are business and rental properties included?)
- What is the cost per return?
- How does this compare in cost to using a tax preparation service which guarantees its work and represents you in case of audit?
- Can you NETFILE with this software package? (See next chapter for details)
- Can you print and file on paper if your return does not qualify for NETFILE?
- Where is the data stored? (In the "cloud" [a remote server] or on your computer?) Which is the best option for you?
- Are there educational tutorials in the software?

- Is there service and support if you run into a problem?
- Look for a free trial—so you can check out the environment for ease of use.
- Are there tax planning screens—opportunities to do "what if" scenarios all year long?

Setting Up Your Tax Software. Because there are so many tax software packages available, the comments in this book cannot be specific to all of their features. We will give you a good overview of how most tax software packages "think" but part of the software set-up instructions for each new tax year is to do the following:

- Familiarize yourself with the new features of the software;
- Import your data from prior-filed returns; and
- Update the identification sections and the "carry forward screens," that show important information from prior years that will be applied to this year's tax computations and/or used in other returns.

Importing Last Year's Data. If you used tax software last year, set up your current year return in the program. What a tremendous asset this is—all of your "carry forward" information is entered into your current year return, including all personal contact and birthdate details, and specific tax provisions that may be available to you from one year to the next.

Do this by opening the current year version of the software and then looking for tax return carry-forward command. Some tax software companies refer to this as importing a prior-year return, transferring a prior year return or converting a prior-year return if you've changed software products.

Carry Forward Information: Your Notice of Assessment or Reassessment. When you received your tax refund or balance due last year, you also received an explanatory note with important information about what changes were made to your tax return, how that affected various lines on your tax return, your current RRSP contribution room, amounts owed to CRA or whether you paid any interest to CRA, your unused capital loss balances and so on. It's important to dig out that documentation now to see if any information needs to be added into your "carry forward" screens.

New Software Users. If you are new to filing your return with software this year, enter all the personal data for each family member on the head person's return. Some software may have a screen for entering family members and other software may require that you create a return for each family member and link the returns together based on each family member's relationship to the head person. Make sure all birthdates and address information is correct.

Then, enter any carry forward information from prior years into the program. If you are switching to a different type of software this year, you will need to import the data from last year's software. Not all software can import data from other software brands and where import is available, be sure to check the imported data for accuracy.

Take a Basic Tax Course. If you would like to take a tax course to help you with "what if" scenarios to better use the full potential of your tax software, do contact **Knowledge Bureau** at www.knowledgebureau.com. We also offer some free course trials that can help you get started using selected tax software options. The beauty of the trial scenarios is you can become familiar with both your tax software and changes in tax law.

Working With Hard and Soft Copy. Developing a consistent process for tax filing is important because you are dealing with several moving parts: the changes in tax law and administrative procedures from government, and the changes in your own life. How you work in entering data is important when you are using software. Most tax software makes the entry of data from T-slips very easy. Just follow along plotting information from the boxes on the slips into the matching info boxes in the software.

However, after this, when the supporting schedules, auxiliary tax forms, worksheets, notes or any other relevant documents saved throughout the year in support of other provisions come into play, you need to follow a consistent data entry plan.

I like to deal with the supporting documents and life events together, addressing them in the order of the line numbers on the actual tax return to make sure nothing is forgotten. This is also how we teach professionals at the Knowledge Bureau. They start by understanding the T1 return and its supporting schedules first. It's a good idea for you to do the same and keep it by your side as a checklist or guide.

 The Bottom Line | Tax software is an important tool in filing your tax returns and in developing a strategic income and capital investment plan. You will do your return more quickly and easily. It can also help you understand the T1 and your supporting hard copy better too, so you can plan to take better control of your after-tax dollars.

3

Forget the Stamp: NETFILE!

It's true, the stamp is out; NETFILING is in. Did you know that of all the millions of tax returns filed in Canada, only about a third of them still are sent to CRA on paper and that number is decreasing each year? In this chapter, you'll learn more about:

- what's required to NETFILE your return electronically;
- when you can't file electronically;
- how much this might cost you; and
- what EFILE is.

What's Required? You'll need to choose software with a NETFILE option. You can find a listing of approved vendors at this CRA weblink: http://www.netfile.gc.ca/sftwr-eng.html. The software packages we reviewed all printed returns, either directly or by creating a pdf file, which is important especially if you are doing returns for those for whom a paper return is required.

Costs. For some tax filers this will be free. For others, costs begin around $10 per return and up. Some software programs or web applications for these purposes, charge by the return but others charge for the tax software, which included, at no extra charge, the opportunity to file a number of returns (up to 20, for example). If your tax return doesn't qualify for free service, you will have to pay whether you print or NETFILE. Transmission is always via the internet using your browser and no transmission fee is involved.

CHECK IT OUT | **When can you transmit for free?** NETFILE restrictions by software vendors may include the following; so check these out carefully:

- For free transmission services, net income on Line 236 is generally low. For some packages it must be less than $25,000, in others, $20,000 or $10,000.
- Several of the software products support only certain provinces.
- For the self-employed and investors, note that many of the choices do not support rental or self-employment income, limited partnerships or tax shelters and non-business foreign tax credits.
- Farmers note that many of the free offerings do not support the forms needed to report income under the AgriStability/AgriInvest programs.

NETFILE Restrictions. CRA also has its own restrictions: you cannot NETFILE if you wish to transmit an amended tax return, a tax return for any year before 2012; or a tax return for another person. Also, you're not eligible if:

- You or one of your dependants is claiming the disability tax credit for the first time or new Forms T2201A and T2201B are required by CRA.
- There are several restrictions if you qualify to claim the foreign tax credit. You must use the full foreign tax credit available or you can't NETFILE, nor can you use the service if you are claiming a non-business foreign tax credit for more than three countries or a business foreign tax credit. Taxpayers with income earned from a prescribed international organization cannot NETFILE either.
- Don't use it if you are filing a tax return for someone who died during the tax year or if you suffered a bankruptcy in the current or immediately preceding tax year.
- Emigrants, non-residents or a deemed resident of Canada may not NETFILE.
- Don't use NETFILE if you are reporting income from a business which has its permanent residence outside your province or territory of residence.

There are other more obscure restrictions on the list, as well. Check it out at this link: http://www.netfile.gc.ca/rstrctns-eng.html#other.

The CRA Transmission Instructions. When you are ready to transmit your return to CRA, most software will take care of the details automatically for you. Here's what will happen next:

- CRA will do a preliminary check of the file and if it meets these tests, you will receive a confirmation number, which means your return has been accepted.
- Rejected returns will be accompanied by a list of errors or corrections required. Corrected returns can be resubmitted.
- Remember: you cannot change your name, address, date of birth or direct deposit information through NETFILE; a paper filed return is required unless you call CRA and get them to change this information on their records before using NETFILE.

- Supporting documents must be retained for six years after the end of the year you filed, in case CRA wants to see them.

Data Storage. As mentioned, there are applications for Windows and Mac computers and also web products. If you choose a web-based product, you should be aware that, in most cases, your data will be stored online and you won't be able to convert your return for use on another tax program in a future year. If you choose an application that you download, your data will be stored on your own hard drive allowing you to review it at any time and possibly switch to a different product next year and convert your data.

 Can you use EFILE? If you are restricted by CRA from NETFILING, your choices are to use a third party transmitter registered for EFILING, or print and mail in your return.

Who Can EFILE? EFILE can be selected by those who file tax returns for others, generally tax professionals. If you seek the services of a pro, select a firm that can EFILE and represent you electronically.

 The Bottom Line | Depending on the various tax filing profiles in your family, you may wish to choose tax software that has few filing or transmission restrictions. The more comprehensive, the better. Most reputable tax software companies will allow you a free demo; many also create tax software for professionals to use, so they are certified by CRA for all types of filing scenarios. Take advantage of the opportunity to try out several. Start early, as you wait for the various T-slips and other documents to arrive. Also consider taking a certificate tax preparation course to get the knowledge a pro has.

4

It Takes Just Seconds!

With your tax software, there are just a few simple steps to doing a tax return, once you have loaded the program, sorted your receipts, refreshed yourself on the tax news and know your way around:

1. Enter all the identification information for the tax filer, including address, birthdate and any dependant information.
2. Ask CRA to compute and forward GST/HST Credits when the tax filer turned 19 and let CRA know about foreign assets.
3. Enter the T-slip information.

Voila! The software effortlessly calculates the federal return. Unless your province of residence offers refundable tax credits, chances are good that the provincial tax calculations have been done as well, without any further effort from you.

You'll be amazed! It can all just take just seconds to do a tax return on your computer... especially if you only have one T4 slip. Try it with the little case study below... it's really fun because you'll see your refund (or balance due) instantly. And, most tax software programs will let you print a one-page summary screen, it may look something like the one on the next page.

Case Study | **John Student**

John Student lives in Saskatchewan and has one T4 slip from his employer. At age 18, he is single and lives at home. Here's a summary of his return:

Knowledge Bureau®	Income Tax Estimator	Tax Year: 2013
Excellence in Financial Education		

Province	Saskatchewan		John Student		
Children:	0	**Single**	**Age:**	18 to 65	

Total income		
Employment Income		$2,400.00
	Total Income	$2,400.00

Net income		
	Net Income	$2,400.00
	Taxable Income	$2,400.00

Refund or Balance owing

Federal tax			$360.00
Federal non-refundable tax credits			
Basic personal amount	$11,038.00		
EI premiums	$45.12		
Canada employment amount	$1,117.00		
Total	$12,200.12		
x Credit rate:	15.00%		
		Total federal non-refundable credits	$1,830.02
		Net federal tax	$0.00
Provincial tax			$264.00
Provincial non-refundable tax credits			
Basic personal amount	$15,241.00		
EI premiums	$45.12		
Total	$15,286.12		
x Credit rate:	11.00%		
		Total Provincial non-refundable credits	$1,681.47
		Net provincial tax	$0.00
		Total Payable	$0.00
Tax deducted, Instalments, or Provincial or other refundable credits			$240.00
		Refund	$240.00

Estimated GSTC: $268.00

Now let's dig a little deeper and zero in on:

- the lines on your return that really matter to you when it comes to tax planning;
- your tax filing approach: what to enter first;
- how to identify your tax filing profile.

Your Tax Summary: Know the Benchmarks. Because the tax software will calculate a new refund or balance due with every number you enter, you will soon become familiar with tax filing benchmarks that are meaningful. For example, circle the important income lines:

- Line 150 Total Income,
- Line 236 Net Income,
- Line 260 Taxable Income,
- Line 350 Total Federal Non-Refundable Tax Credits,
- Line 435 Total Payable,
- Line 484/485 Refund or Balance Due.

You will find Line 350 amounts on Schedule 1; the rest of the lines are on pages 2 to 4 of the T1 return.

 CHECK IT OUT | **What's the most important line on the tax return?** Some might say taxable income or total payable, but always take note of Line 236, Net Income. This figure is used in income-testing for the purposes of refundable and non-refundable tax credits.

Net income is used extensively in tax planning. You can reduce it with an RRSP deduction, for example, resulting in more federal refundable tax credits like Canada Child Tax Benefits or the GST/HST Credit. For seniors, keeping net income below certain "clawback zones," which are also determined at Line 236, can generate more Old Age Security. That helps in planning retirement income. There are several case studies throughout this book to illustrate. Also see *Appendix 3*.

Data Entry Approaches. As you become more confident in using your tax software and get to know the components and lines on the T1, you will note the data entry process may differ for different tax filing profiles discussed below. Software will usually account for this by allowing several data entry approaches. For example:

- **Line-by-Line Approach.** If your software allows you to use the T1 as an option for entering data, start at Line 101 and work in order of the line numbers, entering data from the line to any required schedules, auxiliary tax forms (e.g. T778 *Child Care Expenses*), or worksheets (e.g. Auto Expense calculations).
- **Questionnaire Approach.** If your software has a data entry tab only, or a questionnaire it leads you through, you will need to follow this pre-defined order, at least at the start. Most programs will have you enter all the T-slips first, and you will want to do that carefully, as described below. Once you're done, ask the software to show you a copy of the completed return and review it line by line to make sure nothing was missed. At this point, you may be able to change your data entry approach to be more "profile oriented."

Carefully Enter T-slips First. Most tax returns are simple, requiring no more than a half dozen or so entries which originate from boxes on the T-slips. It's a good idea to enter these first, as you will immediately get a sense of the tax bracket this taxpayer will fall into and whether the withholding taxes deducted at "source" were enough. Common examples are:

- T4 Slips for Employment Income,
- T4A Slips for Superannuation and other pension income, RESP income and TFSA excess amounts,
- T5 Slips for Investment Income, and
- T3 Slips for Trust Income allocations.

CRA will have received one copy of these slips from the employer or financial institution and will cross-check your figures when they run their matching program in the summer. Some taxpayers will receive a tax return that already has the information from those slips on it, in some provinces, so the tax filer simply verifies the amounts and then claims other provisions unique to their financial situation.

That's what's important—you may qualify for so many more provisions that CRA can't know about because of the various life, financial or economic events in your life this past year. So, it helps to think of your tax filing rights in relation to your tax filer profile. Can you find yourself here?

Tax Filer Profiles. Most tax filers will fall into one of these six tax filing profiles, depending on their primary source of income.

1. Credit Filers (these are income-tested; software will calculate allowable credits)
2. Employees
3. Investors
4. Pensioners
5. Self-Employed
6. A recipient of income supplements (Worker's compensation, social assistance, spouse's allowance and Guaranteed Income supplement)

The opportunity is to understand what deductions and credits link to each income profile, so you file the very best returns for your family. Understanding your profile will help you to maximize those you are entitled to and quickly identify any tax changes that may apply to you. See Appendix 3 for a list of the new Refundable and Non-Refundable Tax Credits that may apply to you, for example.

In addition, you may not be aware that your software is in fact calculating some of these claims automatically in the background. Most novices find this quite mind-boggling—but fascinating, as they can often be at a loss to explain how a number appeared on the return. Understanding what tax filing profile you fit into helps.

 The Bottom Line | Every tax filer has a primary tax filing "profile" but for most, this will be a hybrid. For example, you may be an employee with investment income who qualifies for the Canada Child Tax Benefit. Knowing the deductions and credits that belong to your primary profile will help you do a tax return very quickly—often in less than a minute in simple cases—but more accurately. This will create new money for spending and savings.

5

The Many Definitions of Income

What's the definition of income for tax filing purposes? It's an important question, first because there are many definitions, as you have already discovered in the basic elements on the tax return. CRA will penalize you if you understate your income. If you do so intentionally, this is called tax evasion and it could land you in jail and facing expensive penalties when you get out. You'll learn those details at the end of the book. In this chapter, however, you will learn:

- What's considered income and whether a barter transaction or "income in kind" is taxable;
- When income is taxable, and what the cash and accrual methods of accounting are;
- The difference between total, net and taxable income on the T1;
- What "earned income" is: for RRSP/PRPP, child care expense and moving expense purposes;
- What income receipts are tax exempt;
- How the income sources you earn affect your marginal and effective tax rates; and
- Why that's important in planning to pay only the correct amount of tax.

Income. The word "income" has a broad meaning in the eyes of CRA. It covers most amounts (but see exempt list later in this chapter) that are received in cash or in kind within the calendar year for most people. The calendar year is January 1 to December 31. In a very few cases, certain businesses and compounding investments, for example, a different fiscal year is possible for income reporting.

Income received in kind must be included and can include something that has a commercial value, such as a bushel of grain, a gaggle of geese, gold, shares or a variety of services. To record such income receipts requires valuation. The onus of proof for fair market value is on the taxpayer. Therefore, do keep all indicators (appraisals, newspaper clippings, etc.) to justify the price you put on those items.

When is Income Considered to be Received? For most taxpayers, income will be reported when received. This is called the cash basis. It doesn't have to be received in your own hands. It can come through an agent, be deposited in your bank account and so on. In the case of a cheque, it is considered to be received when it is deposited at the post office (i.e. it leaves the hands of the sender). This gives important guidance when you are trying to decide when to report that December-dated cheque received on January 3.

 CHECK IT OUT | **What are penalties for repeated failure to report income?** You should know that if you have failed to report income on the current tax return and in any of the three prior tax returns (2013 and 2010, 2011, or 2012), you will be required to pay a penalty of ***10% of the missed income*** to each of the federal and provincial governments. This is in addition to possible gross negligence and tax evasion penalties (see Part 6).

Cash vs. Accrual. The accrual method of reporting income is used by most businesses and for compounding investments. Notable exceptions are farming and fishing enterprises where the cash method is acceptable. Under the accrual method, income is reported when earned (whether or not received) and expenses are deducted when incurred (whether or not paid).

Income Definitions on the T1. In the previous chapter you have had a good look at the lines that relate to income sources. Take a moment now to better understand the various definitions of "income" on the tax return:

Total Income. Total income is Line 150 of the tax return, and includes income from all sources:

- Employment income;
- Commissions earned by an employee;
- Other employment income including tips, wage loss replacement benefits that were jointly funded by employer and employee, and net research grants;
- Pension income (Canadian and foreign);
- Employment Insurance and Universal Child Care Benefits;
- Investment income from taxable dividends, interest and rental properties;
- Net taxable capital gains (net of current year losses);
- Other income sources, including support payments, RDSP, and RESP receipts;
- Self-employment; and
- Income supplements like Workers' Compensation, social assistance and Guaranteed Income Supplements paid to seniors.

Non-Taxable Income Supplements. You will note that income supplements are taxable and form part of income on Line 150, but in fact, they do not form part of taxable income. That's because there is a full offsetting deduction for these sources on Line 250. Your tax software will automatically calculate that, but do know that in between is Line 236, Net Income. The effect of these calculations is that the income supplements will decrease refundable tax credits.

Net Income. This is Line 236 of the tax return. It is total income less the deductions on Lines 206 to 235 of the tax return and is the income used for income-tested tax credits and social benefits in Canada. For some credits, "family net income" is required—that is, income on Line 236 for both spouses. You'll learn more about that in Part 3 of this book.

Taxable Income. This is the income that is used to compute federal and provincial taxes (except in Quebec). It goes to Schedule 1 for computation of federal taxes, after which non-refundable tax credits are used to reduce the taxes payable.

Earned Income—for RRSP/PRPP Purposes. This is the income that qualifies for building RRSP or PRPP contribution room. This includes employment income, self-employment profits, rental income, CPP disability pension, taxable support payments received as well as a few more uncommon income sources.

Earned Income—for the purposes of claiming Child Care Expenses. This is the income that is used as a limit for your claim for child care expenses. This includes employment income, self-employment profits, CPP disability pension, training allowances, the taxable portion of scholarships received as well as a few more uncommon income sources.

Earned Income—for the purposes of claiming Moving Expenses. This income, if earned at the new location, is used as one of the limits for your claim for moving expenses. It includes employment income (less deductions claimed for employment expenses, union dues, etc.), amounts received under the The Wage Earner Protection Program (WEPP) in respect of your employment at the new work location, self-employment profits, and the portion of scholarships and research grants that must be included in your income.

Exempt Income—very important—these sources will not be taxable:

- Income earned within or withdrawn from a Tax-Free Savings Account (TFSA);
- Income exempt by virtue of a statute, including the *Indian Act*;
- Provincial and Federal Refundable Tax Credits, like Canada Child Tax Benefits, GST/HST credits, including child assistance payments and disability supplements from the province of Quebec;
- Canada Child Tax Benefits;
- Canadian Service Pensions, War Veterans Allowance Act Allowances;
- Compensation by Federal Republic of Germany to a victim of National Socialist persecution;

- Capital gains on publicly traded shares donated to a registered charity or private foundation;
- Foster Care payments;
- Income of Canadian Forces Personnel and Police on High-Risk International Missions;
- Inheritance or gifts;
- Life Insurance Policy proceeds;
- Lottery winnings;
- Military Disability pensions and dependant's pensions;
- MLA and Municipal Officers Expense Allowances;
- Proceeds from accident, disability, sickness or income maintenance plans;
- Payments for Volunteer Emergency Services—up to $1,000;
- *New!* Payments to victims of a criminal act or car accident from provinces or territories;
- Refundable provincial or federal tax credits;
- RCMP Disability Pension or Compensation;
- Service Pensions from Other Countries, as well as a NATO official's income;
- Tax-free benefits of employment, including transportation to a special worksite, certain transportation passes, uniforms supplied to the employee, etc.

Working With Income Definitions. There certainly is a lot to know about your different sources of income. You'll want to understand how to earn and "layer" your income to be taxed by understanding what effective and marginal tax rates apply.

Effective and Marginal Tax Rates. When you divide total income by the taxes payable on Line 435, you will understand the taxpayer's *effective tax rate*—the average rate of tax paid on total income.

 CHECK IT OUT | **What's your effective tax rate?** Let's say a taxpayer's total income on Line 150 is $100,000 and total taxes paid (federal and provincial) are $35,000. This taxpayer's effective tax rate, therefore is 35%.

Your *marginal tax rate* is something different. It is linked to your tax bracket and analyzes how much you'll pay on the next dollar you earn from various income sources. This is an important concept too—not all income sources are taxed alike.

A taxpayer's MTR (Marginal Tax Rate) is a useful tool in measuring tax-efficiency of both actively and passively earned income sources. It will tell you how much tax you'll pay on the next dollar you plan to earn, while measuring the effect of that income on your eligibility for tax credits and social benefits delivered through the tax system.

This is different from the effective tax rate, which reflects the actual tax rate applied to your income after "progressivity" is taken into account. In Canada we have a progressive tax system, which means, the more you earn the more you pay and the less you receive from income-tested social benefits.

To compute your marginal tax rate, you need to understand that your income sources will be classified into several broad categories for tax purposes. For example:

1. **Ordinary income** is fully taxable and includes income from employment, pensions and interest. It may also include alimony and certain social benefits like Employment Insurance, and net rental income—what's left after allowable deductions.
2. **Income from self-employment** is reported on a *net* basis—what's left after revenues are reduced by allowable deductions.
3. **Capital gains** are reported upon the disposition (sale or transfer) of an asset. Only half those gains, net of losses, are reported on the return. Sometimes, gains can be avoided when certain properties are donated to charity. Other gains may qualify for specific exemptions from tax (the Capital Gains Deduction, for example).
4. **Dividends** are the after-tax distribution of profits from private or public corporations to shareholders. Reporting them involves an integration of the corporate and personal tax systems, the end result of which is a preferential tax rate for the dividend recipient.

When you know your marginal tax rate on the next dollars you earn, you can make better choices about your income sources and tax-preferred investments to get the after tax results you want on both income and capital. These results will vary by province, as illustrated on the next page[3].

---

[3] Updates are posted regularly in ***Knowledge Bureau Report***, available free of charge at www.knowledgebureau.com.

Federal and Provincial Marginal Tax Rates for 2013

	Taxable Income Range	Ordinary Income	Capital Gains	Small Bus. Corp. Dividends	Eligible Dividends Large Corps.
BC	Up to $10,276	0%	0%	0%	0%
	$10,277 to $11,038	5.06%	2.53%	2.07%	-6.82%
	$11,039 to $37,568	20.06%	10.03%	4.16%	-6.84%
	$37,569 to $43,561	22.70%	11.35%	7.46%	-3.20%
	$43,562 to $75,138	29.70%	14.85%	16.21%	6.46%
	$75,139 to $86,268	32.50%	16.25%	19.71%	10.32 %
	$86,269 to $87,123	34.29%	17.15%	21.95%	12.79%
	$87,124 to $104,754	38.29%	19.15%	26.95%	18.31%
	$104,755 to 135,054	40.70%	20.35%	29.96%	21.64%
	Over $135,054	43.70%	21.85%	33.71%	25.78%
AB	Up to $11,038	0%	0%	0%	0%
	$11,039 to $17,593	15.00%	7.50%	2.08%	-0.03%
	$17,594 to $43,561	25.00%	12.50%	10.21%	-0.03%
	$43,562 to $87,123	32.00%	16.00%	18.96%	9.63%
	$87,124 to $135,054	36.00%	18.00%	23.96%	15.15%
	Over $135,054	39.00%	19.50%	27.71%	19.29%

The Bottom Line | By understanding CRA's various definitions of income reportable on the tax return, you will be able to avoid tax evasion charges, and plan to "realize" various different income sources for tax purposes at different times that bring you the most advantageous tax results. This can make a big and positive impact, especially if you manage to avoid the next highest tax bracket.

6

Maximizing Your Tax Deductions and Credits

What's the difference between a tax deduction, a non-refundable and a refundable tax credit? You're not alone if these terms confuse you. It's important that you understand them though because the majority of the lines on the return are made up of them and if you are going to miss something, that's likely what it will be.

Deductions and credits work hard for you, so you want to claim them all. But don't over-claim them, because fraud here reaps the same penalties for tax evasion by understating income will. In this chapter you'll find out more about the difference between tax deductions and credits and how to keep your eyes peeled for those that are lucrative for you.

Understanding Tax Deductions. Tax deductions come in two flavours: those which will reduce total income on Line 150 leading to net income on Line 236 and those which reduce net income to arrive at taxable income on Line 260.

Deductions that reduce net income can increase your income-tested credits and benefits. Since all deductions reduce taxable income they reduce your tax bill and, if large enough, they may reduce your marginal tax rate. It's especially important to understand that your marginal tax rate increases, not just because you pay more tax as your income grows, but also as you lose income-tested credits and benefits due to "clawbacks." Therefore, maximizing all deductions is a double benefit.

 CHECK IT OUT | **What are the most frequently missed deductions?** The most frequently missed tax deductions are investment carrying charges; the most lucrative is often moving expenses. All deductions reduce taxes payable and may reduce your marginal tax rate. What are you missing?

Understanding Tax Credits. Tax software does an outstanding job of allocating the various federal and provincial tax credits, many of which you automatically receive. There are three types of tax credits, and people often find this confusing. Often they can't find them and don't know they are receiving them—or could be. So let's begin there:

Federal Refundable Tax Credits. These credits are income-tested, based on the size of your family (both spouses') net income. This means the more you earn the smaller your credit. Check out the Appendices for current income thresholds. What's important is that even if you have no income, you may be eligible for them so always file a tax return.

- GST/HST Credit (paid quarterly starting at age 19)
- Canada Child Tax Benefit (paid monthly the month after your child's birth until they reach age 18)
- Working Income Tax Benefit (may be paid quarterly in advance to supplement expenses of low income earners who start working)

Provincial Refundable Tax Credits. Most provinces have one or more refundable provincial tax credits although most are targeted at specific groups or expenditures that the province would like to encourage. Be sure to print from your software the provincial tax forms that link to Line 479 to make sure you understand the requirements for filing.

Off the Tax Return (benefits sent to you as a result of tax computations on the return). Federally the GST/HST Credit, Canada Child Tax Benefit, Working Income Tax Benefit, and GIS are applied for through the filing of a tax return. Most provinces also provide supplements for low-income families that are paid along with the federal Child Tax Benefit or the GST/HST Credit. Ontario pays several credits monthly rather than including them on the tax return. Therefore even if your income is nil, filing for these benefits is very important.

Non-Refundable Tax Credits. These are credits that reduce taxes payable, therefore if you have no taxes to pay, they do you no good. Everyone qualifies for the *Basic Personal Amount (BPA)* which is just over $11,000 this year so long as you lived in Canada for the full year. This is your "tax-free zone"—income under this amount is not taxable.

The BPA is automatically calculated by your tax software program on Schedule 1. Other non-refundable tax credits, depending on your circumstances, can be claimed to increase your tax-free zone.

 CHECK IT OUT | **Does your province match federal credits?** While both the federal and provincial government share a common definition of taxable income (except in Quebec), they do not have to offer the same non-refundable tax credits. This can make the tax filing process very complicated. Fortunately the tax software program you use will likely enter some of the credits for you on both returns; others are determined by your expenditures and you'll need to find them and address them. The following chart should help:

Name of Federal Non-Refundable Credit	Automatically Entered by Software	Info you must enter	You must have receipts
Basic Personal Amount	Yes	N/A	No
Age Amount	Yes	Your birthdate	No
Spousal Amount	Yes	Marital status and spouse's income	No
Amount for Child Under 18	Yes	Details of dependants	No
Amount for Eligible Dependants	Yes	Details of dependants	No
Amount for Infirm Dependants Age 18 or Over	Yes	Details of dependants	No
Amount for CPP contributions	Yes	T4 slip	No
Amount for EI Premiums	Yes	T4 slip	No
Volunteer Firefighters Amount	No	Eligibility	Yes
Canada Employment Amount	Yes	T4 Income	No
Public Transit Amount	No	Amount paid	Yes
Children's Fitness Amount	No	Expense details	Yes
Children's Arts Amount	No	Expense details	Yes
Home Buyers' Amount	No	Enter the amount	Yes
Adoption Expenses	No	Expense detail	Yes
Pension Income Amount	Yes	Eligible pension income	Yes (Slips)
Caregiver Amount	Yes	Dependant info	No
Disability Amount (self or dependant)	No	Eligibility	Yes (T2201A and B)
Interest Paid on Student Loans	No	Amount paid	Yes
Tuition, Education and Textbook Amount (self and dependant)	No	T2202A info	Yes
Medical Expenses	No	Expense details	Yes
Charitable Donations	No	Amount donated	Yes

 The Bottom Line | Take the time to really dig for every tax deduction, refundable and non-refundable credit you are entitled to. Tax software can claim what it thinks you qualify for, but it won't know about your medical expenses or that you purchased your first home. Don't let that happen at the expense of lucrative amounts that could reduce your taxes this year or in the future.

7

No or Low-Income Filers

No income? File a tax return anyways. You'll need to do that to receive income supplements from the government, often paid monthly or quarterly, including federal tax credits like the Canada Child Tax Benefit, GST/HST credit or the Universal Child Care Benefit.

Approximately 35% of all returns filed in Canada are not taxable. Millions of others have net income levels low enough to qualify for full or partial refundable tax credits. In this chapter you'll learn more about that, plus how incredibly easy software makes the filing of credit-only returns by taking part in a case study for 18-year-old Jill who is filing for her federal and provincial credits.

Eligibility for Refundable Tax Credits. Refundable tax credits can be received from the federal government, and in some cases, provincial governments. The following people *may not* claim refundable credits:

- Those confined to a prison at the end of the year and so confined for six months or more.
- Those who died during the year.
- Diplomats who are not taxable in Canada.

Teenagers Should File for GST/HST Credits. Typical first-time credit filers are 18-year-olds who file for the federal GST/HST Credit, which they will receive the quarter after they turn 19, and at-home single mothers who file for the CCTB and the GSTC.

Filing a Return is Easy. If a GST/HST Credit filer has no income at all to report, filing a return is as simple as counting to five:

1. Enter the taxpayer identification information.
2. Answer the citizenship and Elections Canada questions and address the foreign property lines.
3. Check yes under the GST/HST Credit application in the last box on Page 1 (your software may do this automatically for you).
4. Your software will enter zeros on the key income lines: 150, 236, 260.
5. Your software will determine the amount of credit available to the taxpayer. This will show up on the tax summary as well.

Credit Filers with Income. Many credit filers do have income of some sort so determining the value of deductions they may be entitled to or non-refundable tax credits is the first step in the process of filing the entire tax return.

Because of the importance of net income on Line 236, consider the advantages of an RRSP contribution and deduction even for low-income earners. The objective is to get net income under the "clawback thresholds" so you can get more credits for your family. Clawbacks reduce your available tax credits.

 CHECK IT OUT | **What do low earners need to know about credit filing?**

- No- or low-income adults in most Canadian families should always file a tax return every year to receive their refundable tax credits like the GSTC and the CCTB.
- Both spouses or common-law partners must split certain income sources.
- Both will want to file to receive social benefits like the Guaranteed Income Supplement or Working Income Tax Benefit.

Other Important Issues:

- The "statute of limitations" is shorter for federal refundable credits than for most other provisions. Technically, you can only go back 11 months to recover missed Canada Child Tax Benefits. It is possible to apply for a recovery for a period longer than this, where the appeal is based on circumstances of hardship. See "Voluntary Disclosure Programs" below.
- Provinces also offer tax form based credits or monthly income supplements which are paid to low-income Canadians according to the net income reported on their returns. Look for reference to Line 479 specific to each province.
- The money received from these refundable tax credits can provide a way to save for a child's future education and/or to split the investment income earned on the money.

CHECK IT OUT | **How do you determine if your income is too high for refundable tax credits?** "Family net income" is used to determine the level of refundable tax credits, so you'll need to have your spouse's net income figures from Line 236 of the federal T1 return available to file for refundable tax credits.

If you are using tax software, it will automatically calculate the refundable tax credits you are entitled to, provided you have correctly indicated that you have a spouse or common-law partner and what that person's net income is. For those reasons, families should file together (see Part 3 for details). But this is also where many single parents can make an important mistake. You may not know that your "live-in" relationship has tax consequences.

 CHECK IT OUT | **What if my marital status changes?** If your marital status changes, you must tell CRA about this on *Form RC 65 Marital Status Change* by the end of the month following the month of change, so they can adjust your claim for your refundable credits. Both spouses must sign the form and submit their Social Insurance Numbers. However, if you become separated, they don't want to hear from you until you have been separated for more than 90 consecutive days.

Generally, the Canada Child Tax Benefit will be sent to the female parent, although, it is possible for a male parent to apply for this if he is *primarily responsible* for the care of the child. To establish this, a Form RC66 *Canada Child Tax Benefit Application* must be completed.

There are lots of details that can affect who gets these credits, as you can imagine. We will cover this in more detail in Part 3, but be aware, if you have been filing for credits as a single person, using only your net income for the purposes of applying for your refundable tax credits but you are living common-law, you are offside. To avoid penalties and interest you can voluntarily comply with proper notification to CRA.

Voluntary Disclosures Program. When you voluntarily correct errors or omissions on your tax return, you will avoid penalties and interest. It's easy to do. Simply adjust your tax return using Form T1-ADJ, which you will find in your tax software. You can go back to recover missed provisions for up to 10 years in many cases.

Try It! Use Software to File For Tax Credits

It's a lot of fun preparing your first tax return! The terms are new but using the power of tax software, you'll be empowered to understand how much of your hard earned money you get to keep, and how the opportunities to apply for refundable tax credits and a refund of any overpaid taxes can help you plan investments, too.

Most tax software packages will give you the option to review a "tax summary" similar to the one that follows, to see if you are getting the tax calculation results you should be, based on your tax documentation. It's a great way to check your work. That summary will then be used to match up to the results CRA sends you back on your Notice of Assessment. Your tax summary should also tell you about how much you can expect from various refundable tax credits.

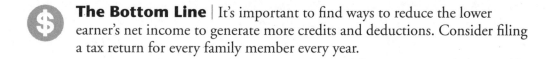

Case Study | Filing For Credits and to Create RRSP Room

The following is a tax summary for a tax return filed for an 18-year-old girl who has part-time income from babysitting and working at the local hamburger joint.

You will see Jill has created RRSP room with her "earned income," and she qualifies for a GST/HST Credit next year. Note total, net and taxable income is circled. Recall the definitions of each type of income.

If Jill will turn 19 before June 1, 2015, she should apply for the Ontario Sales Tax Credit by filing form ON-BEN with her return. The credit will be paid monthly beginning the month after her 19th birthday.

Now think about how you will use the information to plan for financial life events and to increase future income potential for this young woman with investment planning?

The Bottom Line | It's important to find ways to reduce the lower earner's net income to generate more credits and deductions. Consider filing a tax return for every family member every year.

Income Tax Estimator

Tax Year: 2013

Province	Ontario		Jill Student			
Children:	0	**Single**	**Age:**	18 to 65		

Total income

Employment Income		$5,445.24
	Total Income	$5,445.24

Net income

	Net Income	$5,445.24
	Taxable Income	$5,445.24

Refund or Balance owing

Federal tax		$816.79

Federal non-refundable tax credits		
Basic personal amount	$11,038.00	
CPP contributions	$96.29	
EI premiums	$102.37	
Canada employment amount	$1,117.00	
Total	$12,353.66	
x Credit rate:	15.00%	

Total federal non-refundable credits		$1,853.05
Net federal tax		$0.00
Provincial tax		$274.98

Provincial non-refundable tax credits		
Basic personal amount	$9,575.00	
CPP contributions	$96.29	
EI premiums	$102.37	
Total	$9,773.66	
x Credit rate:	5.05%	

Total Provincial non-refundable credits		$493.57
Net provincial tax		$0.00
Total Payable		$0.00
Tax deducted, Instalments, or Provincial or other refundable credits		$544.52
Refund		$544.52

Estimated GSTC: $268.00

8

Avoid Common Errors

Tax software does make tax filing much easier, but you can still make costly errors on your tax return. Most of the software packages will ask you pointed questions about the things you may have forgotten about or bar you from going on unless you enter required information. That's a really good thing!

However there are errors or omissions even your smart tax software can't catch. To avoid them, always follow a process that includes double-checking your data entry to all numbers on the hard copy or other source documents. Pay particular attention to these five "wrap up" principles:

1. **Data entry:** Did you avoid transposition errors (89 instead of 98) and keying information into wrong line or box numbers?
2. **Tax compliance:** Did you report all income—amounts received in cash or in kind—for the calendar year?
3. **Tax theory:** Did you claim all the tax deductions and credits you are entitled to?
4. **Document assembly:** Did you assemble your Permanent File, Working File and Audit Defence file appropriately to communicate with precision in case of audit or adjustment for errors or omissions?
5. **Logic:** Does the outcome make sense? Did you make $20,000 more this year but find you are paying less tax? The year-to-year tax summary comparisons in many software programs are very helpful in this regard. Be sure to find out why. There may be an error.

CHECK IT OUT | **Have you made a common mistake?** Consider this list as you file your return, then check your return carefully before you deliver it—electronically or otherwise—to CRA. You won't want to hold up your refund, or understate it!

Error or Omission	Line
Taxable Benefits Double Reported—remember, taxable benefits are already included in Box 14 of your T4 slip.	101
Missed Premium Deduction on Wage Loss Replacement Benefits Received—get this info from your payroll department.	104
Failure to Report Tips and Gratuities	104
Failure to Report Taxable Foreign Pension	115
Interest income not reported	121
Missed claiming capital losses or capital gains	127
Lost RRSP receipt; claim taken in incorrect tax year	208
Missed GST/HST Rebate on employment expenses	457
Moving expenses—missed real estate commissions	219
Missed safety deposit box fees in carrying charges	221
Missed home office and auto claims by eligible employees	229
Business loss not carried back or forward using Form T1A	252
Prior year capital losses not recorded	253
Spousal Amount—gross rather than net income entered	303
Amount For Eligible Dependants—for single parents	305
Caregiver Amount—missed claim for infirm parent	315
Disability Amount—missed claim for sick child or spouse	318
Tuition, Education and Textbook Credits—missed transfer to parents or other supporting individual	324
Medical expenses—missed claims for self or dependants	330
Donations—claimed on both spouses' returns instead of all on one	349
Tax instalment payments made missed	476

Don't Miss Reporting Other Income on Line 130

Remember, there can be significant penalties for failure to report income sources. But, here is a trap: there are numerous sources of income that are taxable but that may not have their own line on the tax return. That doesn't mean you don't have to report them. These "other income sources" are generally included on Line 130 of the tax return. They can include the following sources:

 New for 2013 | Grants paid to family members who take time off from work to cope with the death or disappearance of a child as a result of Criminal Code activities (PMMC). These amounts would be shown in Box 136 of the T4A slip.

- **Annuity payments** that are not reported on Line 115 Other Pension or Superannuation.
- **Apprenticeship Incentive Grant** received under the Apprenticeship Incentive Grant program provided by the Government of Canada. The AIG is a taxable cash grant of $1,000 per level (maximum of $2,000 per person) and is available to registered apprentices once the first or second level or year of their Red Seal Trade program is completed. It is meant to the apprentice with funds to cover expenses related to tuition costs and/or travel or tools related to their trade.
- **Death Benefits (other than CPP or QPP death benefit amounts).** A death benefit is an amount received after a person's death for that person's employment service. The amount is shown in box 106 of a T4A slip. Tax may not be payable on up to $10,000 of the benefit received.
- **Lump-sum Payments** from a pension or deferred profit sharing plan. If a lump-sum payment was received in 2013 that included amounts earned in previous years, you must include the whole payment on the return for 2013. A reduced tax rate can apply to amounts earned before 1972.
- **Retiring Allowances (Severance Pay).** Include the amounts shown in boxes 026 and 027 of T4A slips.
- **RESP payments.** Look for amounts in Box 040 and 042 of your T4A slips.
- **Retirement Compensation Arrangement payments.** Look for your T4A-RCA Slip.
- **Registered Retirement Income Fund or Registered Pension Plan amounts** if those amounts were rolled over into an Registered Disability Savings Plan.
- **TFSA Payments that are taxable.** Look for amounts in box 134 of T4A slips.
- **Training Allowances**—on a T4A slip; amounts that have not been reported on another line of your return.
- **Trust payments**—Look for an amount in Box 26 of your T3 slips.

Don't Miss Other Deductions on Line 232, Either

Line 232 is used to deduct amounts that reduce net income. That makes these deductions very valuable because they have the effect of increasing refundable and non-refundable tax credits in addition to decreasing taxes. This "catch all" line is for deductions that have not been allocated a special line on the return.

✓ **CHECK IT OUT** | **How many of these other deductions might you qualify for this year?**
- Amounts that were reported as income in 2013 or prior years, that were repaid in 2013; also certain amounts from information slips.
- Accounting and Legal expenses paid, but in the following circumstances only:
  - *CRA Challenges*. Accounting and Legal Fees paid for advice or assistance in responding to a CRA review of income, deductions or credits for a year, or objecting

or appealing an assessment under the *Income Tax Act, Unemployment Insurance Act, Employment Insurance Act* or the *Canada Pension Plan Act.*

- *Retirement.* Legal fees paid to collect or establish a right to a retiring allowance or pension benefit. However, these fees must be reduced by any amounts transferred into an RRSP. There is a seven year carry forward of undeducted amounts.
- *Salary Disputes.* Legal fees paid to collect or establish a right to salaries or wages.
- *Family Law.* Legal fees paid in relation to child support payments may be deductible on Line 221 in some cases; however not legal fees are payable to get a separation or divorce or to establish visitation rights with your child.

• Capital Cost Allowances on Canadian Feature Films.
• Depletion Allowances (attach Form T1229 *Statement of Resource Expenses and Depletion Allowances).*
• Employment Insurance (EI) benefits repaid. This can be tricky because you may have indirectly repaid these amounts by having subsequent EI benefits reduced. What's important to know is the T4E slip you receive in the year will show the net amount after such reductions. However, if you have an amount in Box 30 of that slip, you can take a deduction on Line 232.
• RRSP contribution withdrawals that were previously undeducted (Form T3012A *Tax Deduction Waiver of your Unused RRSP Contributions made in* _____ is required, or Form T746 *Calculation Your Deduction for Refund of Unused RRSP Contributions*) and in some cases:
- The excess amounts of direct transfers between your RPP and RRSP or RRIF that were subsequently withdrawn and included in income,
- Transfers to RRSPs of eligible retiring allowances,
- RRSP commutation payments transferred to an RRSP or RRIF, and
- Refund of RRSP or RRIF premiums or RPP or PRPP amounts rolled over to an RDSP.

• Previously undeducted resource allowances carried forward may be deducted under the debt forgiveness rules. When commercial debts are forgiven, no asset is lost by the debtor and no asset is acquired by the creditor. From the creditor's point of view, the debt is disposed of for nil proceeds. This will result in a capital loss or business deduction, depending on the nature of the debt and the creditor's business. From the debtor's point of view, goods, services or assets may have been acquired at a significant discount. The cost of these goods or services may have already been deducted from income or the acquired assets may already have been disposed of. Since the forgiven amount cannot be allocated to a specific item, the debt forgiveness rules require a reduction in certain "tax preferences" like loss applications. This is a complicated area of tax law and professional advice should be sought.
• Retirement Compensation Arrangement deductions.

Finally, Additional Deductions on Line 256

Line 256 is one of those obscure lines on the tax return on which little know deductions are taken—things like deductions for exempt foreign income. This includes support payments you may have received from a resident of another country that is exempt under a tax treaty. You would first report this amount as income on Line 128 of the tax return (See Part 3).

You may also have received exempt foreign pension income from the United States, Germany, or other foreign country thereby qualifying for a tax deduction for a portion of this income, again due to our tax treaties with those countries. You will learn all about tax reporting for Pensioners in Part 5.

Members of a religious order who have taken a vow of perpetual poverty can deduct the amount of their earned income and pension benefits if these were given to their order. A letter verifying the gift is required.

Assistance paid to cover tuition fees at a primary or secondary school may qualify for a deduction as well; based on income reported in the T4E slip. Students receiving assistance at a post-secondary level may qualify for the tuition, education and textbook amount, which is covered in Part 3.

Finally, if you or a member of your family worked for a prescribed international organization, your *net* employment income will qualify for a deduction as well. However, you will not be able to use NETFILE. The following international organizations and agencies are considered to be prescribed:

- Bank for International Settlements;
- European Fund;
- International Bank for Reconstruction and Development; and the European Bank for Reconstruction and Development;
- International Development Association;
- International Finance Corporation; and
- International Monetary Fund.

 The Bottom Line | Take time to prepare an accurate, audit-proof return, starting with the lowest earner in the family and working to the highest. It's time consuming and therefore vexing to have to correct errors later. Also, be inquisitive: some of the income you earned or expenditure amounts you may have incurred may not fall into a typical tax filing profile. Are they reportable or deductible on the tax return? Even if you use tax software, remember, there are lots of ways to go wrong, so have a consistent process for double-checking your reporting requirements and the final numbers on your tax returns before sending them in to CRA.

9

When to See a Pro

Filing a tax return is a life skill everyone should have. Paying taxes will not go away any time soon, and you need to know how to do three things:

1. Keep more of the first dollars you earn.
2. Hold onto them the longest.
3. Make sure they have purchasing power when you need them.

Knowing more about your tax filing rights and opportunities makes you the master of your money. You will earn more and keep more because you are making tax-savvy decisions. However, that knowledge can be significantly enhanced when you work with a professional advisory team, including a tax professional.

That person, if trained well, should not just be able to do the transaction of filing returns for you. He or she should also be your tax educator, an advocate for your tax filing rights and a steward of your family's money by making sure you only pay the correct amount of tax throughout your lifecycle.

In this chapter learn more about

- Life, financial or economic events for which you should see a tax pro;
- How to use a checklist for finding and interviewing a professional and/or a team; and
- How to think about both in minimizing tax: astute tax planning and tax preparation.

You should be prepared to speak to a pro when you have a "trigger question," that is, there is a financial decision you feel you need to make about life events, financial events or economic events that may affect you. Tax filing time is a good time to do so. There are three types of triggers you may wish to discuss and the following checklists can help you gather your thoughts:

Life Triggers. These age-related tax milestones indicate a new or changed filing status; you might wish to ask your pro about new tax provisions that now will apply to you:

Milestone	Significance for Tax Preparation or Planning
Birth to age 7	• Claim child care expenses and apply for enhanced Canada Child Tax Benefits and Universal Child Care Benefits • Claim non-refundable credits for dependent children under 18 • Children's Fitness Tax Credit and Children's Arts Tax Credit available • Claim Disability Amount for a disabled child • Open bank account and deposit Canada Child Tax Benefit and gifts from non-residents—both are free from the Attribution Rules • Gift investments that produce capital-gains—Attribution Rules do not apply • Open RESP savings accounts to earn up to $500 in Canada Education Savings Grants or Bonds
Ages 7-17	• Claim amount for dependent children under 18 • Child care expense claim reduced but still possible • Children's Fitness Tax Credit and Children's Arts Tax Credit available • Canada Child Tax Benefits reduced but still possible • Create RRSP room by reporting all employment/self-employment • Continue to invest in RESP; CESG eligibility ends at end of the year the child turns 17 • Continue to deposit Canada Child Tax Benefits into untainted savings account
Age 18	• File return so child receives GST/HST Credit starting after 19th birthday • CPP premiums become payable the month after the 18th birthday • Canada Child Tax Benefits end; Eligibility for amount for eligible dependant ends • TFSA contribution room begins to accumulate
Age 19	• GST/HST Credit becomes payable the quarter after turning 19 • Post-secondary school bound: report RESP income, tuition/education/textbook amounts, student loan interest
Ages 20-30	• Conjugal relationships: income splitting, RRSP spousal plans, TFSA • First Time Home Buyers' Tax Credit may be utilized • Use Home Buyers' Plan and Lifelong Learning Plan under RRSP
Age 49	• Last year for earning of Registered Disability Savings Grants and Bonds
Ages 31 to 59	• Peak productivity: RRSP and TFSA maximization; tax efficiency in non-registered savings; business start rules important • Tax-wise employment negotiations important • Family issues: consequences on divorce, illness and death • Charitable gift planning: annual updates required • Parental care: Caregiver Amount, medical expenses

Milestone	Significance for Tax Preparation or Planning
Age 60 plus	• CPP early retirement (age 60 – 64), normal (age 65), or late retirement (age 66 – 70); split income with spouse • Withdrawals from RDSPs must begin after age 59 • Retirement income sources change taxpayer profile • Pension withdrawal planning; clawback zones; pension income splitting • Sale of taxable and non-taxable assets • Transfer of property within the family • OAS begins at age 65 (but may be delayed up to age 70) • Age Credit Amount starting at age 65 • Pension income splitting for RRSP/RRIF starting at age 65 • Withdrawals from RRSP by age 71; make spousal RRSP contribution if spouse is under age 71 and you have contribution room • Check instalment payment requirements

Financial Triggers. Consider seeing a tax or financial pro (or both) if you aren't sure of the answers to these 12 questions:

1. Have I claimed everything I was entitled to in previous tax years?
2. Have I reported all the capital losses I may be entitled to claim in the future?
3. What are the marginal tax rates on our various source of income?
4. How much should each family member contribute to RRSPs this year?
5. When should I make a $2,000 RRSP over-contribution? Is there an excess contribution?
6. How should I structure my employment bonus to pay the least tax?
7. How should I structure my severance package to pay the least tax?
8. Should I defer taking my OAS or CPP pensions or should I begin CPP early?
9. Should I phase into retirement by tapping into my employer-sponsored pension plan early?
10. What is the most tax-efficient way to transfer assets to my spouse or child?
11. Should we be investing in a TFSA?
12. Should we be investing in an RESP or RDSP?

Economic Triggers. A lot is going on in the global economy these days and one of the ways to hedge your investments against the potential of increasing inflation, taxes or volatile economic performance is to make sure you are discussing your tax efficiency strategies today. You may be concerned about how to offset the losses you have in your various investment accounts, or how to shelter your savings from inflation in the future. You may also wonder whether you should remain in equities or bonds. Use the economic circumstances of the day and the following checklist to find a tax and financial advisor to help:

Interview Checklist: Finding A Professional Team

- What are your top three concerns about your taxes?
- What are your top three concerns about your investments?
- Has the professional answered your concerns in plain English?
- Would you consider this person a financial educator?
- How does the professional price his or her services?
- Are they available to help you year round?
- Do they have a "succession" team—juniors they are mentoring so you can get service in case of vacation or illness?
- Is there a guarantee of services—what happens if there is an error or omission that costs you interest, penalties or causes you to lose money?
- Can the professional provide you with three referrals to professionals who have worked with him/her?
- Can the professional provide you with three referrals to clients who have worked with him/her?

It's About Both: Tax Filing and Tax Planning. You may also wish to pick up a copy of the companion book to this one: *Essential Tax Facts: Secrets and Strategies for Take-Charge People* will help you to answer tax planning questions so you can plan your tax efficient investments and income withdrawal choices with the right professional team.

In the meantime, using this book to learn more about filing your own return is an important step in working smarter with tax, investment, retirement and estate planning pros.

 The Bottom Line | Especially if you file your own tax return, a relationship with a financial advisory team, including a tax, investment, retirement, estate and legal advisor, can help you take charge of your wealth and make better decisions about your money. Make sure you deal with competent professionals who can be your financial educator, advocate and steward of your hard earned money. Look for someone who has training as a wealth advisor and can work strategically within a team structure.

PART 2

Reporting Employment Income

You have learned in Part 1 that 70% of Canadians report income from employment and yet most do not understand that various deductions and tax credits can apply to reduce taxes.

Commonly claimed deductions include contributions to employer-sponsored Registered Pension Plans, contributions to Registered Retirement Savings Plans, union or professional dues, and required out-of-pocket employment expenses, especially important to employed commissioned sales people.

Today many more employees are working out of their home offices and can legitimately claim home workspace expenses and auto expenses. But these "mixed use" expenses must be carefully divided between their personal and employment portion.

In addition, child care expenses, moving expenses and other deductions leading to Line 236, Net Income, can be very lucrative because they will help to increase refundable and non-refundable tax credits.

This part of the book will help employees pay only the correct amount of taxes because all the deductions and tax credits they are entitled to are claimed.

What's New
Most years your paycheque will be affected by changes to "statutory deductions"—Canada Pension Plan (CPP) and Employment Insurance (EI), and Income Taxes due to indexing and changes to rates and credits. Tax changes relating to group sickness plans have also increased your taxes this year. If you work offshore check out Form T626. It calculates the lucrative

Overseas Employment Tax Credit, which is being phased out starting in 2013. Contract renegotiations and tax remittance adjustments will be required. Finally, your RRSP contribution room will be impacted by contributions you may have made to a new pension plan: the PRPP. Read on to find out more.

Hard Copy

You'll need to get your employer to sign Form T2200 *Declaration of Conditions of Employment* if you are going to claim employment expenses on your tax return this year. You'll also need Form T778 to claim your child care expenses, Form T1-M to make the claim for moving expenses, Form TL2 if you are claiming meals and lodging as a transport employee and Schedule 8 to make your RRSP contributions deductible.

Software Tips

Your tax software will do many calculations automatically for you but you'll need to avoid data entry traps and common errors to help get the results you want:

- *Enter the Numbers on T4 Slips.* It's easy to slip up so take your time. Your T4s have boxes for the majority of your employment-related deductions and credits, but be careful not to make any transposition errors. If you find another slip after you file, don't file another return. Adjust instead using Form T1-ADJ.
- *Other Employment Income.* Did you receive a research grant? Work only occasionally and didn't get a T4? Perhaps you are a member of the clergy or earned foreign employment income? All of these income sources require some special tax treatment—be sure you know all the reporting traps and tricks to reducing some of them.
- *Employment Expenses.* Working from home? Earning commissions? Be sure to enter out-of pocket employment expenses on Form T777 *Employment Expenses* or the equivalent data entry screens in your software. Make sure Form T2200 *Declaration of Conditions of Employment* signed by the employer is in your file in case of audit.
- *Babysitting.* Use Form T778 *Child Care Expenses* or equivalent data entry screen. But save all your receipts—child care expenses are often audited.
- *Moving to Take a New Job or Go to School.* Claims for moving expenses are entered on Form T1-M or the equivalent data entry screens in your software. Again, audit-proof by having all your receipts on hand.

- *Truckers.* Meals and lodging expenses are entered on Form TL2. To audit-proof you'll need to produce distance logs and your T2200 form, signed by the employer.
- *Blue Cross and Charitable Donations at Work?* Be sure to pull these numbers from your cheque stubs to claim them on the medical expense and charitable donation screens. The numbers end up on Schedule 1 and can reduce taxes payable.

Tax Sleuthing

The most common errors result from lost receipts; it can pay well to hunt them down, as the following are also often audited:

- Employment expenses, which include costs of auto, use of home, promotional expenses for commissioned salespeople, tradesperson's tools, expenses of employed musician and artists, and saws for forestry workers.
- Child care expenses including the cost of nannies, boarding schools and camps; yes you can pay mom to babysit but no claims for payments to anyone you claim as a dependant.
- Moving expenses, including your real estate commissions and hotel costs can be deducted; so can some of the costs at the new location.

Tax Pro Alert

Consider consulting a tax pro if you are:

- Claiming employment expenses for the first time.
- Claiming child care expenses where one spouse is a student or infirm.
- Receiving employee stock options or low-interest loans to make investments.
- Making past service contributions to an employer-sponsored pension plan, or if you have over-contributed to your RRSP.
- Negotiating a job termination or new employment agreement.
- Receiving a lump-sum death benefit for a deceased employee.

10

Employment Income

Most Canadians have been employees at some time or another. By definition, you are considered to be an employee if you are in a "master-servant relationship" with a person who

- controls how and where you work;
- supplies the tools you need to do the work; and
- takes the risk of delivering and getting paid for the work.

Employees can be paid in cash, by way of salary, wages, bonuses, vacation pay or director's fees. They may also enjoy receiving taxable benefits. At tax filing time, these various types of remuneration are all included in Box 14 of the T4 slip. That makes tax filing seem simple—just enter the figures from the boxes on the slip in your software. But there is more to it, as we'll explain. In this chapter, find out:

- How to handle lost, late or multiple T4 slips;
- How to report the perks of your employment and how to reduce their costs;
- News about group health and sickness programs;
- Trick and traps in the reporting of your statutory deductions; and
- How to reduce withholding taxes so you get your refund all year long!

The T4 Slip. The T4 slip is the source document issued by employers to report your employment income and taxable benefits as well as statutory and other deductions withheld by or through the employer. You will receive a T4 slip by the end of February from each of your employers. It's easy to deal with them in your tax software. Just gather them all together and enter the numbers methodically. Yet there are a few circumstances that can trip you up.

CHECK IT OUT | **Did you make a transposition error?** T4 slip filing data entry errors can delay your return, so be sure to know how to avoid them... double check each figure as you enter it from the slips.

• **More Than One T4.** If there is more than one T4 slip, your tax software will lead you through a T4 slip summary to better manage the information.
• **Lost T4 Slips.** If you are missing a slip, contact the employer for a replacement or log on to your My Account page at CRA and view a copy of the slip as it was submitted to CRA. If the slip is not on your My Account page and you cannot locate the employer then take the information from your cheque stubs to estimate the amounts.
• **Late T4 Slips.** If you receive a T4 slip you forgot about after the return has been filed, don't file another return. Just send in a copy of the slip with a *T1 Adjustment Request* (Form T1-ADJ—you may or may not find it in your tax software as it cannot be filed electronically). You'll have to mail in the printed form to ask CRA to add the information to the return or you can request an adjustment online through your "My Account" page.
• **Employer Errors.** If the employer has made an error on the T4 slip, don't fix it on the return! CRA has been provided with a copy of that slip by the employer and will adjust your return to coincide with the slip they received. Errors on slips, including T4 slips, must be corrected by the company which issued the slip by filing an amended slip.

Perks. The perks of employment can make you wealthier, but don't double-report them on your tax return. Some are taxable; some are not.

 CHECK IT OUT | **What perks of employment are taxable?** Employees may receive taxable or tax-free perks, which should form part of every employment negotiation. Look for them in the "Other Information Section" of your T4 Slip.

Figure 2.1 Perks of Employment

Taxable Benefits*	Tax-Free Benefits
Board and lodging	Board and lodging at a remote worksite; limited meals or meal allowances for overtime
Rent-free and low-rent housing	Discounts on merchandise and subsidized meals; travel passes for the exclusive use of a transit company's employees
Free or discounted travel passes for a transit employee's family	Transportation to a special worksite or for security reasons, frequent flyer points unless converted to cash

Taxable Benefits*	Tax-Free Benefits
Personal use of employer's vehicle	Recreational facilities, including social or athletic club memberships
Gifts in cash or those that exceed $500	Non-cash gifts under $500; $500 more in cash for birthdays, anniversaries for an annual $1,000 max.
Value of holidays, prizes and awards	Employee counseling services for health, retirement or re-employment
Premiums for a provincial health or hospital plan	Premiums for a private health plan or lump sum wage loss replacement plan
Tuition paid for courses for personal benefits	Tuition paid for courses for the employer's benefit
Interest-free and low-interest loans	Certain moving expenses if required by the employer
Group sickness, accident or life plans	Employer's required contribution to provincial health and medical plans
Gains and income under employee stock option plans	Employer-paid costs of attendant for disabled employees or to cover away-from-home education due to work in remote worksites

* If these amounts include GST/HST, employees who are allowed to claim employment expenses may be able to claim a rebate on Line 457 by filing form GST/HST 370. If you receive this rebate, claim it as income in the following tax year on Line 104.

 New for 2013 | Employer's contributions to group accident and sickness plans will be taxable. These tax changes will not affect contributions made to a wage loss replacement plan that provides for periodic payments or contributions to a private health services plan.

Reducing Taxable Benefits. Taxable benefits can be reduced in certain cases. Note two in particular:

- *Personal use of employer-provided vehicle.* This is also known as a "standby" charge. Employees may elect to reduce this taxable income if personal driving is less than 1,667 kilometres per month. Reimbursements for supplementary business insurance, parking or ferry/toll charges are tax free.
- *Interest-free or low interest loans.* If the loans is used for investment purposes, including investment in an employer's stock, a deduction for the amount shown as a benefit is possible on Schedule 4 under carrying charges.

Other Employment Income. Perhaps you worked only occasionally and no T4 slip will be issued. In this case report your employment earnings on Line 104 Other Employment Income. This line is also used to report the following income sources:

- **Tips and Gratuities.** These sources are taxable and must be self reported. Don't make the mistake of missing this as tax auditing can be painful—often going back two or three years at a time—it's easy for CRA to determine what should have been reported when they check the records of the restaurant you worked for. After all, most tips are recorded right into the debit or credit card machines at the end of your meal. Also see below for information about electing to contribute to the CPP on these earnings.

- **Foreign Employment Income.** Report this income in Canadian funds. Any foreign taxes paid may qualify in Canada for a foreign tax credit. This is automatically calculated by your tax software. However, some restrictions may apply to NETFILING in these cases—if you are claiming less than the maximum foreign tax credit available to you for example.

- **Research Grants.** If you receive a grant to do research, my need only report your net income from your research. In other words, you can reduce the amount you report by any reasonable expenses to conduct the research. You can't, however, report a loss if your expenses exceed your income.

Statutory Deductions. Employment income is paid periodically—usually every two weeks, by cheque or direct deposit. A pay stub reports the gross and net earnings received, in an envelope or via direct deposit. In either case, keep a hard copy of your pay stubs in your tax files, as sometimes T4 slips get lost in the mail, employers go bankrupt or for any other reason, you may not receive yours. When this happens, you'll need to estimate your earnings and deductions. Tax time will be less frustrating in these cases if you have hard copy.

Statutory source deductions, those required under law, are contributions to the Canada Pension Plan (CPP), premiums for Employment Insurance (EI) and, of course, Income Taxes (IT) withheld to cover the taxes you owe on what you've earned.

It's possible to make an overpayment to CPP, EI and IT, especially if you worked for more than one employer. Your software will automatically calculate those overpayments and show the excess amounts on Line 435 for IT, Line 448 CPP premiums and Line 450 for EI premiums.

Note, if you lived in Quebec, you will receive a separate information slip for the provincial tax withholdings (PIT) and the Quebec Pension Plan (QPP).

CPP Premiums. CPP contributions must be made by employees between age 18 and 70 unless they opt not to contribute as described in "Optional CPP Contributions" below. The first $3,500 of employment income is exempt. Beyond that, premiums are 4.95% of earnings to the maximum contributory earnings. (This is $51,100 for 2013; the maximum CPP contributions for the year for employees amount to $2,356.20.)

CPP Proration. CPP contributions will also be prorated in the year the taxpayer turns 18 or 70, starts receiving CPP disability benefits or turns 65 while receiving CPP retirement benefits and opts not to continue contributing. This will also be the case in the year of death. Most tax software will calculate this automatically if you enter the correct year of birth.

Optional CPP Contributions. If you are receiving a CPP retirement pension and are also working, you must contribute to CPP at least until you reach age 65. If you're over 65, your employer will continue to deduct CPP premiums until age 70 unless you opt out of contributing by completing form CTP30 and submitting it to your payroll department. Contributions made after you begin receiving your CPP retirement pension will result in an increase in your CPP pension (called a **Post Retirement Benefit**) beginning in the following year. See Part 5 for more information.

You may also elect to "Opt In"—that is make CPP contributions on income sources from which your employer did not make those remittances. This includes your tips and gratuities, casual earnings, employment by a person registered under the *Indian Act* who received tax exempt salary, or income that you may have earned abroad for a Canadian employer, if CPP contributions were not made. See form CPT20 *Election To Pay Canada Pension Plan Contributions* and make this election by June 15, 2015. If your software includes this form, the amounts required to be paid will be automatically entered on Line 421.

EI Premiums and Exemptions. EI premiums must be paid by employees, regardless of age. The rate applicable for 2013 is 1.88% of insurable earnings to a maximum of $891.12 for the year. If you have more than one employer in the year, you may have more than the maximum deducted. Your software will calculate the overpayment using Form T2204 and apply for a refund of your overpayment for you.

Part-Time Worker? If your total insurable earnings for the year are $2,000 or less, you are not subject to EI premiums and any amounts withheld from your wages are refundable. The refund of excess premiums deducted is claimed on Line 450 of your tax return. Your software will calculate this automatically for you. This is often the case for students.

Software Tips. Your EI insurable earnings are shown in Box 24 of your T4 slip and most often match Box 14 unless your income exceeds the maximum insurable earnings ($47,400 for 2013). If Box 24 is blank, do not key zero into your software unless you are exempt, which is indicated by an "X" in Box 28 of your T4 slip.

Reduce Income Tax Withholding at Source. While most people are happy to get a refund at tax time, the government makes no interest payments on the use of your money all year long. That makes overpaying your taxes a bad investment. You will want to change that as you become more tax savvy. Here's what you should do to keep more of your money throughout the year:

1. *File your TD1 personal tax credits return.* Most of you will remember these forms—one of the first things you complete when you start a new job. There is both a federal and a provincial Form TD1. Your employer will deduct your tax based on your entries.

   Ideally these two forms should be given to you annually for review, because your changing personal circumstances and tax laws can affect your tax withholding rates.

The TD1 forms will tell the payroll clerk whether you are able to take advantage of non-refundable tax credits that could reduce your withholdings, like the age amount, pension income amount, tuition, education and textbook amounts, disability amount, caregiver amount or amounts transferred from spouse. Be proactive; it's your money.

2. *File Form T1213 to further reduce tax withholding.* A lesser known form rarely provided by the employer is Form T1213 *Request to Reduce Tax Deductions at Source.* You need to initiate this. It tells CRA that you qualify for deductions that will increase your tax refund like, for example, RRSP contributions, child care expenses, employment expenses, investment carrying charges, rental or business losses, deductible spousal support or non-refundable tax credits like charitable donations and medical expenses. By filing this form, you can get that refund with every pay, instead of waiting until spring.

    Here's what to do: Send the signed T1213 form to CRA, (attach details of your eligibility for the write-offs) who, in turn, will send the employer permission to reduce your withholding taxes.

3. *File Form TD1X if you earn commission income.* Commissioned sales employees may also adjust their tax withholdings to take into account their related expenses. The form to use is *TD1X Statement of Commission Income and Expenses for Payroll Tax Deductions.* It must be provided to the employer by January 31 or one month after start date.

    This requires an estimate of net commission earnings for the year and a reduction of those earnings by either last year's expense claim (*Form T777 Statement of Employment Expenses*) or an estimate of this year's expenses. Completing this form gives the employee the benefit of reducing the taxes remitted by the employer all year long, rather than waiting for a refund after filing the return. We will discuss employed commissioned sales people and their expenses later in this section.

Non-Statutory Deductions. Non-statutory deductions can also be important to the outcomes on your tax return—examples are contributions to your employer-sponsored pension plan (Registered Pension Plan), group health premiums paid through the employer, charitable donations made at work and union dues deducted. Your software will claim the appropriate deductions based on the entries you make from your T4 slips.

Employment Expenses. Most employees are not allowed to claim out-of-pocket expenses for the costs of going to work. Items such as the cost of driving to and from work, eating out at lunch or dry cleaning are not deductible. However, a non-refundable tax credit is provided for these purposes. It's called the ***Canada Employment Amount (CEC)*** and it's described in more detail in Chapter 18.

Other Itemized Expenses. Perhaps you're a commissioned salesperson who is required to negotiate contracts on behalf of your employer. Or you are required to work out of the family home and are eligible to claim home office expenses or perhaps, the family pays for child care in order for you to work. If any of these apply to you, they can result in additional deductions on your tax return. These deductions are covered in this part of the book.

Overseas Employment Tax Credit. If you are employed overseas for a period of more than six consecutive months beginning or ending in the taxation year and work for an employer resident in Canada or a Canadian-owned foreign affiliate and perform services outside Canada in connection with a contract for either the exploration for natural resources, or in any construction, installation, agricultural or engineering activity, you may be eligible for the Overseas Employment Tax Credit. This credit exempts a significant portion of your employment income from taxation in Canada. Note however, that this credit is being phased out. For 2013, the exempt portion is 60% of your foreign income to a maximum of $60,000. The maximum credit is reduced to 40% and $40,000 for 2014; 20% and $20,000 for 2015; and is reduced to zero for taxation years after 2015.

To claim this credit, use Form T626 *Overseas Employment Tax Credit* which must be certified by your employer.

 The Bottom Line | Employees have a great opportunity to use their employer's capital to cover current income needs and to save for future income requirements through various perks and benefits. The spending and saving decisions, however, are up to you.

11

RPP Contributions

Your employer can help secure your future income in retirement by offering an employer-sponsored pension plan. This can also be known as a Registered Pension Plan (RPP).

Not only does your employer contribute to the plan with you, the earnings in the plan accumulate on a tax deferred basis, so they grow exponentially. Having an RPP, though, can impact your ability to save separately in a private Registered Retirement Savings Plan (RRSP). Consider the following opportunities:

- How to make up for missed past service contributions to your RPP;
- Whether interest costs on loans for making those contributions are deductible; and
- What a PA, PSPA and PAR is and how they affect your RRSP contribution.

By knowing more about the tax strategies above, entering the right data in your tax software and then making good decisions about supplementing the employer's plan by contributing to your privately held RRSP, you'll be richer, sooner.

 CHECK IT OUT | **How do I maximize my employer-sponsored pension?** When you contribute to your employer-sponsored RPP, there will be deductions withheld and remitted into the plan for you. You will be able to deduct certain amounts based on your current year services, as shown in Box 20 on the T4 slip. Your software will post this amount to Line 207 of your tax return to claim a deduction.

Past Service Contributions. Sometimes you'll be able to make past service contributions, too. If you make contributions to top up prior years after 1990, those contributions are also deductible in the year and will be included in Box 20.

If you made past service contributions relating to years prior to 1990, those contributions will be shown on your T4 slip in Box 74 (if you were a contributor) or Box 75 (if you were not a contributor). Your claim for such contributions is limited as follows:

- You cannot claim more than $3,500 for past service contributions while you were not a contributor (Box 75).
- For contributions shown in Box 74, you cannot claim more than $3,500 less any other contributions deducted in the current year (current and past service while not a contributor).

Any amount contributed that cannot be deducted in the current year may be carried forward and claimed in a future year according to these same rules.

Software Tips. Each software package will have its own worksheet dealing with past service contributions for years prior to 1990, so follow the worksheet and make sure your claim follows the above rules. Also note any carry-forward amounts because you'll need to know them when you prepare next year's return. Your software may have a carry-forward form or screen that takes care of this for you.

Carry-forward Provisions on Restricted Deductions. While we see fewer of these claims now, it's important to note that if your deduction for past service contributions before 1990 was limited on your prior year return, you may be able to deduct those contributions in the current year. Undeducted contributions from prior years may be deducted following the same rules as outlined above for current year contributions. You'll have to add these amounts to the worksheet in your software for claiming prior-year contributions. This is a complicated process and it may be a good idea to *get some professional help* in this case to ensure future claims are maximized.

Interest Costs. Any interest you paid because you elected to make those past service contributions in instalments is handled as follows: the interest is deductible for tax purposes as if it were part of the past service contributions and deductions are limited to the rules outlined above for past service contributions.

 CHECK IT OUT | **How do I best manage my RRSP if I have an RPP?** You may not be able to contribute to your own RRSP, depending on how much was contributed to your RPP. You'll need to understand what the PA, PSPA and PAR acronyms are if you want to understand how the RPP and the RRSP provisions interact, so you can maximize contributions to each.

- **What's the PA?** When you contribute to a Registered Pension Plan or your employer contributes to your plan, your RRSP contribution room for the year is reduced. The amount of the reduction is called a Pension Adjustment (PA). The amount of your pension adjustment is shown in Box 52 or your T4 slip. This will not affect your current-year RRSP contribution limit as it is based on your 2012 income, but it will reduce your RRSP contribution room earned in 2013 and available in 2014.
- **What's a PSPA?** If you make past service RPP contributions, those contributions will also reduce your RRSP contribution room earned in the year. The reduction is called a Past Service Pension Adjustment (PSPA). You'll receive a T215 slip showing the amount. This will affect your RRSP contribution room for the following year and will be reflected in your RRSP contribution limit as indicated on your Notice of Assessment. Most software does not include the T215 form as it does not affect the current year.
- **What's a PAR?** In some cases, when you cease to be a member of a RPP and the benefits you receive from the plan are less than your accumulated pension adjustments, you'll receive a Pension Adjustment Reversal (PAR). The PAR is reported on a T10 slip and increases your RRSP contribution room for the next year.

The Bottom Line | Becoming wealthier has as much to do with maximizing your take-home pay as it does with negotiating employment benefits to create a future income in retirement. In addition, your employment income level and your contributions to your employer-sponsored pension contributions will affect how much you can contribute to your privately funded RRSP. Tax-astute employees will make sure current and future needs are adequately met with the help of Registered Pension Plans.

12

Should You Contribute
to an RRSP or PRPP?

Should you contribute to an RRSP (Registered Retirement Savings Plan) even if you have an RPP at work? Should you do so if you have contributed to the new PRPP (Pooled Retirement Pension Plan)? What is the difference between an RRSP and a PRPP?

An RRSP is a retirement savings plan registered by CRA. The contributions you or your spouse make to an RRSP are deductible on the tax return and all income earned within the plan is tax deferred until withdrawal. At withdrawal both principal and earnings are added into your income as pension income, fully taxable.

 The PRPP | A new type of private pension plan is available in federal workplaces this year and some workplaces in the Yukon, Nunavut, and North West Territories: the Pooled Retirement Pension Plan (PRPP). Other provinces are slowly following suit in passing enabling legislation. The amount that can be contributed is determined by your RRSP contribution room, and so the two plans are "joined at the hip" when it comes to understanding the tax rules on contribution.

However, on withdrawal, the PRPPs act like an employer-sponsored pension plan. That is, if benefits are paid as a life annuity, pension income splitting is possible with spouses and the pension income amount of $2,000 is claimable. Those withdrawal options will be discussed in more detail in Part 5.

Key Benefits. There are many benefits to making contributions to RRSPs and PRPPs, not the least of which is getting a larger tax refund so you can put away the most money possible to work for your own future. Consider these pluses:

- RRSP/PRPP contributions result in an immediate tax deduction for the principal, which reduces your tax bill in the current year, as well as your net income on Line 236.
- By reducing your net income, you will limit reductions of tax credits or social benefits you may be entitled to, including Employment Insurance.
- RRSP/PRPP deposits accumulate and grow on a tax-deferred basis (that is, earnings within the plan are not taxable until they are removed from the plan).
- Withdrawals of RRSP funds in a year when your marginal tax rate is lower will result in a net tax saving.
- Money may be borrowed on a tax-free basis from your RRSP to fund the purchase of a new home under the *Home Buyers' Plan* or to finance post-secondary education under the *Lifelong Learning Plan.*
- Starting at age 65, RRSP pensions may be split with your spouse to reduce the taxes payable on the receipt.
- PRPP pension income can be split with your spouse regardless of your age.

In this chapter, learn more about whether you qualify to make RRSP/PRPP contributions in order to take a deduction now or in the future, how you can get into some tax trouble with over-contributions, and participate in a case study in which you'll clearly see how lucrative an RRSP/PRPP deduction can be for you this year.

 CHECK IT OUT | **What are restrictions on RRSP/PRPP contributions?** You must have "earned income" to contribute. There are some rules to follow, as described below.

- **RRSP/PRPP Earned Income.** If you earn income from employment, self-employment, net rental income, CPP disability income or taxable support payments last year, you have "earned income" for RRSP/PRPP purposes this year. Many software packages will show you how this is computed in detail.

How Much Can You Contribute? Each year that you have earned income, you create RRSP/PRPP contribution room which you can use the following year. The contribution room you generate is the lesser of:

- 18% of your earned income for the prior year to an indexed annual dollar maximum ($23,820 for 2013; contributions based on 2012 income), less

- any pension adjustments (PA) from your employer-sponsored plans in the prior year. This is shown on Box 52 of the T4 slip and ends up on Line 206 of the return.

 New for 2013 | Your contribution room will also be reduced the following year if your employer made to a PRPP on your behalf. These amounts will be shown in the "employer contribution amount" box on your PRPP receipts and must be reported on line 205 of your return.

Do You Need to Use the Contribution Room? RRSP/PRPP contribution room is cumulative so if you generate contribution room and don't use it by making your maximum RRSP/PRPP contribution, the amount carries forward and you can make a larger contribution in a future year.

Maximum RRSP/PRPP Contributions. Each year your Notice of Assessment or Reassessment from CRA will show the maximum contribution that you can make for the next taxation year. This will include the "unused" room from the past, 18% of your earned income to the current dollar maximum, and adjustments due to changes in your RPP contributions or employer contributions to your PRPP. Your tax software will also keep track of this for you in your carry forward screens, provided you have entered all the numbers properly. You can contribute throughout the year, or within 60 days of the year end to make a tax deduction on this year's return.

Reporting RRSP/PRPP Contributions. You'll enter the information about the RPP and the PA on your employer-provided T-slips in the appropriate T4 screens; but you'll enter the information about your RRSP/PRPP contribution receipts on a different screen, which will link to Schedule 7. This screen will vary in name and composition by software. Start by entering your RRSP/PRPP contribution limit as shown on your Notice of Assessment or Reassessment for the prior year.

Next follow the screen to enter all of your RRSP/PRPP contribution receipts for the period from March 2, 2013 to March 3, 2014. The contribution date is important and that will be clear as you review the receipts. Any contributions made in the first 60 days after the tax year can be deducted on Line 208 of the T1 in either the prior tax year (2013 in this case) or the year of contribution (2014). For 2013 only, enter any PRPP contributions you made in January or February 2013 as these could not be entered on your 2012 return.

The deductible amounts will show up in two places on your return: Schedule 7, as mentioned and Line 208.

Undeducted RRSP Contributions From Prior Years. If you have undeducted RRSP contributions from prior years, you will need to enter those too. These amounts can be carried forward indefinitely for use in reducing income anytime in the future.

Example: Thomas contributed $5,000 to his RRSP last year because he had some extra money, but it turned out that he didn't need to claim the deduction. He has carried forward the undeducted contributions and plans to deduct them this year.

RRSP/PRPP Overcontributions. If you are at least age 18 you may overcontribute up to $2,000 above your contribution room to your RRSP. Otherwise, it's best to take overcontributed amounts above this out of the plan as soon as possible to avoid expensive penalties. See a tax professional to help you with this.

RRSP/PRPP Excess Contributions. If your RRSP overcontribution exceeds $2,000 at any time or you overcontribute to your PRPP, you are considered to have made an excess contribution. Excess contributions are subject to a penalty tax of 1% of the excess contribution per month for each month that they remain in your RRSP/PRPP.

Therefore, you should remove excess contributions as soon as possible after they are discovered. Contributions that are withdrawn will not be taxable if they have not been previously deducted. You'll have to file a Form T1-OVP *2013 Individual Tax Return for RRSP Excess Contributions* to calculate your overpayment tax. If you find that you have an excess RRSP/PRPP contribution, it's best to get professional advice to minimize your penalty tax and get your RRSP/PRPP contributions sorted out.

RRSP Home Buyers' Plan and Lifelong Learning Plan. If you participated in the *Home Buyers' Plan* or the *Lifelong Learning Plan*, you'll need to enter details on the appropriately names screen as well so your RRSP deduction can be claimed. The result will be posted to Schedule 7 for reporting to CRA. This information will be carried forward to assist with proper repayment scheduling as well. If you fail to repay amounts as they become due, the unpaid amounts will be added to your income.

Reducing Your Source Deductions: Recall that when you contribute to your RRSP, you can reduce your withholding taxes at source so you essentially get your tax refund with every paycheque.

✓ **CHECK IT OUT** | **How do I figure out what my take-home pay will be?** You can use the *Knowledge Bureau's Take Home Pay Calculator* to figure this out for yourself. Sign up for a free trial at http://www.knowledgebureau.com/calculators. Then figure out how an RRSP deduction can help you put more money in your pocket sooner, using your tax software.

Case Study | **How an RRSP Can Reduce Your Taxes**

Consider Rupert, who is single and 45 years old. In 2013, his firm closed and he found himself out of a job. His T4 slip shows $65,000 employment income, $2,356.20 in CPP contributions, $891.12 in EI premiums and $15,000 of income tax deducted. He is able to claim $4,500 in employment expenses.

He also has a T4E Slip showing the $10,000 EI in benefits he received. Because Rupert was on EI back in 2004, he is required to repay 30% of the EI he received. But, he may be able to avoid that repayment. How can making an RRSP contribution help?

You will see on the summary below that by making a $10,000 RRSP contribution, Rupert has changed his $1,990.46 tax bill into a $2,931.86 tax refund. The tax savings of $4,922 represents a 49% immediate return on his RRSP investment! Note, these figures will vary depending on province of residence.

 The Bottom Line | Remember, you're only required to pay the correct amount of tax, no more. Do all you can to minimize over-withholding, then invest the after-tax increases in your net pay in a tax-efficient investment like an RRSP, accelerating your journey to financial freedom. Need help? Ask your tax advisor before you finish with your tax filings for this year.

Knowledge Bureau® Excellence in Financial Education

Income Tax Estimator   Tax Year: 2013

Identification: Rupert					W/O RRSP	With RRSP
Province: Ontario		Children: 0		Age:	18 to 65	18 to 65
Total income						
Employment Income					$65,000.00	$65,000.00
Employment insurance benefits					$10,000.00	$10,000.00
				Total Income	$75,000.00	$75,000.00
Net income						
RRSP deduction					$0.00	$10,000.00
Employment expenses					$4,500.00	$4,500.00
Social benefit repayment (EI / OAS)					$3,000.00	$375.00
				Net Income	$67,500.00	$60,125.00
				Taxable Income	$67,500.00	$60,125.00
Refund or Balance owing						
				Federal tax	$11,800.73	$10,178.23
Federal non-refundable tax credits						
Basic personal amount	$11,038.00	$11,038.00				
CPP contributions	$2,356.20	$2,356.20				
EI premiums	$891.12	$891.12				
Canada employment amount	$1,117.00	$1,117.00				
Total	$15,402.32	$15,402.32				
x Credit rate:	15.00%	15.00%				
			Total federal non-refundable credits		$2,310.35	$2,310.35
Social benefit repayment (EI / OAS)					$3,000.00	$375.00
				Net federal tax	$12,490.38	$8,242.88
Provincial tax					$4,547.61	$3,872.79
Provincial non-refundable tax credits						
Basic personal amount	$9,575.00	$9,575.00				
CPP contributions	$2,356.20	$2,356.20				
EI premiums	$891.12	$891.12				
Total	$12,822.32	$12,822.32				
x Credit rate:	5.05%	5.05%				
			Total Provincial non-refundable credits		$647.53	$647.53
Provincial surtax (plus OHP)					$600.00	$600.00
				Net provincial tax	$4,500.08	$3,825.26
				Total Payable	$16,990.46	$12,068.14
Tax deducted, Instalments, or Provincial or other refundable credits					$15,000.00	$15,000.00
				Refund		$2,931.86
				Balance Owing	$1,990.46	

13

Employment Expenses

Do you spend money in the course of your work that's not reimbursed by your employer? Certain employees may, in fact, claim out-of-pocket expenses on their tax returns. However, the *Income Tax Act* is very specific about the expenses that may be claimed. Read on to find out more about:

- Claiming out-or-pocket expenses on Form T777 *Statement of Employment Expenses*;
- The required completion of Form T2200 *Declaration of Conditions of Employment*, by your employer;
- How the deductible expenses can differ depending on whether you are employed, an employed commissioned salesperson or self-employed;
- How artists and musicians, forestry workers, and tradespeople can benefit from limited claims, too.

Claiming Employment Expenses. The deduction for these costs will ultimately show up on Line 229 of the T1. It's a good idea to use the T777 as a guide to the receipts you need to look for. You'll also need to have the T2200 signed by your employer.

 CHECK IT OUT | **What out-of-pocket expenses can I claim?** This depends on whether or not you earn commissions under your contract of employment.

Employees may claim certain specific expenses of employment, depending on whether the employer will verify this was a necessary condition of employment. Commissioned sales people can claim more expense categories—sales and promotion expenses for example— because they are expected to foster relationships with clients in their negotiation of contracts for their employers. Let's discover who can claim what.

Employees on Salary Only. Those who earn salary only may deduct the following out-of-pocket expenses:

- accounting, but not including income tax preparation, except if you are a commissioned sales person
- legal fees may be claimed if incurred to establish a right to collect salary, wages or a retiring allowance or pension benefits, but these costs may not exceed the amount of those sources that you report in income. Any non-deductible components may then be carried forward and deducted in any of the seven subsequent tax years in which further income from these sources is reported. When pensions or retiring allowances are transferred to an RRSP, the deductible legal expenses must be reduced by the amount of the transfer.
- motor vehicle expenses (including Capital Cost Allowance (CCA)—the tax equivalent of depreciation, interest or leasing costs, as well as operating costs), but only if the employee is not in receipt of a non-taxable allowance for the use of the motor vehicle
- travel expenses, including rail, air, bus or other travel costs
- meals, tips and hotel costs, providing the excursion is for at least 12 hours and away from the taxpayer's metropolitan area. Meals and tips are subject to a 50% restriction.
- parking costs (but generally not at the place of employment)
- supplies used up directly in the work (stationery, maps, etc.)
- salaries paid to an assistant (including spouses or children if a salary equivalent to fair market value is paid for work actually performed)
- office rent or certain home office expenses (discussed later)
- Note: the cost of tools acquired by employed mechanics are generally not deductible, however a special rule exists for new tool costs incurred by apprentice vehicle mechanics and tools acquired by tradespersons.

Salary and Commission. Employees who earn their living negotiating contracts for their employers or selling on commission may claim for the expenses itemized above, as well as income tax preparation costs, legal fees incurred to defend charges incurred in the normal course of business, and auto and travel expenses.

This is allowed only if they are required to pay their own expenses and regularly perform their duties away from their employer's place of business. However, the expenses are categorized into two groups: deductible travel and deductible sales expenses. This is because you cannot claim sales expenses that exceed commissions earned in the year.

A. *Deductible travel expenses* allowed include:

- Auto operating expenses like gas, oil, repairs and fixed costs like licenses, insurance, interest, leasing and capital cost allowance. The latter three expenses are limited to annual maximums if a passenger vehicle is used. See Auto Expenses in the next section.

- Travelling expenses such as the cost of air, bus, rail, taxi or other transportation, which takes the employee outside the employer's metropolitan area. However, travel expenses are claimable only if the employee does not receive a tax-free travel allowance.

Note that when these two types of expenses only are claimed, the amounts may exceed commissions earned (as reported in Box 42 of the T4 slip) and excess expenses may be used to offset other income of the year. Your software will do that automatically for you.

B. *Deductible sales expenses* allowed include the expenses above plus:

- promotional expenses;
- entertainment expenses (subject to a 50% restriction for the personal component of the expense);
- home office expenses.

When you are claiming expenses under category B above, your claim *may not* exceed commissions earned in the calendar year (Line 102) *except* for interest and capital cost allowance on a motor vehicle.

Because your tax software will calculate this automatically, you may be at a loss to understand why the claimable amounts have been reduced. Worse, any restricted expenses are lost and cannot be claimed in a future year. New sales people are at risk.

Example: Sarah started her career selling real estate as an employed commissioned salesperson in November, and was so excited that she purchased $2,400 in promotional gifts for her future clients and prospects, a new computer and an iPhone. Her first commissions did not materialize until the next spring and to her dismay, her expenditures were not deductible. She could not carry them forward for use next year, either.

 CHECK IT OUT | **What errors do I need to avoid on asset purchases?** Deductible equipment costs are also subject to special rules. Employees are not allowed to make a claim for capital expenditures, like a computer or cell phone at all. However, leasing costs are deductible. In the case of the cell phone, air time is deductible.

The reason is this: the employer is expected to provide those assets for the employee. There are three exceptions: the purchase of vehicles, musical instruments or aircraft used in performing the duties of employment. Therefore, it is wise tax planning to lease computers, cell phones or other equipment.

Artists and Musicians. Artists and musicians may claim expenses for items specific to their profession, including capital cost allowance on musical instruments. These claims are limited to the lesser of $1,000 and 20% of the employee's income from related employment. Claims may be for such items as ballet shoes, body suits, art supplies, computer supplies, home office costs as well as rental, maintenance, insurance and capital cost allowance on musical instruments.

Forestry Workers. Employees working in the forestry industry may claim the actual costs of operating a power saw, including gas, oil, parts and repairs providing an itemized statement is prepared and saved in case of audit requests. The power saws may be written off in full but, in the case of a new saw, the claim must be reduced by trade-in value or sales proceeds received from the disposal of the old saw during the year.

Apprentice Vehicle Mechanics. Apprentice vehicle mechanics may claim expenses incurred in purchasing tools in excess of $1,500. If the taxpayer does not take the maximum deduction in the tax year, the unused portion may be carried forward to apply against income earned in a future year. Apprentice vehicle mechanics may also claim the Tradesperson's Tools deduction.

Tradespersons. Tradespersons are also able to claim a deduction (to a maximum of $500) for the cost of tools in excess of the *Canada Employment Amount* (CEA) for the year. If the cost of tools is less than the CEA, then no deduction is allowed. Electronic communication devices and electronic data processing equipment do not qualify as tools for the purposes of this deduction (i.e., a cell phone, PDA, tablet, or laptop is not a "tool").

Your software will likely have a section of the screen for claiming employment expenses dedicated to claims by musicians, artists, apprentice vehicle mechanics and tradespersons. Also see instructions for long distance truck drivers later in this section.

✓ CHECK IT OUT | **Can I get a GST/HST rebate on my employment expenses?** Employees who claim deductible employment expenses may be able to receive a rebate of the GST/HST paid using Form GST370 *Employee and Partner GST/HST Rebate Application* and make the claim at Line 457. Rebates received are added to income (on Line 104) in the year received, unless they apply to capital assets, in which case the cost base of the asset will require adjusting. These claims are often missed and can be complicated! Be sure to file an adjustment to prior-filed returns if you have missed it, with the help of a tax pro if necessary.

$ The Bottom Line | Employees may claim certain unreimbursed expenses of employment but Form T2200, *Declaration of Conditions of Employment, signed by the employer,* is required for each year in which tax-deductible expenses are claimed. This form must be kept on file for CRA to review. In addition, employees are subjected to a restricted list of possible expenses; your software will be programmed to account for these.

14

Auto Expenses and Home Office

Auto and home office expenses are common deductions for self-employed individuals, and certain employees who work from home offices. They are often audited, however, and the tax filing rules can be complicated. Tax software can do many of the calculations in the background, so you may wish to take some time now to find out how it's done.

We'll start with the simpler of the two: the expenses of the home workspace, and then take you through a case study in claiming auto expenses, too.

Home Workspace Expenses

To qualify to make home workspace expense claims, the space must be

- the place where the individual principally (more than 50% of the time) performs the office or employment duties, or
- used exclusively in the period to earn income from the office or employment and, on a regular and continuous basis, for meeting customers or other persons in the ordinary course of performing the office or employment duties.

The home workspace must be separated from other living areas in the home, but does not need to be a separate room. The home may either be owned by the taxpayer or rented. To determine the amount of deductible home office expenses, total expenses for the costs of maintaining the home are pro-rated by the following fraction:

$$\frac{\text{Square footage of the home workspace}}{\text{Square footage of the entire living area}} \times \text{Total Eligible Expense} = \text{Deductible Expenses}$$

Example: Jona is required to work out of his home as he manages his territory for a manufacturer. His total home expenses are $5,000. The office space is 200 square feet and the entire home is 2000 square feet. Jona can claim 200/2,000 x $5,000 = $500.

 CHECK IT OUT | **Can employed and self-employed people claim the same expenses?** The answer is no. Whether you are employed or self-employed matters, when claiming home office expenses, as described below:

Employees who do not earn commission may claim:

• utilities;
• maintenance and repairs, including light bulbs and cleaning supplies; and
• rent.

Commissioned sales employees can claim:

• utilities;
• maintenance and repairs, including light bulbs and cleaning supplies;
• rent;
• insurance; and
• property taxes.

Self-employed people can claim:

• utilities;
• maintenance and repairs, including light bulbs and cleaning supplies;
• rent;
• insurance;
• property taxes;
• interest; and
• capital cost allowance (although this is not a good idea if the home is your principal residence). CCA claims will compromise the principal residence exemption.

Claims are Limited to Income. An employee may not claim home office expenses that exceed income from the employer. A self-employed person may not create or increase a business loss with a claim of home office expenses. But the good news is that non-deductible home office expenses may be carried forward (indefinitely) to reduce income from that employer (or business) in subsequent years.

Example: Marcel is a commissioned salesman (no salary) who is required to provide his own office space in his home and pay his own expenses. He started his new position in December. He incurred $5,000 in qualifying home expenses, but only earned $200 commission in the tax year: His office comprises of 200 of the 2,000 square feet in his home.

The business use of home expenses are equal to $500 [200 sq ft/2000 sq ft) x $5,000]. As this is more than his employment income from that employer, he may only deduct $200. The remaining $300 may be added to the following year's home office expenses and deducted against income in the following year (if that income exceeds the expenses).

Documentation Requirements. It's important to gather all receipts and print the following from your software and keep on hand for audit:

- A completed *Form T2200 Declaration of Conditions of Employment*, on which the employer certifies that the employee is required to maintain the home office and pay the expenses of operating it. This form must be signed by your employer.
- Employees' claims for home workspace expenses are made on *Form T777 Statement of Employment Expenses*. It's a good idea to attach receipts in order behind this printed form.

Auto Expenses

The rules of claiming these costs are similar for both employed and self-employed people, and they are also among the most frequently audited. Taxpayers will want to keep proper documentation and make the claims correctly.

Eligibility. Automotive expenses can only be deducted if they are not reimbursed by the employer. An employee who receives a reasonable allowance for the use of the vehicle may not claim the related expenses. Otherwise, employees can deduct auto expenses when they pay their own auto expenses and are required to use their vehicle in carrying out their duties of employment.

For any expenses of employment to be allowed, the employer must sign Form T2200 *Declaration of Conditions of Employment*, stating the employee must use the auto for employment and is responsible for paying auto expenses, does not receive a reasonable allowance for auto expenses, and will not be reimbursed for them (if there is a partial reimbursement this must be accounted for).

Business vs. Personal Driving. For those who use their vehicle for both personal and business/employment purposes, it is necessary to keep an auto log that records distance driven for both purposes, for at least one year (the base year). After this you can keep the records for as few as three consecutive months. So long as your driving patterns do not vary on either side by more than 10%, you will be able to claim the ratio determined by the formula:

$$\frac{\text{Current year ratio for log period}}{\text{Base year ratio for same period}} \times \text{Base year full-year ratio}$$

Case Study | Plan Logbook Entries to Calculate Percentage Claimable

June's auto log book for 2011 shows that she drove her car 5,427 kilometres for business use and 3,414 kilometres for personal use (for a total use of 8,841 kilometres). She was able to deduct 61.38% of her auto expenses (5,427/8,841 x 100%). In 2012 June kept a logbook for three months and used that to estimate her business usage for the year.

For 2013, June must again keep a logbook for at least three consecutive months. Her logbook for the months of January, February and March 2011 showed 1,410 km business use and 850 kilometres personal use (total 2,260 km)—62.39% business use.

Her log book for the same three months in 2013 shows 1,842 km business use and 945 personal use (2,787 total)—66.09% business use.

Since the difference between the 2011 and 2013 usage was less than 10%, her business use percentage for 2013 is 66.09%/62.39% x 61.38% = 65.02%

Personal use includes vehicle use by other family members, friends, etc. In other words, total personal use of the vehicle is assessed, not just the use by the person using the auto for business or employment.

When there is a "*mixed use*" of the car, the expenses are first totalled. This is based on your actual receipts and a log of cash expenditures, like car washes or parking. Then the total costs are pro-rated by the allowable business use ratio, as calculated above.

Total Allowable Expenses x Allowable business use ratio

Your tax software will have a place for this calculation on an automobile expense screen.

 CHECK IT OUT | **What can I claim for my auto expenses?** There are two types of auto expenses that can be claimed: fixed and operating, and this can have an important effect on the type of car you buy or lease and how much money you spend.

A. Fixed Expenses include:

- Capital Cost Allowance (subject to a maximum cost of $30,000[4], plus taxes)
- leasing costs (subject to a maximum of $800 a month, plus taxes)
- interest costs (subject to a maximum of $300 a month)

---

[4] These maximums in effect at the time of writing.

B. Operating expenses include:

- gas and oil, tires, maintenance and repairs
- car washes (keep track of coin operated washes)
- insurance, license fees
- auto club memberships
- parking (generally parking expenses while on business are fully deductible and not subject to a proration for personal component)

In addition, you should know that in general, "cents-per-kilometer" claims are disallowed except in specific instances where a "simplified method" is allowed. These include claims for medical travel or certain moving expenses, but not employment expenses.

Cost of Car Matters. How much you can claim for fixed expenses is restricted, as you can see, and this depends on the cost of the car you drive and for what purposes. More complexity here: there are two types of vehicles for tax purposes, which depends on cost and use:

A. Passenger Vehicles (sometimes called luxury vehicles) are designed to carry no more than nine passengers and are not on the "specifically excluded" list below. The maximum claim for depreciation is $30,000 plus taxes if purchased or $800 a month plus taxes for leasing costs if leased. Interest will be restricted to $300 a month.

B. Motor Vehicles are vehicles that are not passenger vehicles. There are no restrictions on the deductible amount for depreciation, leasing or interest expenses. Vehicles are passenger vehicles if they are designed to carry nine or fewer passengers unless they fall into a specifically excluded list:

- ambulances, taxis, busses used in the business of transporting passengers;
- hearses and other vehicles used in the transport of passengers in the course of a funeral;
- any clearly marked emergency medical vehicle which is used to transport paramedics and their emergency medical equipment;
- motor vehicles acquired to be immediately sold, rented or leased;
- pick-up trucks that are used more than 50% of the time to transport goods;
- vans that are used more than 90% of the time to transport goods; and
- extended cab pick-up trucks used primarily for the transportation of goods, equipment or passengers in the course of earning or producing income at a work site at least 30 kilometres from any community having a population of at least 40,000.

Buying Your Car. Because of the rules above, the first rule to remember when buying a car "for tax purposes" is that you may not be able to write off the full cost if it is a luxury or passenger vehicle.

CHECK IT OUT | **How do I account for depreciation on my car?** The rules for claiming wear and tear or depreciation on an asset like a car can be complicated, as for tax purposes you will claim a deduction on a Capital Cost Allowance (CCA) Schedule, which applies a specific rate to specific classes of assets. If you're claiming the cost as part of your employment expenses, this CCA schedule will likely be associated with the T777 form. Set up your schedule as follows:

• **Motor Vehicles and Passenger Vehicles that Cost Less Than $30,000 Belong to Class 10.** A 30% Capital Cost Allowance (CCA) rate is used. CCA is used at your option, so if your income is not high enough, you can save your "*Undepreciated Capital Cost*" (UCC) balance to make a larger claim next year. Note, in the year that the vehicle is purchased, the claim is limited to 50% of the normal CCA allowed. This is known as the "half-year" rule.

Things get complicated when you dispose of these assets. If, for example, it was the last asset in the Class 10 pool of assets, the remaining balance must be deducted as a *Terminal Loss.* If other assets exist in the Class 10 pool, then the reduced CCA balance is used to calculate the CCA claim for the year.

If after removing the amount from the Class 10 pool, the balance in negative, this negative amount is taken into income as *Recapture*. This means you have taken too much for your CCA deduction over the years and must include the over-deducted amounts in income.

• **Passenger Vehicles Belong in Class 10.1 if They Cost More Than $30,000.** If your car cost $30,000 (plus taxes) or more, it is listed in a separate Class 10.1 and again qualifies for a 30% Capital Cost Allowance (CCA) rate, which your software will compute automatically. If your car cost $50,000 claim only $30,000 plus taxes. There is a "half-year rule" on acquisition: only 50% of the normal CCA is claimed in the year you acquire the luxury car.

Again, it gets more complicated: when you dispose of a Class 10.1 asset, there is another half-year CCA calculation. There is no terminal loss or recapture of capital cost allowance on the disposition of a Class 10.1 vehicle. This restriction reflects the fact that the class never included the full capital cost of the vehicle to begin with.

Change of Use Rules. If the use of a vehicle changes from business to personal use, the CCA pool must be adjusted. The estimated Fair Market Value of the vehicle at the time of the change must be removed from the CCA pool as a deemed disposition and this could cause some of the tax consequences described above (recapture or terminal loss for a motor vehicle or the half-year limitation for a passenger vehicle).

Interest Costs. Remember that your claim for interest costs will be restricted to $300 a month if you own a passenger vehicle. In a low-interest rate environment, this shouldn't be a big problem, but your software will be calculating the restriction, and you need to know why.

Leasing Costs. These costs will be restricted to $800 a month plus taxes on your tax return, something to think about before you lease the Bentley.

 The Bottom Line | Is it better to own or lease a car for tax purposes? Use your tax software to project forward your after-tax results for at least three years to work out any CCA restrictions, including the "half-year rules."

15

Claiming Child Care Expenses

Child care is expensive. Fortunately, you can look to the tax return for relief. The cost of paying a babysitter or nanny for the care of the children is tax deductible. This applies to costs incurred while the parent(s) works in employment or self-employment or attends school, full or part time. Grab a java now, sit back and enjoy as you learn more about:

- Claiming child care expenses on Form T778;
- Who the eligible child care providers can be—can you claim your mom, for example?
- Who the eligible children are—will your disabled adult child be claimable?
- What the eligible expenditures are and the maximum limitations for claiming them;
- What's not deductible;
- When higher earners can make the claim; and
- Who claims child care in the case of separated couples.

Making the Claim for Child Care. Use Form T778 *Child Care Expenses Deduction*; your software will then make the claim on Line 214, usually on the supporting individual with the lower net income, in the case of couples.

 CHECK IT OUT | **What expenses are deductible for babysitting costs?** Expenses are deductible for the care of dependent children who were under the age of 16 (at any time during the year) or who are physically or mentally infirm. An eligible child must be

- a child of the taxpayer, the taxpayer's spouse or the taxpayer's common-law partner's; or
- a child who was dependent on the taxpayer, or the taxpayer's spouse or common-law partner.

The definition of a child includes an adopted child or the spouse of a child of the taxpayer. If the child is not the child of the taxpayer or the taxpayer's spouse or common-law partner, then the child's net income must be less than the Basic Personal Amount.

Eligible Child Care Providers. Child care must be for services provided in Canada, although deemed residents living abroad qualify as well. The services must be provided by any of the following and receipts must be available to support the claim:

- a day nursery school or daycare centre;
- a day camp or day sports school;
- a boarding school or camp (including a sports school where lodging is involved);
- an educational institution for the purpose of providing child care services; or
- an individual who *is not*
  - the child's father or mother, or a supporting person of the child;
  - a person in respect of whom the taxpayer or a supporting person of the child has claimed a personal amount; or
  - a person who is under 18 years of age and related to the taxpayer.

Note: A deemed or factual resident of Canada who is not physically present in Canada may claim these expenses even though the services are not provided in Canada. There is also an exception to the residency requirements for commuters who live near the Canada-U.S. border as long as the child care expenses were provided at a location that was closer to the taxpayer's place of residence than any place in Canada where such child care services are available.

Eligible Child Care Expenditures. The following are expenses that may be claimed:

- babysitting costs;
- daycare costs;
- costs of a live-in nanny; which may include advertising, salary and benefits including the employer's portion of CPP and EI;
- lodging paid at boarding schools, day camps, overnight sports school and overnight camps to a maximum of:
  - **$100 per week** for each child age seven to sixteen for which the Disability Amount cannot be claimed; plus
  - **$175 per week** per child under seven for which the disability amount cannot be claimed; plus
  - **$250 per week** for each disabled child.

Ineligible Child Care Expenditures. The following may not be claimed as child care:

- medical or hospital care;
- clothing, transportation;
- tuition fees;

- board and lodging expenses except when they are included in the total charges for a boarding school, day camp or overnight sports school and do not exceed the weekly limits; and
- expenses which were not actually paid or which were or will be reimbursed.

Earned Income Limitation. The child care deduction is limited to two-thirds of the claimant's earned income. This includes:

- salaries and wages;
- net profits from self-employment;
- training allowances;
- income received under the Apprentice Grant program;
- the taxable portion of scholarships, bursaries, fellowships and research grants;
- disability pensions under Canada or Quebec Pension Plans;
- apprenticeship incentive grants received under the Apprenticeship Incentive Grant program administered by Human Resources and Social Development Canada; and
- any earnings supplement received under a project sponsored by the Government of Canada to encourage employment or sponsored under Part II of the *Employment Insurance Act* or any similar program.

On EI? No babysitting claimable. Note that Employment Insurance is not listed here. This means that child care cannot be claimed if this is your only income source.

Maximum Child Care Claims. The maximum claim you can make is the least of:

- the eligible child care expenses paid to eligible child care providers,
- two-thirds of your earned income, and
- the following limits:
  - **$4,000 for each child age seven to age sixteen** for which the Disability Amount cannot be claimed
  - **$7,000 for each child under age seven** for which the Disability Amount cannot be claimed
  - **$10,000 for each disabled child**

Form T778 *Child Care Expenses Deduction* does not apply the limit on a child-by-child basis. Therefore, if the taxpayer has two children under age seven and pays $10,000 for child care for one and $4,000 for the other, the entire amount may be deducted (if earned income is sufficient).

Students. In addition to the limitations for all taxpayers, students have the following limitations on their child care expense claims. *Full-time students* are limited to:

- $100 for each child age seven to age sixteen for which the Disability Amount cannot be claimed, plus

- $175 per child under age seven for which the Disability Amount cannot be claimed, plus
- $250 per disabled child

times the number of **weeks** of full-time attendance.

Part-time students are limited to:

- $100 for each child age seven to sixteen for which the Disability Amount cannot be claimed, plus
- $175 per child under seven for which the Disability Amount cannot be claimed, plus
- $250 per disabled child

times the number of **months** of part-time attendance.

Who makes the claim? Generally, child care expenses may only be claimed by the supporting person with the lower income. A supporting person includes:

- The child's parent.
- The spouse or common-law partner of the child's parent.
- Anyone making a claim for the Amount for Eligible Dependants, Amount for Infirm Dependants Over 18, or Caregiver Amount in respect of the child.

Separated Families. If you were married or living common-law during the year but separated and did not reconcile, each parent may claim child care for the time the expense was incurred and the child lived with the parent. The common-law couple will be considered to be separated if they lived apart for a period of 90 days or more during the tax year and did not live together any time during the first 60 days of the new year. Otherwise, if you live together and support the child, you are considered to have a conjugal relationship in which net income levels are compared.

Child Care Claims by Lower Earners. The person who usually makes the claim for child care is the one whose net income is the lowest, before claiming child care expenses, EI repayments payable or OAS clawbacks. In the unlikely event that two supporting persons have identical incomes, no deduction may be made unless the taxpayers jointly agree which one will make the claim.

Child Care Claims by Higher Earners. The higher income person may only claim child care expenses during periods in which:

- the lower earner was a full- or part-time student
- the lower earner was incapable of caring for the children because of mental or physical infirmity
- the lower earner was confined to a prison or similar institution for at least two weeks

- the higher income spouse was separated from the lower earner due to a breakdown in their relationship for a period of at least 90 days but they have reconciled within the first 60 days after the taxation year.

The claim for babysitting costs when the lower earner is a student will depend on whether you study full or part time:

- When the lower-income taxpayer is a part-time student, the limits to part-time students apply to the claim made by the higher-income taxpayer.
- When the lower-income taxpayer is a full-time student, or was incapable of caring for the children because of the three circumstances above (infirmity, imprisonment or separation), the limits to full-time students apply to claims made by the higher-income taxpayer.

Restrictions to Disability Amounts. Amounts claimed for child care expenses have a negative effect on the Disability Amount. The Disability Amount for a dependant who is under 18 includes a "child supplement" which is reduced by any child care expense claim in excess of an indexed amount. See the Appendices for the current supplement amount and the current child care expense limitation.

Receipts for Expenses. Receipts for child care expenses do not have to be filed with the return but should be maintained for inspection by CRA. These claims are often audited. Receipts for amounts paid to individuals must include the caregiver's social insurance number unless they are paid to individuals who are not Canadian residents.

 The Bottom Line | The child care expense deduction reduces net income and therefore, like Registered Retirement Savings Plan (RRSP) contributions, is a valuable contribution in increasing tax credits like Canada Child Tax Benefits and the Working Income Tax Benefit. It also reduces taxes payable, so be sure you save all babysitting receipts.

16

Claiming Moving Expenses

The deduction for moving expenses is possibly the most lucrative on the tax return—often in the five figures—so you'll want to be sure you take advantage of it. This deduction is claimed on Line 219 and Form T1-M *Moving Expenses Deduction*. It is available to employees, self-employed persons and students. In this chapter, find out more about:

- The required distance of the move;
- Whether you need to move to a job, or if retirement moves qualify;
- What expenses qualify—will staying en route at a hotel, for example, count?
- What expenses don't qualify;
- Whether students can make the claim;
- What happens if income is too low to benefit from the deduction;
- How to salvage a claim if you've lost your receipts; and
- What to claim if you've received a reimbursement from your employer.

What Moves Qualify? To be eligible, the new home must be at least 40 km closer to the new work location than the old home. The distance is measured by the shortest normal route open to the travelling public. Generally the move must be within Canada, although students may claim moving expenses to attend a school outside Canada if they are otherwise eligible.

Expenses may be claimable on moves to Canada if the taxpayer is a full-time student, or a factual or deemed resident. Moves from Canada may also qualify if the student is a full time student, or a deemed or factual resident.

CHECK IT OUT | **Do I have to earn income at the new location to qualify?** The answer is yes and it must be actively earned. That means moves to a retirement home won't qualify unless you work or are self-employed at the new location. Certain students may also make the claim. Income includes:

- salary, wages (including amounts received under the *Wage Earner Protection Program Act* in respect of work at the new location); or
- self-employment income.

In addition, the taxpayer must establish a new home where the taxpayer and family will reside. The following income sources earned at the new location are **not** qualifying income for the purposes of claiming moving expenses:

- investment or pension income
- Employment Insurance benefits
- other income sources, except taxable student awards (see below).

What this means is that if you are unemployed and move to get a job in another province, you'll have to earn qualifying income before moving expenses are claimable. In another example, those who move and retire will need to get a job or start a business, at least for a little while, if they want to have qualifying income against which to deduct moving expenses.

Carryover Periods. If the taxpayer's income at the new location is not sufficient to claim all moving expenses in the year of the move, they may be carried forward and applied against income at the new location in the following year or years.

Since 1997, expenses relating to the move that are not paid until the next taxation year may be deducted in the year paid if income at the new location is sufficient or they may be carried forward to the following years.

Eligible Moving Expenses. Most expenses for moving to the new location are eligible and include the following:

- **Selling the Old Home.** Costs of selling the former residence, including
  - real estate commissions,
  - penalties for paying off a mortgage,
  - legal fees, and
  - advertising costs
- **Waiting to Sell the Old Home.** Costs of keeping a vacant old residence (to a maximum of $5,000) while actively attempting to sell it, including
  - mortgage interest,
  - property taxes,

- insurance premiums, and
- heat and power

- **Purchasing the New Home.** Expenses of purchasing the new home (as long as the old home was owned), including
  - transfer taxes, and
  - legal fees
- **Costs en Route.** Temporary living expenses, (meals and lodging) for up to 15 days
- **Removal and Storage Costs** including
  - insurance for household effects, and
  - costs of moving a boat, trailer, or mobile home (to the extent the costs of moving the mobile do not exceed the costs of moving the contents alone)
- **Transportation and Other Costs:**
  - costs of meals en route (100%—no 50% restriction),
  - cost of cancelling an unexpired lease, and
  - cost of revising legal documents to show the new address, replacing driver's licenses and auto permits, cost of utility connections and disconnections.

Ineligible Moving Expenses. The following expenses are not deductible moving expenses:

- expenses to make the former property more saleable,
- losses on the sale of the former property,
- expenses incurred before the move (such as house hunting or job hunting),
- value of items that could not be moved (plants, frozen foods, paint, cleaning products, ammunition, etc.),
- expenses to clean a rented residence,
- replacement costs for items not moved such as tool sheds, firewood, drapes, etc.,
- mail forwarding costs,
- cost of transformers or adaptors for household appliances,
- GST on new residence, and
- expenses that are reimbursed.

Home Relocation Loans. Sometimes an employer will require an employee to relocate to another part of the country. In such cases, it is not unusual for a low-interest or interest-free housing loan to be granted to cushion the costs of the move. That benefit (the difference between the *prescribed rate of interest* and the interest rate the employee paid) is a taxable benefit. However a home relocation loan deduction may be taken to offset such a benefit on Line 248. The employee must move at least 40 km. closer to the new work location to qualify.

The maximum annual tax-free benefit is equivalent to the benefits arising from an interest-free housing loan of $25,000 x the prescribed rate of interest, and this will available for the first five years of the loan. The prescribed rate at the time the loan was taken will remain in effect for the full five-year period, so in the current low interest rate environment, it is important to compute the net tax liability being incurred on this arrangement. The amount of the benefit that you are eligible to deduct will be shown in Box 37 of your T4 slip. Your software will post this amount to Line 248 automatically.

The prescribed rate of interest is set quarterly by CRA and is calculated as the average yield on the three-month Treasury Bills sold in the first month of the preceding quarter, rounded up to the nearest percentage point. For the first three quarters of 2013, the rate was 1%; for the last quarter it was 2%.

Special Rules for Students. Students moving to attend full-time courses at a post-secondary school (or to work as a co-operative student in an industry relating to academic studies), qualifying income against which to claim moving expenses may be the taxable portion of research grants, or other awards (e.g. prizes for achievement). Students may also claim moving expenses against income earned at summer jobs or employment/self-employment.

A full-time student is defined as someone who regularly attends college, university or other educational institution at a post-secondary level and is taking at least 60% of the usual course load. Correspondence or a few evening courses will not be sufficient to qualify for these purposes.

Moves Outside Canada. Expenses for moves between two locations outside Canada may be possible if the taxpayer is a deemed resident or factual resident of Canada and the move was taking place from the place the taxpayer ordinarily resided, to a new place where the taxpayer will ordinarily reside.

Simplified Method. Travel expenses may be calculated using a "rate per kilometre" basis rather than claiming the actual amount spent and saving receipts. This method requires a record of the distance traveled during the move. The rate is calculated based on the province in which the move began. The rates allowed for the prior year are announced by CRA in January. Meals en route may also be charged at a flat rate per meal ($17.00 currently) with a maximum of three meals per day (total $51.00). Subscribe to *Knowledge Bureau Report* for a free update at the start of every year, or check the CRA website.

Reimbursements by Employers. Taxpayers who receive reimbursements for moving expenses may only deduct expenses if the amount received as a reimbursement is included in income, or if the amounts claimed are reduced by the amount of the reimbursement.

 The Bottom Line | Moving expenses are very lucrative. Enter your earned income at the new work location in order for your software to calculate the allowable amounts. Be sure to keep a record of the carry forward amount if there is no income at the new work location. You'll need to enter that claim next year, too, unless your software does that for you.

17

Special Situations: Truckers and Others

In this chapter, we would like to take a closer look at employees for whom there are special tax deductions on the T1:

- Line 229—Transport Employees,
- Line 244—Canadian Forces Personnel and Police,
- Line 249—Employee Stock Options, and
- Line 255—Northern Residents.

Transport Employees

Transport employees may deduct board and lodging expenses on *Form TL2 Claim for Meals and Lodging Expenses* and report the deductions on Line 229 if they incurred them in the course of their employment. The employer must verify the status of employment and the requirement for the employee to pay expenses by completing the *Employment Information* section and signing the TL2 form and the employee must keep trip logs to support claims for meals and lodging. Qualifying employees must work for:

- Airline, railway, bus and trucking company employees, or
- Be hired as employees whose employer's principal business is to transport goods, passengers, or both.

In the course of their work, they also must:

- regularly travel away from the municipality and, if there is one, the metropolitan area where their home terminal is located,
- use vehicles provided by their employers to transport goods or passengers.

✓ **CHECK** | **Do I have to keep receipts to make my meal claims?** Truckers may
IT OUT | make claims for meals using one of two methods:

- *the "simplified method"* which allows one meal every four hours from checkout time, to a maximum of up to three meals per 24-hour period. Claims can be made for a flat rate per meal, without being required to produce receipts. The amount that can be claimed is $17 per meal (maximum $51 per 24-hour period). For trips in Canada, the $17 limit is in Canadian dollars. For trips in the U.S., the amount is $17 U.S.
- *the "detailed method"* whereby claims may be made for the amount shown on actual receipts.

Day Trips. Workers who are regularly required to travel away from their municipality but are occasionally scheduled on runs of 10 hours or less are expected to eat before and after work and therefore may only claim one meal per day on such runs.

Work Crews. Special rules apply for crews of workers who are provided cooking facilities. Under the batching method, receipts are not required but the claim is limited to $34 per day.

Restrictions for Claiming Meals. The 50% meal restriction is modified for long-haul truck drivers who may claim 80% of meal costs, but only if they qualify as long-haul drivers. Your software will do the calculations, but based on your proper theory selections.

The 80% claim is limited to an employee whose principal duty or an individual whose principal business is to drive a long-haul truck in transporting goods, and to employers who pay or reimburse such expenses. In addition, the following criteria must be met:

- a long-haul truck is one with a gross vehicle weight rating in excess of 11,788 kg;
- the enhanced deductibility percentage applies only to eligible travel, which is a period during which the driver is away for at least 24 continuous hours from the employer's municipality or metropolitan area to which the employee reports (employed drivers) or the municipality where the driver resides (self-employed drivers);
- the trip must involve the transport of goods to or from a location at least 160 km from the location described above.

Claiming Lodging Expenses. Claims for lodging must be made using the detailed method—i.e. the actual amounts spent must be claimed. All claims must be supported by receipts.

GST/HST Rebate Possible. There is more good news. Employees who claim deductible expenses such as the Claim for Meals and Lodging Expenses may be able to receive a rebate of the GST/HST paid using Form GST370 *Employee and Partner GST/HST Rebate Application* and making the claim at Line 457. Rebates received are added to income in the year received.

The Bottom Line | Long distance truck drivers are in a good position to make lucrative claims for meals and lodging with a variety of filing options. However, these claims are frequently audited; be sure trip logs are available and if the claims are too complicated—especially the GST/HST Rebate, do see a tax pro for help.

Canadian Forces Personnel and Police

Certain members of the Canadian Forces or a Canadian police force serving on a deployed operational mission will be entitled to deduct from taxable income the amount of employment earnings from that mission.

The income is reported on Line 101 as usual and is therefore included in the taxpayer's net income, which is used to calculate non-taxable and refundable credits like the Canada Child Tax Benefits (CCTB), Goods and Services Tax Credit (GST/HSTC), several provincial credits, etc. The deduction is claimed at Line 244. The income is also included in earned income for RRSP purposes with no adjustment for the deduction.

Software Tips. Your tax software will handle this claim by automatically claiming the deduction when you enter the amount shown in Box 43 of your T4 slip.

 CHECK IT OUT | **Can all military personnel make this claim?** The employee must be serving on a deployed operational mission that is assessed for risk allowance 3 or higher (as determined by the Department of National Defence) or a prescribed mission. Lower-risk missions may also qualify if designated. The deduction will be limited to the lesser of

- the employment income earned while serving on the mission, and
- the maximum rate of pay earned by a non-commissioned member of the Canadian Forces (approximately $6,000 per month) to the extent that the employment income is included in computing the taxpayer's income for the year.

Selected Canadian Forces missions assessed for risk allowance 2 (as determined by the Department of National Defence) will be *"prescribed missions"* under *Income Tax Regulation* 7400, including the following:

- Operation Calumet (Middle East—Sinai);
- Operation Jade (Middle East—Jerusalem and Damascus);
- Operation Hamlet (Haiti);
- Operation Gladius (Golan Heights); and
- United Nations Mission in the Sudan—Civilian Policing Component (Sudan—Kartoum)

The Bottom Line | Taxpayers who qualify for this deduction and have other sources of income may want to adjust the tax withholding on that other income or any instalment payments they may have been planning to make as they will likely be in a lower-tax bracket as a result of this deduction.

Employee Stock Options

An employer may provide its employees the opportunity to purchase shares in the employer's corporation at some future date, but at a price that is the current market price when the option is granted (the exercise price). There are no tax consequences when the option is granted.

However, when the employee exercises these security options (also referred to as stock options) it will give rise to a taxable benefit. The benefit is calculated as the difference between the market value of the shares purchased and the exercise price. This benefit is included in income then, but may qualify for a Stock Options Deduction on Line 249.

 What can I claim as a deduction? The amount of the security options deduction is one-half of the taxable benefit and will be detailed in Box 39 (for a CCPC) or Box 41 of the employee's T4 slip. The tax treatment differs, however, depending on whether a Canadian Controlled Private Corporation (CCPC) or a public corporation grants the options.

- *Options Granted by a CCPC.* The taxable benefit included in employment income is deemed to have arisen only when the employee disposes of the shares. The security options deduction is available provided only that the employee held the shares for at least two years before disposing of them.
- *Options Granted by a Public Corporation.* Where the option is granted by a public corporation or by a private corporation that is not Canadian-controlled, the taxable benefit is deemed to have arisen when the employee exercises the option.

For options exercised after February 27, 2000 and before March 5, 2010, employees who would otherwise be taxed on stock option benefits in the year the option is exercised could elect to defer a portion of the security options benefit (up to $100,000) until the shares were disposed of by filing Form T1212 *Statement of Deferred Security Options Benefits* with the tax return each year.

However for options exercised after March 5, 2010, this deferral opportunity is not available. The following rules now apply:

1. When an employee has deferred stock option taxable benefits and subsequently disposes of the securities, the taxable benefits must be reported on Line 101. If the employee is still employed by the same employer, the benefit may be included in Box 14 of the T4 slip. If the employee is no longer employed with the same employer, the amount is calculated on Form T1212.

2. In a year in which a taxpayer is required to include a deferred securities option benefit in income, it will be possible to elect to pay a tax equal to the taxpayer's proceeds of disposition of the optioned shares. (In Quebec the tax is 2/3 of the proceeds.) This election is made on form RC310 *Special Tax On Disposition Of Securities Acquired Under An Employee Securities Option Program* and will make sense when the proceeds are less than the taxes payable on the deferred benefit—that is when the value of the stocks has decreased by more than 80% since the option was exercised.

Software Tips. In all cases except the RC310 election, your software should post the amounts to the proper lines based on your entries for Box 39 or Box 41 on your T4 slip and your entries on Form T1212 if you have deferred benefits.

 The Bottom Line | It's wonderful when an employee can participate in an employee stock option plan. However because of recent complexity, consult with a tax pro to ensure you are claiming your benefits and later, the capital gains and losses on disposition properly.

Northern Residents Deduction

If you lived in a prescribed northern or intermediate zone for a period of at least six consecutive months beginning or ending in a taxation year, you may claim the Northern Residents Deduction on Line 255 by filing Form T2222 *Northern Residents Deductions*. These zones are published in CRA's website at http://www.cra-arc.gc.ca/tx/ndvdls/tpcs/ncm-tx/rtrn/cmpltng/ddctns/lns248-260/255/zns-eng.html.

This claim may also be made on the final return of a deceased taxpayer if the deceased lived in a prescribed zone for six months prior to death.

There is no requirement to make income to make this claim; however, because it's a deduction, it will only benefit those with taxable income. It cannot be carried back or forward if you don't use it this year.

CHECK IT OUT | **What is the amount of the Northern Residents Deduction?** Two types of deductions are available: a residency deduction and a travel deduction, and your software will usually calculate these amounts for you.

The residency deduction is equal to the lesser of:

- 20% of the individual's income for the year, and
- a percentage of:
  - $8.25 for each day in the year in the period in which the individual resided in the prescribed zone (the basic residency amount), plus
  - $8.25 for each day in the year in the period that the individual maintained and resided in a self-contained domestic establishment in the prescribed zone and no other individual residing in that dwelling claimed a residency deduction for that day (the additional residency amount).

For taxpayers who lived in a prescribed northern zone, the percentage applied is 100%. For taxpayers who lived in a prescribed intermediate zone, the percentage applied is 50%. Employees in prescribed zones may also receive a tax-free benefit for the cost of housing. See *Perks* in earlier chapters in this section.

The travel deduction is provided to an employee or a member of the employee's household for travel expenses incurred in connection with:

- any trips made to obtain medical services not available locally, and
- a maximum of two trips per year for other reasons, to the extent that the value of the benefits is included in employment income.

For trips that begin in one year and end in the next, the claim should be made in the year that the taxable benefit appears on the taxpayer's T4 slip. If the amount will not appear on the T4 slip, claim the trip in the year that the trip began and include the value of the benefit provided by the employer in income. The maximum claim for each eligible trip is a percentage of the lowest of the following amounts:

- the travel benefits received from the employer for the trip (and included in the taxpayer's income),
- the total travel expenses for the trip, and
- the cost of the lowest return airfare available at the time of the trip between the airport closest to the taxpayer's residence and the nearest designated city. The following cities are designated for this purpose:

  - Calgary, AB
  - Edmonton, AB

- Halifax, NS
- Moncton, NB
- Montréal, QC
- North Bay, ON
- Ottawa, ON
- Québec City, QC
- Saskatoon, SK
- St. John's, NL
- Toronto, ON
- Vancouver, BC
- Winnipeg, MB

Travel expenses include any of the following amounts:

- air, train, and bus fares;
- vehicle expenses (actual expenses or a prescribed per kilometer amount);
- meals; hotel and motel accommodations, and camping fees; and
- other incidental expenses, such as taxis and road or ferry tolls.

For taxpayers who lived in a prescribed northern zone, the percentage applied is 100%. For taxpayers who lived in a prescribed intermediate zone, the percentage applied is 50%. For many taxpayers living in a prescribed intermediate zone, it may make more sense to claim the medical travel as a medical expense. Note, however, that no claim may be made for medical travel if the same expenses are claimed by anyone as a medical expense. See Chapter 26.

 The Bottom Line | Use the power of your tax software to help you claim every deduction an employee is entitled to: from sales expenses to auto and home office, to the specialized deductions for those who live in the north, move or have babies. Print each "auxiliary" tax form and attach receipts for use in case of audit.

18

Schedule 1 Tax Credits: Claiming Costs of Going to Work

Employees will often qualify for non-refundable tax credits that are not specific to their expenditures at work. In this chapter we will discuss three of them: public transit costs, medical expenses and charitable donations. They are found on Schedule 1 of the T1.

Canada Employment Amount

Anyone who reports employment income is entitled to claim the Canada Employment Amount. This amount, which is the lesser of the employment income reported on lines 101 and 104 and $1,117 (for 2013) is designed to help offset the normal expenses of earning employment income which cannot be claimed. Such expenses include the cost of diving to and from work, the cost of normal work clothes and their maintenance (such as dry cleaning). Your software should automatically claim the Canada Employment Amount on Schedule 1, Line 363 if you enter employment income.

Amount for Public Transit Passes

Riding the bus or subway these days? Keep your receipts because a non-refundable tax credit is available on Schedule 1, Line 364 for the cost of an eligible public transit pass. If your employer paid for your passes, the amount you can claim is shown in Box 84 of your T4 slip (you can also claim the amount shown on your spouse's T4).

CHECK IT OUT | **Who can claim it?** Either spouse may make the claim for eligible transit costs of the two parents and the dependent children under 19 years of age at the end of the year, or one person can make the claim for all. If the claim is split between two taxpayers the total amount claimed may not exceed the maximum allowed.

An eligible public transit pass includes:

- a document issued by or on behalf of a qualified Canadian transit organization that identifies the right of an individual to use public commuter transit services of that organization on an unlimited number of occasions and on any day during which the services are offered during an uninterrupted period of at least 28 days,
- an electronic payment card, provided the card provides at least 32 one-way trips in a period not exceeding 31 days, or
- a weekly transit pass covering a period of 5 to 7 days, so long as the taxpayer purchased at least four consecutive weekly passes.

A qualified Canadian transit organization is one that is authorized under a law of Canada or of a province to carry on a business in Canada (through a permanent establishment in Canada) that is the provision of public commuter transit services.

"*Public commuter transit services*" have a specific definition:

- the services must be offered to the general public to and from places in Canada;
- the individual would return daily to the place of their departure; and
- the services have to be offered ordinarily for a period of at least 5 days per week by means of a bus, ferry, subway, train, or tram.

A transit pass will qualify if it displays all of the following information:

- an indication of the duration pass;
- the validation date or period;
- the name of the transit authority or organization issuing the pass;
- the amount paid for the pass; and
- the identity of the rider, either by name or unique identifier.

If the above information does not appear on the transit pass, the taxpayer should obtain a dated receipt, or retain cancelled cheques or credit card statements, to support the claim.

Is There a Maximum Claim? There is no maximum dollar limit for these claims. The cost of the passes must be reduced by any reimbursement received from an employer unless that reimbursement was included in income.

Medical Expenses for Employees

Almost everyone misses claiming medical expenses every year. You want to avoid this because there is a very lengthy list of provisions that can make a difference on your return.

For employees this begins with claiming the group medical expenses you might be paying for every two weeks. This is one of those tax credits where your tax software will rely on you to give it full and complete information. It can then do the calculations in the background properly, and even optimize the claim.

As long as the taxpayer is a resident of Canada, expenses incurred abroad are also claimable, including Blue Cross and other travel or private health insurance premiums. Blue Cross and similar private health insurance premiums are often deducted by the employer; the amount paid by the employer and included in the employee's income will be shown on the T4 slip; amounts paid by the employee will likely be shown on pay stubs.

For more on claiming medical expenses, see Chapter 26.

Charitable Donations on the T4 Slip

A non-refundable tax credit for charitable donations may be claimed to reduce taxes payable. If you are employed, you may have given a donation at work. Look for this on your T4 Slip, box 46. Your software will have automatically entered it on Schedule 9 *Donations and Gifts*, and to the non-refundable credits on Schedule 1 *Federal Tax,* Line 349. Enter other donations you make outside of work, on the Donations data entry sheet. What's important is to consider combining these donations with your spouse's for a higher claim.

For more on claiming charitable donations, including the new First-Time Donor's Super Credit see chapter 29.

 The Bottom Line | The non-refundable tax credits which apply at work: public transit costs, medical and charity expenditures will help you to reduce your federal and provincial taxes payable. You can combine these claims with the costs your family members incurred too.

19

Severance and Unemployment

Losing a job—especially unexpectedly—can be a difficult life event. You should know how to keep the most of a lump sum that might come your way. The taxes on this lifeline can rob you of precious resources while you look for new work or arrange for your retirement income. There are also investment planning decisions to be made.

Begin by answering the common "trigger questions" most people in this situation have:

- Is termination payment acceptable?
- Will you want to contest the termination?
- Do you need to be introduced to a broader professional team that may include lawyers and accountants, recruitment services, or credit counselors?
- How can you develop new networks of potential influencers to assist in seeking the next opportunity?
- Will you be employed or self-employed in your future?

If illness is a reason for job termination, financial relief may be available by applying for the Canada Pension Plan disability benefits, Worker's Compensation or Wage Loss Replacement Plans.

In this chapter we will discuss two important income sources to those who lose a job: severance or retiring allowances and Employment Insurance and take you through a case study to illustrate some tax strategies.

Retiring Allowances

Employees who are leaving their jobs and who receive job termination payments or retiring allowances should do some tax planning perhaps with RRSP contributions and other income splitting or deferral options.

 CHECK IT OUT | **How can I keep more of my severance package?** An RRSP contribution can help you keep more of your retiring allowance. If adding your retiring allowance to your income brings you into a higher tax bracket, you should consider transferring at least enough of the retiring allowance to your RRSP so that you don't go into that higher tax bracket. The case study in Chapter 12 provided a good planning example.

RRSP Rollovers. You may receive an "eligible" retiring allowance or an "ineligible" allowance, and this will show up on your T4 slip. Here's what this means:

- *Eligible Allowances.* The portion of your retiring allowance that is "eligible" (shown in Box 66) can be transferred into your RRSP, even if you don't have any contribution room. The effect of such a transfer is that you won't have to pay taxes on that portion of the retiring allowance until you take that money out of your RRSP.
- *Ineligible Allowances.* The portion of your retiring allowance that is "ineligible" (shown in Box 67) can also be transferred to your RRSP, but only if you have enough contribution room to cover the contribution.

Avoid Lump Sums. Whenever possible, avoid adding a lump sum to income in one tax year. You might be able to take your severance over two tax years, for example: part in December and part in January. That will often bring a better tax result.

If your only option is to accept a lump sum, check out your RRSP contribution room and contribute as much of your severance to your RRSP as possible. This will offset taxes owing on the severance in the current tax year. You'll get to keep more money, earn investment income on a tax deferred basis and reserve for yourself the opportunity to time RRSP withdrawals in the future to get a better tax result as a family. There may even be an opportunity to split RRSP withdrawals with your spouse.

 Case Study | When Edward left his employer late in 2013, he had already earned $65,000 for the year and received a severance settlement of $100,000.

Had Edward done nothing, the full $100,000 would have been added to his income in 2013 adding more than $42,000 to his tax bill! To minimize the income tax consequences, Edward made an RRSP contribution of $100,000 (having not maximized his RRSP contributions in the past he had sufficient RRSP contribution room). The RRSP deduction eliminated that extra $42,000 in taxes.

If Edward needs to use those funds over the next two years, he could withdraw $50,000 each year and (assuming no other income sources) his tax bill would be about $8,700 per year. This strategy would save Edward $24,600 in taxes simply by parking the money in his RRSP for a year or two. If possible, withdraw money from the RRSP only when other taxable income sources are exhausted to maximize your retirement.

Legal Fees. If you incur legal fees in order to collect money owed to you for severance, pension benefits, or a retiring allowance, you may claim those expenses as Other Deductions on Line 232 so long as those expenses were not reimbursed and the amount collected is included in income. Your claim for legal fees may be reduced if amounts are transferred into your RRSP. If unabsorbed by the severance income they can be carried forward for seven years.

Unemployment and Your T4E Slip

For those who become unemployed, EI benefits received in the year are taxable. They are entered from the T4E slip onto your tax return. Be careful to watch for any income tax deductions so you can enter these, too.

The EI benefits received may be subject to repayment, if you have received regular benefits in the previous 10 years, and your income exceeds the annual income threshold for these purposes.

 CHECK IT OUT | **How can I keep more of my EI benefits?** Tax planning with RRSP contributions can help avoid this. Your software will calculate the repayment automatically and add it to the amounts you need to pay for the year. Be sure to check whether you have to repay prior to the RRSP deadline so that you can minimize this clawback by making an RRSP contribution.

Other types of EI benefits which are not considered "regular benefits" and are not subject to repayment include:

- EI-funded financial assistance paid while you are taking part in an approved employment program (Box 17),
- Tax exempt benefits received by status Indians (Box 18),
- Tuition assistance (Box 20 or Box 21),
- Maternity benefits, Parental benefits,
- Sickness benefits, and
- Compassionate care benefits.

EI and the Self-Employed. You may find at the end of your employment that you want to earn your living as a self-employed person. Small business owners can now opt in for certain restricted employment benefits available including maternity benefits, parental/adoptive benefits, sickness benefits and compassionate care benefits.

However, there is a trap. Once you opt in, you have 60 days to change your mind. After the 60 days, you are in the program for the calendar year. Assuming you do not collect any EI benefits, you may choose to opt-out at the beginning of any calendar year. If you do receive EI benefits, however, you are no longer eligible to opt-out of the EI program on self-employment earnings, ever. Once you receive a benefit you will continue to remain in the program and have to pay annual premiums on your self-employment income.

 The Bottom Line | If you are leaving your job, reduce any lump sum amounts received with an RRSP contribution if possible. Your legal fees may also be tax deductible.

20

When to See a Pro

Use the following checklist in anticipation of filing your returns if you are an employee. Consider getting the advice of a professional to answer the following about your employment contract:

- ☐ **Working from Home.** Am I (or the family members who work for me) employed or self-employed? How can I tell? I have a home office, for example, and my wife helps me with the accounting.
- ☐ **Negotiating a New Contract.** I am negotiating a new employment agreement that includes both a cash raise and some benefits my employer will pay for. Which benefits are taxable and which are tax free? Also:
  - My employer wants me to move to a new city. What expenses can be claimed for moving to a new location and what are the restrictions?
  - What are the income tax consequences of receiving a low-interest or no-interest loans from my employer for my mortgage or other expenses?
  - My employer is offering me stock options as part of my compensation. How much tax will I pay if accept them and later if I sell the securities ?
- ☐ **Understanding Your Pension Options.** Find out how much is accumulating in your RPP and how you can supplement your pension income with an RRSP without overpayments. Also discuss the new PRPP with your tax pro, especially if you are self-employed, or thinking about starting a new small business.
- ☐ **Losing Your Job.** My employer is terminating my job. What do I need to know about taxable severance payments? When should I take them? Can I claim my legal fees for challenging my settlement? Will I have to pay Employment Insurance benefits I am

receiving? When is the best time to tap into other savings like my RRSP? What if I am suddenly disabled?

☐ **Claiming Out-of-Pocket Expenses.** What expenses can I claim against my employment income? If I am a long haul trucker? A teacher? An artist? A forestry worker? Working on oil rigs? What if I am with the military? A cross-border worker?

☐ **Made an Excess RRSP or PRPP Contribution.** If you find that you've contributed an excess amount to your RRSP (more than $2,000 more than you're allowed) or PRPP, seek help from a tax pro to get these excess funds out of your RRSP and file the required forms to report and pay the penalty tax on the excess contributions.

☐ **Paying Child Care Expenses and Either You or Your Spouse is a Student.** Claims can get complicated when the lower-income spouse is a student. A tax pro can help you make the best claim possible.

PART 3

Families and Children

Family life is changing significantly in Canada. Consider that in 1961, just over 50 years ago, about 92% of families were headed by a married couple. By 2011 this had dropped to 67%, according to the Canadian Census. Meanwhile significant growth in conjugal relationships includes common-law couples, blended families as well as same-sex couples.

It's not surprising then, that the tax system has had to keep up with those changes. Common-law couples are now treated in the same way as married couples for tax purposes. That means, however, you'll need to take a second look at your tax filing obligations any time you and your partner start living together and understand the definition of "common-law" for tax purposes.

There are numerous tax deductions and credits that can be shared within the family and opportunities to accumulate and split income and capital now and in retirement to your best tax advantages. Even the rules for those who adopt children improved, starting in 2013.

But, be aware that those who live common-law, like married couples, must combine "net family income"—Line 236 on both returns—to claim certain refundable tax credits. That will mean a smaller benefit, if one exists at all, in many families.

What hasn't changed, however, is that "optimizing" all income reporting, deductions and credits is important to get the best results for the family unit as a whole. That's the subject of this section.

What's New

Most of the changes for families are in the indexed refundable and non-refundable tax credits.

To encourage new donors, the government has introduced a new First-Time Donor's Super Credit which adds an additional credit of 25% on the first $1,000 of cash donations to the normal donation credit amounts for those who have not claimed a donation credit since 2007.

There are also changes to the rules behind Registered Disability Savings Plans, as well as the maximum amounts to be contributed to Registered Pension Plans and RRSPs.

Hard Copy

When you gather the hard copy this year, remember to organize all the receipts for the entire family, starting with the lowest income earner and working your way up to the highest. From T4 slips to tuition, subway passes to medical expenses—it's all important—and may be transferrable from one family member to another.

Software Tips

Your software may automatically link all the family returns together. That's a great option, if you can find it, as it helps you to optimize transferrable deductions and credits which you'll learn about in this section.

Also, you will find that many of your personal tax credits will be automatically calculated by your software after you enter details about birthdates and net incomes.

Tax Sleuthing

Review the summaries of all tax returns and do some "reverse engineering." Do you understand all the numbers? Are they on the right return? What is the net result for the family—have you paid the least taxes possible? Maximized refundable and non-refundable tax credits, too?

Tax Pro Alert

Do you qualify for income splitting? Can you transfer assets—legitimately—to your spouse or children? Be sure you understand the "Attribution Rules" before you do either. A tax professional can help you plan to achieve the most tax efficient results for family income and capital in future years.

21

Conjugal Relationships: Filing With Your Spouse

The number of common-law couples has risen 13.9% in Canada between 2001 and 2006. This compares with a 3.1% increase for married couples in the same period. Lone-parent families increased 8% over the same period. Growth was higher for male lone-parent families (+16.2%) than for female lone-parent families (+6%).

– Statistics Canada Census Data, Sept. 2012

In Canada, we are taxed as individuals. We each qualify for our own Basic Personal Amount (just over $11,000). We have our own marginal tax rates on our various sources of income. And we individually are subject to a progressive tax system; that is, the more we earn, the more we pay, and the less we receive from income-tested benefits like refundable tax credits or the Old Age Security.

However, most families make financial decisions as one economic unit. Frankly that's how the government redistributes income, too. They look at the size of "net family income" for certain provisions like the refundable tax credits. But that "joint filing" requirement for some provisions but not others can make tax filing and the communications of vital information between family members challenging.

Just when, for example, do families have to declare their relationships and add incomes together? When is income splitting possible? How many tax-exempt residences can a family unit own? You need to know the answers to these important questions before you start filing your family's tax returns, especially if you are:

• **married to someone**, with no children just yet,

- **living common-law** with your partner of the same or opposite sex,
- **parents of children** together,
- **adoptive parents of a child**, including your spouse's or common-law spouse's child,
- **a supporting individual** to a sibling, parent, grandchild, aunt, uncle, niece, nephew or any other person whose care you are responsible for, including in-laws, or
- **a single parent**, or perhaps one who is recently separated or divorced with joint custody or summer visitation rights to your children.

In each case, you will need to discuss joint tax provisions for family members, even though each individual might be filing their own tax return. In this chapter you will learn:

- Who a spouse is for tax purposes;
- Who should claim income provisions to reduce taxes;
- What tax deductions and credits can be claimed by either of you; and
- Why optimization of income, deductions and credits can save you money.

Lower Earner First. I am suggesting you file these two tax returns together... starting with the lower income earner; then enter the data of the higher earner. Be aware that your tax software may automatically "optimize" your net family results, with the right information.

But to begin with, you must tell the software whether you have a spouse—legally married or otherwise—or others to be claimed on your return.

 CHECK IT OUT | **What is the definition of a spouse?** A spouse or common-law partner is someone with whom you are living in a *conjugal relationship* (that is, "as married"). You must mark your marital status as "married" or "common-law partner" in the identification area of the tax return, as the following circumstances apply:

- *A spouse*, for tax purposes, is someone of the same or opposite sex to whom you are legally married.
- *A common-law partner*, is someone who is not your spouse but is someone who qualifies under **one** of the following conditions:
  - someone of the same or opposite sex who has been living with you in a conjugal relationship for at least 12 continuous months (separations of less than 90 days do not affect the 12-month period), or
  - someone you have resumed living with and your current relationship has lasted at least 12 continuous months, or
  - someone who, at the end of the tax year, was the actual or adoptive parent of your child, or
  - someone who has custody and control of your child, or did so immediately before the child turned 19, and who wholly supported that person.

As a general rule, any tax provisions that apply to a spouse apply equally to a common-law partner. Unless specifically noted otherwise, you may assume throughout this book that any time the term "spouse" or "spousal" is used, that the provision applies to both legally married spouses and to common-law partners of the same or opposite sex.

When you indicate you have a spouse whose net income is below the Basic Personal Amount, your software will automatically claim the "Spousal Amount." However, just because your spouse has little or no income, doesn't necessarily mean he or she shouldn't file a tax return.

Filing Together Counts. There are several "joint filing" provisions for couples that can bring home tax benefits for your family unit.

Quite often your tax software will do this for you automatically in the background. This might confuse you, as you may not understand where the figures have come from or why. The tax reporting guidelines below should help you decipher some of the reporting rules.

Spouse Not Filing? If you don't know what your spouse's net income is because you are not filing at the same time, you must report on your return, the net income that your spouse would declare if your spouse is filing at the same time. Do so, even if the amount is zero.

Average Tax Downward. Over time, the object is to develop strategies to "average down" the income tax you pay as a family by splitting income sources with family members , (although special Attribution Rules may prohibit this—see Chapter 30). Lower individual income levels could increase the tax benefits governments have waiting for you, as well.

Income Reporting. Sometimes there is a choice when it comes to reporting certain income sources. Other times, you may be unsure, but the results are quite specific. Consider the following common traps experienced by average tax filers, to make sure you get it right:

Line 117 The Universal Child Care Benefit (UCCB). One of the ways the tax system addresses the extra expense of raising children is with a *universal* monthly payment—that is, everyone gets it regardless of income level. The amount is $100 per month for each child under 6. If you're in a conjugal relationship, this must be reported by the spouse with the lower net income.

Note, however, this income will not reduce your family's refundable tax credits, like the *Canada Child Tax Benefit (CCTB),* or related provincial credits.

UCCB Bonus for Singles. If you are a single parent, you may also choose to report this income on the return of a child you are claiming as an "Eligible Dependant", if that is to your tax advantage. Do a couple of "what if" solutions with your software to find out for sure. Single parents will be discussed in more detail in Chapter 31.

Line 114 Canada Pension Plan Benefits. One spouse may assign up to half of the Canada Pension Plan benefits to the other, so that each receives some of the benefits the other is entitled to. The result is that the couple will usually pay lower taxes as a unit, than they would if one person reported a high income and the other a lower one. To qualify your spouse must be at least age 60 and not a contributor; otherwise you must make the assignment for both retirement benefits if you both receive them.

Line 115 Pension Income Splitting. Spouses have a fantastic opportunity to split income from qualifying employer-sponsored or private pensions. In these cases, a lower level of income between the two may also reduce the clawback of Old Age Security and quarterly tax instalments. We'll discuss this and the CPP opportunities in more depth in Part 5.

Line 120/121/126/127 Investment, Revenue Property and Capital Gains Income. Who reports the income from joint accounts? Can I claim the dividends this year instead of spouse? Unfortunately, the tax department generally frowns upon higher income earners transferring capital, including investments and revenue properties to lower earners in the family to avoid taxes on the income these assets generate. For that reason, the "Attribution Rules" disallow most loans and transfers.

 CHECK IT OUT | **What are the Attribution Rules?** When income is earned on property that is loaned or transferred to a spouse or minor child, it must generally be reported by the transferor. There are some exceptions, for example, an investment in a TFSA or a Spousal RRSP. These rules will be discussed in more detail in Chapter 31.

However, properly documented, income from assets held in the hands of each family member can substantially reduce family tax burdens.

Line 135 Self-Employment Income. If your spouse has income from a proprietorship, *Form T2125 Statement of Business Activities* will be completed to self-report income and deductions as well as the ongoing cost of assets used in a business. If the business is a corporation, a separate T2 tax return will be filed to report that income and the owner-manager will likely report on the T1 return any salary, wages or dividends drawn out of the corporation.

Businesses must be more than a hobby run out of the basement. There must be a reasonable expectation that a profit will result from a business activity, profession, calling, trade or other activity. While this is a large subject and the focus of my book *Make Sure It's Deductible* (available at www.knowledgebureau.com), an example of the income splitting opportunities appear at the end of this chapter together with a checklist of common write-offs to discuss with your tax professional. You'll also find a great overview of tax filing tips for proprietors in Chapter 43.

Claiming Deductions. There are numerous deductions leading to individual net income on Line 236 of the T1, and many of these contain rules that require a look at both spouse's tax returns to make allowable claims. Recall, the refundable tax credits you may be entitled to from the federal or provincial governments are based on your combined "net family income," which is Line 236 of both spouses' returns, or in some cases, Line 234.

 CHECK IT OUT | **Why is net income so important?** The lower your family net income is, the more tax credits and social benefits you'll receive.

Common Tax Deductions that Reduce Net Income

Line 208 RRSP/PRPP Contributions	You may contribute to your own RRSP or to a "Spousal RRSP" or to your PRPP based on your own "earned income." You'll get the tax deduction, but it's a good idea to accumulate equal amounts in your RRSPs, so you get better tax results with you make retirement income withdrawals. See Part 5, Reporting Pension Income. The RRSP/PRPP deduction is claimed on Schedule 7.
Line 214 Child Care Expenses	Make this claim on Form T778. Usually this must be claimed by the person with the lower net income on Line 234, but in some specific instances the higher earner may make the claim, as described later.
Line 215 Disability Supports Deduction	Receipts are required for supports that enable a disabled person to go to work and earn income at a place of employment or business, or to carry on research or to study at a post-secondary school. This includes the cost of an attendant who assists a severely disabled person. The attendant must be an unrelated person and over 18. Some of the same expenses may qualify as medical expenses but, of course, can't be claimed twice. Claiming the deduction on this line will generally get a better result because it reduces net income.
Line 219 Moving Expenses	Form T1-M is used to claim this lucrative tax deduction. Either spouse can claim moving expenses, if the move was at least 40 km closer to employment or self-employment. There must be income at the new location and in general the person with the higher income will get a better result. A carry forward of the expenses is also possible if there is not enough income earned in the year at the new location.
Line 221 Carrying Charges	Receipts are required for all amounts claimed here including safety deposit boxes (2013 and prior years) and the details of loans taken for investment purposes. Any dual-purpose loans must be prorated (e.g. lines of credit used for both a personal and investment purposes). Either spouse may claim the safety deposit box, one of the most commonly missed deductions for couples.

Refundable Tax Credits. Once you know how much your net income on Line 236 will be for each spouse, your tax software will combine the incomes to calculate many tax credits automatically, including the three federal refundable tax credits below; review their values and income thresholds in *Appendix 3 Refundable Tax Credits Summary.*

- Canada Child Tax Credit (CCTB)
- GST/HST Credit
- Working Income Tax Benefit (WITB)

Planning RRSPs Will Reduce Family Net Income. In Chapter 12, you may recall Rupert, who was single and saved over $4,500 by contributing to an RRSP. The RRSP is equally effective for couples. The following case study illustrates the effect on family net income and credits.

 **Case Study** | **Planning to Increase Tax Credits with an RRSP**

Sarah and Brett live in Vancouver and have two children under age 5; her income is $55,000 and his net income from his consulting business is $25,000.

Without an RRSP contribution, their Canada Child Tax Benefits are $1,454; with a $5,000 contribution based on Sarah's contribution room, they increase to $1,654, plus the couple's tax savings are $1,485. The contribution saves them in total $1,685, a return on their RRSP investment of 34% by way of tax savings.

Non-Refundable Tax Credits. Take a good look at Schedule 1 in your software, where you'll find your federal credits; then visit Appendix 3 for detail about all the non-refundable tax credits claimable on your tax returns. You will note that most of them have been indexed to inflation over the years, and an enhanced series of credits is possible if a family member is disabled.

✓ CHECK IT OUT | **What is the Family Caregiver Amount (FCA)?** When the dependant is infirm, this credit provides a $2,040 "bump" in the value of four tax credits:

- the Spousal Amount (available if you are legally married or living common-law),
- the *Amount for Eligible Dependant* (an "equivalent-to-spouse" amount for families headed by a single parent),
- the *Amount for Children Under 18,* and
- the *Caregiver Amount.*

Note that the Amount for Infirm Adults (18 and over) includes the FCA. In order to claim the FCA, a statement signed by a medical doctor is required showing what the impairment is, when the impairment began and what the duration of the impairment is expected to be. The impairment must be prolonged and indefinite. For 2013 and future years, this letter is not required if there is an accepted disability certificate on file with CRA.

We will discuss the non-refundable tax credits available to families with children, singles and caregivers in more detail later; now, let's discuss non-refundable credits for spouses.

Line 303 Spousal Amount. For 2013, the maximum claim is $11,038 (the same as the Basic Personal amount), plus the FCA if your spouse is infirm. This credit is reduced by each dollar your spouse makes, as per the example below:

 CHECK IT OUT | **How does the FCA work with the Spousal Amount?** Charles and Jennifer are a common-law couple. Charles earns $46,000 at his job and Jennifer is a student. Jennifer's net income for 2013 was $6,500. She is infirm. Charles would usually claim the spousal amount of $11,038 − $6,500 = $4,538 for Jennifer if she were not infirm. But in this case, his claim would be $13,078 − $6,500 = $6,578.

Your software will calculate this automatically when you add your spouse's income details and indicate that your spouse is infirm. For these reasons, it may be wise for your spouse to contribute to an RRSP, as it will reduce net income, thereby potentially increasing or creating a Spousal Amount on your return.

Credits Either Spouse May Claim, Depending on Income. Note that there are three non-refundable tax credits that spouses can potentially claim on either tax return, based on where the best benefit lies:

Line 364 Public Transit Amount. This credit was discussed in detail in Chapter 18. Eligible monthly passes for buses, subways, street cars, commuter trains, and ferries may be claimed by either spouse, or one spouse can make the claim for the whole family. There is no maximum claim.

Line 326 Amounts Transferred from Spouse. Individual taxable income is used to determine whether you can make a transfer from spouse on Schedule 2, for five non-refundable credits:

- *Line 303 Age Amount* (available if your spouse is 65 or older);
- *Line 367 Amount for Children Under 18* (available if the child lives with both of you throughout the year);
- *Line 314 Pension Income Amount* (a $2,000 credit for periodic benefits from a qualifying pension—this amount is not indexed;
- *Line 316 Disability Amount* (if your spouse is markedly restricted due to a physical or mental infirmity and has a Disability Tax Credit Certificate signed by a doctor; and

- *Line 323 Tuition, Education, and Textbook Amounts* (when your spouse is a student at designated educational institute).

If one spouse's taxable income is too low to benefit from these credits, it's best to transfer these amounts to the higher income earner, which your software will do automatically for you.

Line 330 Medical Expenses. Individual net income is used to determine who should claim the medical expenses for the family.

 CHECK IT OUT | **Why should the lower earner claim medical expenses?** Because medical expenses are reduced by 3% of net income (to an upper maximum of $2,151 in 2013). That means the lower income earner generally gets the better result, provided that person is taxable.

Your software may figure that out for you. If there is no benefit this year, you may be able to claim them next year. You can claim medical expenses for the best 12-month period ending in the tax year, so group larger amounts together over two calendar years. The detail for what is claimable is discussed in Chapter 26. However, for couples, pay particular attention to the following specific costs, when health issues arise:

- **Moving to a New Home.** The additional costs for moving into a new primary residence that will accommodate the special needs of a newly disabled spouse. Note that the *RRSP Home Buyers' Plan* can be tapped immediately without waiting for the normal four-year period after owning another home.
- **Travel Insurance.** Claim any additional premiums paid for private health care or travel insurance.
- **Van Modifications.** Write off up to 20% of the costs of a van that has to be adapted to accommodate a disabled person to a maximum of $5,000, on acquisition or within six months of acquisition. This includes conversion kits to allow the disabled person access into and for driving the van. Reasonable costs of modifying a driveway for greater access to a bus or Handi Transit services qualify.

Combined Tax Credits. Depending upon the size of your expenditures; a greater benefit is possible when spouses combine certain contributions together on one return in the case of following two multi-tiered tax credits:

Line 349 Donations and Gifts. Individual net and taxable income levels are taken into account in determining who should claim the Charitable Donations Amount. Particularly if total gifts are $200 or more, it is usually best to group donations on one return (usually the higher earner's) to maximize the claim, which is calculated as follows:

- 15% of the first $200 gifted and
- 29% of the balance on the federal return;
- provincial governments will add value to this.

 First-Time Donor's Super Credit | For taxation years 2013 to 2017, if neither spouse has made a claim for the donation credit since 2007, an extra 25% credit is available for cash donations up to $1,000.

Maximum Claims for Donations. The claim is generally limited to 75% of net income, and so the limitation is rarely a factor in claiming the credit. (Note that in the year of death and the year immediately before death, that 75% limitation is raised to 100%.)

Your tax software will do all the calculations in the background. "Total charitable gifts" include gifts made in the current year or in any of the immediately preceding five years and not previously claimed. That means, you may elect not to claim anything for charitable gifts made in the current year, if it's not to your advantage.

Carrying Donations Forward. Carry the unclaimed gifts forward for five years, especially if you are not taxable this year. The details of these claims, including the First Time Donor's Super Credit will be discussed in Chapter 29.

Line 409 Political Contributions. When you give to your favourite federal political party, you'll need sufficient federal taxes payable to absorb this non-refundable tax credit. Good news is that spouses can claim each other's credits or, better, one spouse can claim for both for a better result if the spouse cannot use the credit. The credit is calculated as follows:

- 75% of the first $400, plus
- 50% of the next $350, plus
- 33⅓% of the balance to a maximum credit of $650, which is reached when a total of $1,275 is given.

Tax Calculations on Spouses' Returns. You will discover, when you review the results of the tax calculations that that one person making a high income, let's say $104,000, will pay a lot more tax than two people making $52,000 each. There are some good opportunities in particular when income is split by families who operate a small business (see Chapter 43 for more details) or in cases where there is significant pension or investment income.

 Keep an Eye on Your Tax Brackets | What tax bracket does each spouse's income fall into? Often there is significant income room until the top of a bracket is reached. That's significant because after-tax income taxed in the lower brackets is larger. When you have the choice, you may wish to add certain income sources to your tax return this year, especially if your income is below $43,561, as shown below:

2013 Federal Tax Brackets	2013 Federal Tax Rates
Up to $11,038	0
$11,039 to $43,561	15%
$43,562 to $87,123	22%
$87,124 to $135,054	26%
Over $135,034	29%

There are some potential pitfalls to consider: Seniors will want to be aware of clawback zones that reduce their Age Amount or Old Age Security benefits. (See Part 5 and Appendix 3 for more information.) Clawbacks will factor into results for other refundable and non-refundable tax credits, which will decrease or be phased out, depending on income level.

Higher incomes also require the pre-payment of taxes on a quarterly basis in some cases. Use your tax software to do "what if" scenarios to avoid this. However, if your income is lower today than it will be on a future tax return, "topping up to bracket" may be a good strategy for reducing your taxes over time. Spouses who are in a position to split income sources can minimize taxes using this strategy.

 The Bottom Line | The family unit that files together saves tax. You'll be able to control the level of net family income to increase refundable and non-refundable tax credits. And, if your goal is to keep more money in the family—both income and capital—you'll optimize the tax provisions that allow you to file as one economic unit. When you know net and taxable family income—both yours and your spouse's—you are in a better position to make important investment and lifestyle decisions: should we pay down the mortgage or invest in an RRSP? Should we borrow money to invest in the stock market? Should we consider buying life insurance or invest in a TFSA instead? Should we take more money out of our RRSP or RRIF?

22

Filing for Kids

When you add kids to the family mix, another dimension emerges on the tax return: there are more refundable and non-refundable tax credits to claim, and great opportunities for your family to save money for future generations.

You have learned that the refundable tax credits you file for will be based on your and your spouse's "net family income." However, the amount of non-refundable tax credits you can claim for your child (or other dependant) will depend on two things:

(a) whether or not *the dependant* has *taxable* income; if so they must file their own return to report this and

(b) what your *dependant's net income* is, which could affect the size of some of the non-refundable tax credits you can claim for them.

Blended Families. In the case of blended families, it's possible to make choices about who claims certain credits for the child who lives in different homes. Generally, that will be the parent who claims the Amount for Eligible Dependant (an "equivalent to spouse" amount). See Chapter 31, where we discuss single parents, separations and divorce.

In this chapter you'll learn:

- Who is a dependant for tax purposes?
- Whether your dependant has to file a tax return;
- How to report income, deductions and tax credits for dependants; and
- Why income levels on your dependants' tax returns matter.

Who is a Dependant for Tax Purposes? A dependant is a person who, at any time in the year, is dependent on the individual for support and is either the child or grandchild of the individual or of the individual's spouse or common-law partner; or, if resident in Canada at any time in the year, the parent, grandparent, brother, sister, uncle, aunt, niece or nephew of the individual or of the individual's spouse or common-law partner. The taxpayer's spouse is also a dependant if their income is low enough that they rely on the taxpayer for the basic necessities of life.

Is Your Dependant's Income Taxable? Because your dependant will qualify for a *Basic Personal Amount* which is just over $11,000, the answer is usually no: most children will not make enough money during the year to be subject to tax. Therefore, you will make a claim for various tax credits on your tax return as the supporting individual. (Some credits can be transferred to your spouse as we will discuss below.)

 CHECK IT OUT | **Whose tax return should be completed first?** *Always do the lowest earners tax returns first.* In that way you can immediately see whether income is low enough to claim the dependant on your return.

It's a good idea to print out your child's tax summary to guide you to important figures: the child's net income, any tuition, education and textbook amounts, and so on.

Next, determine whether the child qualifies for any tax deductions that will reduce net income, so you can make claims for deductions and credits for that child on your returns. Here are some guidelines for you.

Filing Tax Returns for the Kids

We'll discuss this topic in the order of the basic elements of the tax return: income, deductions, refundable credits, non-refundable credits and tax calculations.

Income. Always file a tax return for children who have any earnings from active employment or self-employment. It really doesn't matter how old they are. You may have a 12 year old, for example, who earns babysitting money, or a 16 year old who works at the local hamburger joint. There are several reasons:

- *Create RRSP Contribution Room.* This notional account records 18% of earned income, which is the amount eligible for RRSP contribution purposes. Your software will take note and carry the RRSP Contribution Room forward for future use. RRSP contribution room is accumulated by CRA and shown on the Notice of Assessment each year. The records in your software should be compared with this. This contribution room can provide a valuable planning tool to parents once children go to postsecondary school, if the student earns too much for the parents to transfer Tuition, Education, and Textbook credits. More about that later.

- *GST/HST Credits Require Filing by 18 Year Olds.* When your child turns 18 it's important to file for the purposes of making Canada Pension Plan contributions on qualifying earnings (there is a $3,500 exemption, so that means earnings above this are subject to CPP contributions the month after the child turns 18.) In addition, 18 year olds should file so they can start receiving their quarterly GST/HST refundable tax credit the month after they turn 19.

    Example: Justin was born February 15, 1996 so he turned 18 in 2014. His parents will receive any GST/HST credit payable for him until he turns 19. However payments after February 15, 2015 will not be made to his parents. Instead, the credit payment on April 5, 2015 will be paid to Justin but only if he files a 2013 return to apply for the credit.

- *Report Investment Earnings.* Your child will not qualify to invest in a *Tax-Free Savings Account (TFSA)* until he or she turns 18; at which time this should be strongly encouraged to do so. However, in the meantime, your child may have enough savings based on their own earnings to open a non-registered savings account. Resulting investment earnings are reported by the child. Be aware that a T-slip may not have been issued if the earnings are under $50; they must be self-reported in that case.

    You can also run afoul of the *Attribution Rules* introduced in the previous chapter. This can happen when adults loan or transfer capital they have earned to the child. Resulting investment income is attributed back to that adult, so keep the birthday money in a separate account. You'll also learn in Chapter 30 about an exception here: capital gains (but not dividends and interest) earned on capital that has been loaned or transferred to a child will not be subject to the Attribution Rules.

Deductions Your Working Child Can Claim. Some of the common ones that apply to a working child include the following:

RRSP Contributions. If your child's taxable income exceeds the Basic Personal Amount, and the child has the required RRSP Contribution Room, you may wish to make a contribution to the child's RRSP in order for the child to take an RRSP deduction. Note that children under 18, however, are not allowed to make an RRSP overcontribution, which is only permissible (up to $2,000) in the case of adults.

Depending on income level, the RRSP deduction may help the child avoid taxation, but in addition, if the child is attending post-secondary school and qualifies for a tax credit under the Tuition, Education, and Textbook Amounts, a lower net income may open up a transfer of up to $5,000 of that credit to your return. See Chapter 25.

Undeducted RRSP Contributions. If the child's income is too low to be taxable, carry forward the undeducted RRSP contributions to the future when income is higher. In the meantime, your child benefits from the power of tax-deferred compounding of investment earnings in the RRSP. That means the investment will grow faster.

In addition, if you are claiming Child Care Expenses for a child (other than that of yourself and your spouse), as described in Chapter 15, making an RRSP contribution may reduce net income below the Basic Personal Amount, so you can claim child care for that child, if under 16 or if over 16, disabled.

Moving Expenses. Your child may take a deduction for moving expenses on Line 219 if they have moved at least 40 kilometers closer to a new work location or to begin self-employment. Look for Form T1-M on which to make the claim and see Chapter 16 for details.

In addition, students who move to attend a post-secondary school in Canada or abroad full time, may claim moving expenses to offset income at the new location, including taxable awards such as research grants, as long as one of the residences was in Canada (before or after the move). Registration for regular full-time attendance in an academic year is required, even if, for post-graduate studies, required attendance is minimal. In the case of "co-op" courses that have a work component attached to them, only those months of attendance at the school qualify as "full-time" attendance.

A good guide for deciding whether attendance is full or part-time is that at least 60% of a normal course load is required to meet the full time rules. Students will be addressed in more detail in Chapter 24.

Business Income and Losses. It's not unusual to fill in a business statement for children who are making money babysitting, doing lawn care or other activities of self-employment. In fact, do file Form T2125 reporting this income for that entrepreneurial child because it will help to create unused RRSP contribution room. See Chapter 43 for tips on claiming income and expenses for a small business.

In the unlikely event that your child has incurred losses from a business (the lemonade stand may not cut it—unless it had a reasonable expectation of profit), or the sale of a capital property, a tax writeoff is possible.

Request for Loss Carry Overs. In the case of the unincorporated business, a non-capital loss will offset other income of the year, or if unabsorbed by income, the loss may be carried over (three years back and 20 years into the future to offset income in those years). So you can see, this can be valuable in offsetting future income. Use Form T1A *Request for Loss Carry Over.*

In the case of capital losses from the disposition of investment assets, other capital gains of the year would first be offset with the loss; then, the net capital loss remaining would be applied to the carry over years against capital gains in the prior three years or they can be carried forward indefinitely. Claim capital losses on Schedule 3 first; then use Form

T1A. Your software will do much of this for you in the background, but you'll need to specify how much of the losses to claim in each year. Remember to print off the carry over schedules for your permanent records.

Refundable Tax Credits. Minor children don't normally qualify for refundable tax credits, as it is assumed their parents will be claiming federal and provincial tax credits for them: the Canada Child Tax Benefit, GST/HST and Working Income Tax Benefit all have provisions for children. This is true of most provinces who distribute refundable tax credits as well. However, in some instances, for example, if the minor has a child of his or her own, filing for refundable tax credits is possible. Single parents are discussed in Chapter 31.

Non-Refundable Tax Credits for Children. Your minor child will commonly qualify for these credits:

- **Line 300** Basic Personal Amount;
- **Line 312** Employment Insurance Premiums Paid (no premiums are payable if employment income is $2,000 or less); and
- **Line 363** Canada Employment Amount on T4 earnings.

Note that the amounts below are transferrable to supporting individuals or in some cases may be carried forward if the child is not taxable:

- **Line 318** Disability Amount (if a Disability Tax Credit Certificate is available—transferrable to supporting individuals);
- **Line 319** Interest Paid on Student Loans (can be carried forward five years if the child not taxable);
- **Line 323** Tuition, Education and Textbook Amounts (up to $5,000 can be transferred to a supporting individual if the student is not taxable);
- **Line 330** Medical expenses, although this is usually claimed by the supporting individual; and
- **Line 349** Donations and gifts made personally or through employment (these can be carried forward five years if the child not taxable).

Note that students and children with infirmity will be cover in later chapters.

Tax Calculations. Your child's tax refund will generally relate to any withholding taxes at part time jobs or a return of Canada Pension Plan premiums deducted in error for those under 18.

Refundable Tax Credits for Children. For children reporting T4 income, CPP contributions and EI premiums are often over-deducted by the employer. This is because the first $3,500 of earnings is exempt from CPP and employees who earn less than $2,000 are not required to pay EI premiums. Your software will automatically do the calculations required on Form T2204 *Employee Overpayment of 2013 Canada Pension Plan Contributions and*

2013 Employment Insurance Premiums and any overpayments calculated will be posted to lines 448 and 490 of the return.

 What's the Kiddie Tax? The "kiddie tax" is a punitive tax on dividends paid to children from corporations owned by their parents as well as on certain capital gains from the sale of shares in such corporations. The tax is payable at the highest marginal rate to discourage income splitting with minor children using a corporation.

Use Form T1206 *Federal Tax on Split Income* to compute this. To avoid this tax, be sure to consult a professional before paying dividends to children from your corporation.

 The Bottom Line | The level of income on your child's return matters. If it's high enough, of course, the income level will determine the taxes payable on that income but for many children, the income level determines how much of their non-refundable credits are available for transfer to their parents. Transferrable credits include the Tuition, Education, and Textbook Amount and the Disability Amount. See the next chapter for details of transferring credits from the child's return to the parent's.

23

Claiming the Kids
on Your Return

Let's turn now to a discussion of family-filing provisions on your and your spouse's returns, beginning with deductions and then moving to tax credits. In this chapter you will learn:

- What deductions are important in reducing your net income;
- About the numerous non-refundable tax credits you should be claiming for your dependants; and
- How the resulting tax calculations can help you plan for the future.

Child Care Expenses. You may have enrolled your little ones in activity day camps while you work over the summer, with a babysitter in your home, or you may take your little ones out for daycare. If so, you'll want to claim Child Care Expenses on Form T778 and Line 214. Child Care Expenses must usually be claimed on the return of the lower earner, but some exceptions exist. They reduce net income, which means refundable tax credits like the Canada Child Tax Benefit are increased. And so because there is so much to know to make a proper claim, please see Chapter 15 for a complete discussion of claiming Child Care Expenses and what needs to be entered on the appropriate auxiliary tax form: T778.

Disability Supports Deduction. This will be discussed in more detail in Chapter 27 for the same reasons—there is a lot to know. However, for now, the deduction is used to account for supports required by a disabled person to go to work or to school. Many of these items also qualify for the medical expenses credit. Only the disabled person can make this claim, so if your child doesn't need the deduction, it may be best to claim the supports as medical expenses which can be claimed on your return.

Non-Refundable Tax Credits. There are numerous non-refundable tax credits that could be claimed for your family members, and that's where the focus will be in this chapter.

Remember that non-refundable tax credits are claimed on Schedule 1 of the federal tax return. Your software will make many of these claims automatically for you in the background, but for some of the provisions, you'll need to enter data yourself.

 CHECK IT OUT | **What are the non-refundable tax credits available for your dependants?** Check these out on Schedule 1 of the T1 return:

- Amount for Eligible Dependant (claimed by single parents for one child),
- Amount for Dependent Children under 18,
- Amount for Infirm Dependant Age 18 or Older,
- Adoption Expenses,
- Amount for Children's Fitness,
- Amount for Children's Arts,
- Disability Amount Transferred from Dependant,
- Tuition, Education, and Textbook Amounts Transferred from a Child, and
- Medical Expenses.

For the purposes of the discussion in this chapter, we will assume your child lives with you in a home you share with your spouse, and that you do not share custody of this child with anyone else.

Line 367 Amount for Children Under 18. This amount, for children under 18, shows up on Schedule 1 of the T1 General as the *"Amount for children born in 1996 or later"* (the year changes annually to reflect the right age). Available since 2006, this credit may be claimed by either parent. The amount has been indexed each year to a formula linked to the Consumer Price Index, and it's not income-tested.

If there are multiple children under 18 in the family, one spouse must claim all of them. If that parent is not taxable, any unused amounts are then transferred to the other spouse using Schedule 2. When your returns are linked, your software will generally do all of this in the background for you, but it's best for you to check to be sure you get the intended results.

CHECK IT OUT | **What is the maximum claim for a minor child?** The amount of the credit is $2,234 for 2013. This amount is increased by $2,040 to $4,274 if the child is infirm. A child is considered infirm only if he or she is likely to be, for a long and continuous period of indefinite duration, dependent on others for significantly more assistance in attending to their personal needs and care when compared generally to persons of the same age.

Line 306 Amount for Infirm Dependants Age 18 or Older. When you support a dependant age 18 or over, it is assumed the person will file their own return, and receive their own refundable and non-refundable tax credits to offset any taxes payable. However, if that person is dependent on you by reason of mental or physical infirmity, it is possible to claim this non-refundable tax credit. You'll do so on the details of dependants form in your software or your software may allow you to enter details right on Schedule 5 and the numbers will end up on Schedule 1 to offset taxes payable. Some things to watch for in making this claim:

- *Qualifying Dependants.* If anyone else claims any tax credits for this infirm adult, you cannot do so. Otherwise, claim it for an adult you are supporting who is at least 18 at the end of the year and dependent because of their infirmity. This can include:
  – your child or grandchild, or that of your spouse
  – your parent, grandparent, brother, sister, uncle, aunt, niece or nephew or that of your spouse but in these cases, the dependent must have been resident in Canada at any time in the year.
- *Infirmity Definition.* The adult dependant does not need to be "markedly restricted" by their infirmity for the purpose of claiming this credit. That definition is used to qualify for the Disability Amount, described later. Rather, CRA's Interpretation Bulletin 519 describes the term as "lacking muscle or mental strength or vitality."

✓ **CHECK IT OUT** | **What is the maximum claim for an infirm dependant for 2013?** The claim is $6,530 per dependant but it is reduced by the dependant's net income in excess of $6,548 so if the dependant has net income in excess of $13,078, the claim is reduced to zero. If your qualifying dependant is a senior, for example, your parent, it's possible that person may be receiving income from the CPP and OAS, which could knock out the claim. However, you may get relief from the Caregiver Amount on Line 315, if the dependant resides with you.

Example: Beth and Tom take care of Tom's mother, Sophia, who lives with them. Sophia's only income for 2013 was a taxable foreign pension of $15,000 CDN. While Sophia's income is too high to claim the amount for infirm dependants, they can claim the caregiver amount of $4,490.

Line 364 Public Transportation. Described earlier, don't forget to save those transportation travel passes for a federal non-refundable tax credit of 15% of your monthly expenditures. All the travel pass costs for every member of the family (who is under age 19 at the end of the year) can be claimed by one parent. There is no maximum claim.

Line 365 Children's Fitness Amount. Claimable since 2007, this credit recognizes eligible expenses for sports and fitness activities taken by each child under age 16, up to a maximum of $500. (Parents of a disabled child under 18 get to claim $500 more if they spend at least $100.) Some interesting activities qualify—sailing, bowling and golf lessons, for example, in addition to the more typical hockey and soccer.

 CHECK IT OUT | **How much can you claim for the Children's Fitness Amount?** You'll save 15% of every dollar you fork out, up to the maximum limits above. That's a maximum of $75 for each healthy child. Because this is a non-refundable tax credit, it offsets federal taxes you otherwise pay. No benefit, in short, for those who pay no federal tax.

Line 370 Children's Arts Amount. A federal tax credit for costs of participation in artistic, cultural, recreational or developmental activities should be claimed for the costs of enrolling children in literary, visual and performing arts, or music or language lessons, too. Costs of instruction, equipment, uniforms, facility rental and administration costs included in the registration or membership fees will qualify.

 CHECK IT OUT | **How much can you claim for the Children's Arts Amount?** It is structured much like the Children's Fitness Credit, so expect your refund to grow by up to another $75 as described above. Again, that's a maximum of 15 per cent of $500 (up to $1,000 if your child is disabled), used to offset other federal taxes payable. If your children participate in fitness and arts activities, you can make two claims: one for each credit. Not allowed: fees paid for programs that are part of a regular school curriculum. Nor are costs for travel, meals and accommodation.

Be careful to choose programs of the right length, too. For both the Children's Fitness and Children's Arts Amount, the program must last at least eight consecutive weeks if it is a weekly program or in the case of children's camps it must last at least five consecutive days.

Line 313 Adoption Expenses. Either parent may claim the costs of adopting a child or they may split the costs as long as no more than the actual amount spent is claimed.

 CHECK IT OUT | **What is the maximum claim for Adoption Expenses?** Allowable expenses include:

- fees paid to a provincially or territorially licensed adoption agency,
- court, legal and administrative expenses,
- reasonable travel and living expenses for the child and adopting parents,
- document translation fees,

- mandatory fees paid to a foreign institution, and
- any other reasonable expenses required by a provincial or territorial government of a licensed adoption agency.

 The adoption period is the period that begins at the earlier of the time the adoptive parent makes an application to register with a licensed adoption agency or province and the time the application is made to a Canadian court, if earlier, and ends at the later of the time the file is acknowledged by the Canadian government or the moment the child begins to reside with the adopted parents. The maximum claim for 2013 is $11,669 and must be made in the year that the adoption period ends.

An eligible child for whom the credit is to be claimed is an individual who has yet to turn 18 years old at the time the adoption file was acknowledged by the Canadian government. You'll need to enter the amounts paid into your software, which will then calculate the credit against taxes payable. There are no provisions for carrying over expense claims where the parent is not taxable.

Line 316 Disability Amount for Children. It is possible your child will qualify for the Disability Amount if there is a severe and marked restriction in daily living activities due to a physical or mental infirmity, as confirmed by a qualified medical practitioner on a signed Disability Tax Credit Certificate (old T2201 for newer T2201B).

 CHECK IT OUT | **How much can you claim for a disabled child under the Disability Amount?** Children qualify for the normal disability amount of $7,697 (for 2013). Also, for children under 18, the disability amount will be increased by a *Disability Amount Supplement*. This adds $4,490 to the value of the Disability Amount. However, Child Care Expenses (Line 214) and the Disability Supports Amount (claimed at Line 215 or as medical expenses on Line 330) claimed in excess of $2,630 by anyone for the child will reduce the Disability Amount Supplement.

Your medical practitioner must assess how the impairment of the child affects the ability to perform one or more basic activities of daily living where the child is three years of age or older. From birth to three the assessment is different: the development progress of the child as it relates to a normal range of development is observed. If the child's impairment is obvious and medically proven, the credit may be allowed.

Note that children who require therapies administered to them 14 hours a week or more, including kidney dialysis and insulin injections and other care for diabetics, will qualify for this claim. *See Chapter 27 for more details on this credit.*

Line 327 Tuition, Education, and Textbook Amounts. Because this claim is made for post-secondary education at a designated educational institution leading to a diploma or degree, there are few claims available for those with younger children under this provision. However, it is possible in some cases. See Chapter 24 for more details.

Line 330 Medical Expenses. A parent or other supporting individual will generally claim medical expenses incurred for the child. An extensive list will be shared in Chapter 26, but specifically, allowable medical expenses can include the following for children:

- Medical devices and equipment such as braces, glasses, artificial limbs, wheelchairs;
- Costs of medical practitioners such as speech therapists, language pathologists, audiologists, sign language interpreters;
- Costs of caring for a physically or mentally disabled person, including children suffering from behavioural problems and attendance problems and dyslexia in an institution;
- Costs of care for those addicted to drugs or alcohol for outpatient or care in detoxification centres; and
- Premiums paid for tutoring and textbooks for a person with learning disabilities if certified by a medical practitioner.

Note that the cost of maternity clothes, diapers or diaper services is not deductible.

Allowable expenditures must be supported by hard copy and will normally be entered on the return with the lower net income. That's because total medical expenses must be reduced by 3% of net income, and claiming them on the lower earner's return will generally result in a better family benefit. However, if that person is not taxable, and the spouse's returns are linked, many software packages will provide the opportunity to transfer the amounts to the higher income earner or optimize the credit by carrying forward the amounts for use next year.

Tax Calculations. Your tax software will calculate your federal and provincial taxes for each family member in the background, automatically claiming any of the federal and provincial tax credits that result from all the net income thresholds. You'll find this quite remarkable, especially if provisions like tuition fees and medical expenses magically appear on the right returns in the right amounts. Your software is "smart" but you'll need to explain it all to a tax auditor, so be sure you get the intended results on the right returns and have the documentation in your files to back the numbers up.

 The Bottom Line | An RRSP for each family member with RRSP contribution room can work wonders to increase refunds and tax credits. Try some "what if solutions" and look at the difference. also, remember to save all your receipts for discretionary claims like the RRSP, child care and moving expenses, as well as Tuition, Education, and Textbook amounts, medical expenses and charitable donations as these are often subject to review after tax season.

24

Filing for Students in the Family

Filing a tax return for a student can involve several provisions and they are all quite important because they generate transferred credits to supporting individuals in some cases, or they can be carried forward for the student's use to reduce taxes payable in the future.

Tax software does an impressive job of both optimizing these claims between family members and keeping track of the carry forwards. Especially if students study abroad, the amounts can be large. In addition, several provinces provide rebates to graduates of their tuition fees paid to attract them to stay in the province. Therefore, this is an important tax filer profile.

Because of the joint filing requirements between family members, we will discuss the rules for students according to the basic elements of the tax return: income, deductions, tax credits and tax calculations specific to students and then, in the next chapter, the returns for the parents or supporting individuals will be discussed.

Income. Students report employment or self-employment income in the normal manner, but you should be aware of the following income sources commonly earned by students working their way through a post-secondary educational experience and some special rules:

Line 104 Other Employment Income. There are two income sources common to students you'll want to report here:

- *Tips and Gratuities.* Waiters and waitresses often turn into doctors, lawyers and teachers. Along the way they can make lots of money in the service industry to pay their way through school. That can become a problem if the income is not reported as required, especially when the employer is audited and credit card chits are reviewed for average tips left. You will want to avoid this.

Be sure to report those tips on the tax return and build RRSP contribution room, which can be very valuable to you along the way, as you'll see in this chapter. If you can afford to do so you can also voluntarily contribute to the Canada Pension Plan, using form *CPT 20 Election to Pay Canada Pension Plan Contributions*. Because youth brings with it a long period of compounding, these opportunities will serve you particularly well over the years as your money compounds on a tax deferred basis. In addition, saving within an RRSP allows you tax-free access to the money later, under the *Home Buyers' Plan* or the *Lifelong Learning Plan*.

Finally, be sure to open a Tax-Free Savings Account (TFSA) when you turn 18. It's a great place to "park" money and earn tax-free income too, possibly to fund next year's tuition.

• *Line 104 Net Research Grants*. If you receive a research grant, you'll be taxable on the net amount—that is, you can deduct any costs of completing the research. There is no special form for deducting your costs, simply report the net amount on Line 104. The net amount is considered earned income for both RRSP and child care purposes. If the grant is received in relation to a post-secondary program leading to a degree then the research grant may qualify as exempt scholarship income (see Line 130 below).

Line 119 Employment Insurance (EI). Sometimes, people who lose their jobs can apply for EI to help them go back to school. Know that those amounts may be taxable and that, for those who make more than a single claim in a 10-year period, the regular benefits received may be subject to a clawback if net income is above $59,250 in 2013. An RRSP contribution can help you avoid this clawback.

Line 126 Rental Income. Parents will sometimes buy a property for the university-bound child as a principal residence. That's a good way to avoid the Attribution Rules, as some or all of the future capital gains will be tax exempt. If the child rents out some of that residence to help pay for its upkeep, the rental income is reported by the child. In general, there is no attribution of income reporting back to the parent as the child is now an adult and there is likely no profit motive—the income will cover the expenses in most cases. See Chapter 36.

Line 130 Scholarships, Bursaries and Fellowships. Great news! Students who win awards to go to school now qualify for full tax exemptions, if they qualify for the full-time education amount. This credit is discussed in more detail below.

Review the list of rules below, to adjust prior filed returns if you made any errors or omissions:

• **Prior to tax year 2006**, up to $3,000 of income from scholarships, fellowships and bursaries was exempt from taxable income.

- **Since 2006**, the full amounts of these awards are excluded from income if the recipient qualified for the full-time education tax credit.
- **No Education Amount—$500 Exemption Only.** If the student does not qualify for the education amount, a $500 exemption applies; you'll report the rest as income on Line 130 Other Income. Your software may simply call this "Other Income" on your selection screens.
- **Elementary or Secondary School Awards.** For 2007 and later years, scholarships and bursaries that relate to attending elementary or secondary school programs will also be exempt from tax if the student qualifies for the full-time education amount.
- **Part-Time Students.** Beginning in 2010, students in part-time programs will limit their scholarship exemption to tuition paid plus costs of program-related materials. An exception is where they also qualify for the Disability Tax Credit, in which case the full scholarship is exempt.
- **Research Leading to a Degree.** Where the scholarship is received in respect of a program that consists mainly of research, the education amount (and therefore the scholarship exemption) is allowed only if the program leads to a degree.

Line 130 RESP Income. Many families save for years within a Registered Education Savings Plan (RESP) for their child's education. When it comes time to take money out of the plan, here's what will happen:

- The student will report the Educational Assistance Payments (EAPs), which include investment earnings on the principal contributed by the benefactors, as well as the Canada Education Grants and Bonds on Line 130.
- The capital contributed may be withdrawn tax free.

Enrolment Time Required. The maximum amount of EAPs is $5,000 until the student has completed 13 consecutive weeks in a qualifying education program at a post-secondary educational institution (3 weeks if the student is studying abroad). Once the 13 weeks have been completed, there is no limit to the amount that may be withdrawn from the plan.

However, if, for a period of 12 months, the student does not enrol in a qualifying education program, the 13-week period and the $5,000 limitation will be imposed again. There are no restrictions on how the EAPs are actually spent so long as the student is enrolled in a qualifying educational program.

Line 135 Self-Employment. The student may have a variety of self-employment income sources; for example, tutoring others, marking exams or providing consulting services. Be sure to report these amounts on Form T2125 *Statement of Income and Expenses*. Auto and home office expenses may be claimable and certain equipment, like computers depreciable on Capital Cost Allowance schedules. For tips on claiming income and expenses in a small proprietorship see Chapter 43. Business ownership is discussed in more detail in my book *Make Sure It's Deductible*. Do know that any allowable business losses can be used to offset other income sources of the year; if there is a net profit, it will build RRSP contribution room. In addition, CPP premiums may be payable.

Deductions. Students may qualify for a number of deductions on the tax return, which may reduce net income on Line 236 or taxable income on Line 260.

Of note is the RRSP contribution, based on the student's unused RRSP contribution room built up over the teenage years by smart parents who have filed tax returns for their children. This deduction will reduce net income, which in turn will make it possible for the parent or supporting individual to claim a transfer of the Tuition, Education, and Textbook amounts the student may qualify for.

Case Study | Using an RRSP Contribution to Generate a Tuition Transfer

Irene is a full-time student at university. Working part-time during the winter and full-time during the winter, she earned $14,000 in 2013. She has a Tuition, Education, and Textbook amount of $3,500. Her RRSP contribution room for 2013 was $2,500 based on income in prior years.

Without an RRSP contribution, she will need $1,062 of her federal Tuition, Education, and Textbook amount and could therefore transfer the remaining $2,438 to her father. If her father gave her $1,000 to make an RRSP contribution, her taxable income would decrease by $1,000 and she'd only require $62 of her federal Tuition, Education, and Textbook amount. This would, allow her to transfer an additional $1,000 of the credit to her father. Provincial credit transferred would be increased as well but the amount depends on Irene's province of residence.

Refundable Tax Credits. All students should file a tax return to claim their *GST/HST Tax Credit*. In addition, some students may qualify for the *Working Income Tax Benefit (WITB)*, which is provided to those who earn at least $3,000 and have an eligible dependant. Your software will calculate this automatically, but to illustrate, please see the case study below.

Case Study | Planning to Maximize Student Credits

Jonathan is a 19-year-old part-time commerce student living in Ontario. He works part time as a waiter and reports T4 income of $5,000 and tips of $6,000 on his tax return. His wife Amanda is not a student and has no net income because she stays at home to look after their son Joshua. He receives both a GST/HST Credit and a WITB.

GST/HST Credit. Jonathan can claim the GST/HST credit for himself, his wife, and his son. The total credit for July 2014 to June 2015 is approximately $676.

WITB. Because Jonathan has an eligible dependant and employment income—he qualifies for the Working Income Tax Benefit. With a combined family net income of only $11,000, Jonathan qualifies for a WITB of $1,797.

Non-Refundable Tax Credits. Students will qualify for two specific tax credits: The *Amount for Interest Paid on Student Loans* and *the Tuition, Education and Textbook Amount,* described below.

Line 319 Interest Paid on Student Loans. Taxpayers who pay interest on student loans under the *Canada Student Loans Act,* the *Canada Student Financial Assistance Act* or a provincial statute that governs the granting of financial assistance to students at a post-secondary level, may claim a non-refundable credit against taxes payable for the interest paid. You should have official receipts for the amount paid. Keep these in case CRA asks for them.

Student Loan Forgiveness | Starting in 2012-13, the government will also forgive a portion of the federal component of Canada Student Loans for new family physicians, nurses and nurse practitioners who agree to work in under-served rural and remote communities.

Five Year Carry Forward. Although not transferable to another person such as a spouse or common-law partner, any credit not claimed in one year may be carried forward for up to five years. Keep back-up documentation on file.

Line 323 Tuition, Education and Textbook Amounts. This is a combo of three great tax credits in one! Post-secondary students may claim the Tuition amount, the Education amount and the amount for Textbooks.

The student must make the claim on his or her tax return first, but if not taxable, or if the full amount is not needed, this credit may be transferred from a student to the supporting individual. Alternatively, the student can decide not to transfer the amount and instead carry any unused amount forward to be used in future years to offset income tax payable.

 CHECK IT OUT | **Where is the Tuition, Education and Textbook Amount claimed?** The claim for these credits originates on the student's Schedule 11 *Tuition, Education, and Textbook Amounts.* But then, depending on who claims the amount, you may have to check out three different lines:

- Claim the credit for the student on Line 323 of Schedule 1 on the Federal T1.
- Claim the amounts transferred from a child on Line 324.

- If the transfer is to the student's spouse, complete Schedule 2 *Federal Amounts Transferred From Your Spouse or Common-law Partner.*

Qualifying Programs. The educational institution will issue an official receipt or Form T2202A *Tuition, Education, and Textbook Amounts Certificate* showing the amount of tuition paid. Qualifying institutions in Canada post-secondary institutions like universities or colleges or private designated educational institutions.

Universities outside Canada. These may qualify too. They will send the student Form TL11A *Tuition, Education, and Textbook Amounts Certificate—University Outside Canada*, TL11C *Tuition, Education, and Textbook Amounts Certificate—Commuter to the United States* or TL11D *Tuition Fees Certificate—Educational Institutions Outside Canada for a Deemed Resident of Canada.* Flying schools may send Form TL11B *Tuition Fees Certificate—Flying School or Club.*

Qualifying Course Duration. The required study period for claiming the Tuition and Education amounts as well as qualifying to withdraw Education Assistance Payments from an RESP is 13 weeks. However, if the student is studying abroad, that duration has been shortened to three consecutive weeks effective the 2011 tax year.

Tax Calculations. Students will want to file their no or low income returns to transfer their Tuition, Education, and Textbook Amounts to supporting individuals. This is the subject of the next chapter.

In addition, from a provincial perspective, it's important to file to take advantage of tuition rebates or provincial tax credits. The following tuition rebate programs are refundable (i.e. do not require tax provincial taxes be payable to the student):

- Saskatchewan Graduate Retention Program Tuition Rebate,
- Manitoba tuition fee income tax rebate, and
- The NB Tuition Rebate is claimed on a separate application form (NBTR(1)) and is not integrated into the NB provincial tax forms.

 The Bottom Line | Students should be filing returns for several reasons, even if they are not taxable. They should report income to build RRSP contribution room. They should claim only the Tuition, Education, and Textbook Amounts that they need to eliminate their taxable income and either transfer the unused credits to a supporting person or carry them forward to be claimed in a future year. Students who are taxable may find that an RRSP contribution may reduce their need for their Tuition, Education, and Textbook amounts and allow them to transfer the unneeded credits to a supporting person.

25

Claiming Students

When filing a tax return for a student in the family, it's important to know who qualifies as a supporting individual to the student. This can be a spouse, parent or grandparent. In each case it's important to file the tax return of the student first, to understand that person's level of net and taxable income. Then it can be determined what non-refundable tax credits can be claimed on each return: the student's and the supporting individual's.

In this chapter we are primarily concerned with a parent or grandparent who is eligible to transfer the Tuition, Education, and Textbook Amount to his or her return. However, in the case of spouses who support their partners who are students, recall that it is possible for the higher earner to claim Child Care Expenses for any children the couple may have (see Chapter 15), and make claims for the Spousal Amount, Public Transit Amount, and charitable donations for the family.

Where the student who qualifies for the Tuition, Education, and Textbook Amount is under 18, other provisions may be claimed for that minor, including Universal Child Care Benefits as income, and a variety of non-refundable tax credits summarized later in the chapter. If the student is disabled, even more tax preferences emerge. See Chapters 27 and 28.

Transferring Tuition, Education, and Textbook Amounts to Supporting Individuals. In order to make this transfer, several circumstances must be present:

- The student must not need this credit to reduce taxable income. That's why the student's return is completed first, and why it's a good idea to create RRSP contribution room for the student along the way. Recall, this is done by filing tax returns to report babysitting, lawn care or paper route earnings during the teenage years. This opportunity to make an RRSP contribution will create a deduction that could make the difference in allowing the transfer of Tuition, Education, and Textbook Credits to offset the supporting individual's taxes payable.

- The student must "sign over" the credits to the supporting individual, by completing the back of the T2202A slip.
- If there is a spouse who claims the student as a dependant, the transfer must be to the spouse, even if the young couple lives at home.
- Schedule 11 *Tuition, Education, and Textbook Amounts* is completed.

Eligible Amounts to Transfer. When all of these steps are properly completed, here's what the supporting individual will be able claim: up to $5,000 of the following:

- **Tuition fees paid in excess of $100** to each individual qualifying post-secondary institution can be claimed. This includes admission fees, charges for the use of library or laboratory facilities, examination fees and ancillary fees that exceed $100 including the cost of identification cards and certain prerequisite study materials.
- **Education amounts** of $400 per month for full-time students and $120 for part-time students are possible.
- **Textbook amounts** claimable are $65 a month more for full time students and $20 a month more for part time students.

Unused Credits in Excess of $5,000. What happens if neither the student nor the supporting individual can use up all the Tuition, Education, and Textbook Credits? Here are the rules:

- The amount that is not claimed by the student and not transferred can be carried forward to the following taxation year.
- If carried forward, the unused amount must be used by the student—it is not eligible for transfer to a supporting individual in that year.

 Case Study | **Carry Forward of Tuition, Education, and Textbook Credits**

In 2012, Kyle's taxable income was less than $10,000 so he could not use any of his $6,000 Tuition, Education, and Textbook Amounts so he transferred $5,000 to his mother and carried forward $1,000.

In 2013, Kyle's taxable income was $14,500 and his Tuition, Education, and Textbook Amount was $6,500. With non-refundable credits of $13,006, Kyle needed to use $1,494 of his Tuition, Education, and Textbook Amounts. He will use $1,000 of the amount carried forward and $494 of his 2013 amount leaving $6,006 unused. He can transfer $5,000 − $494 = $4,506 to his mother for 2013 and carry forward the remaining $1,500 to next year.

Other Provisions. If your student is under 18 or infirm, a host of other tax provisions may be claimed on your return. Some of them will be affected by the size of the student's income. For these reasons, it's a good idea to reduce net income with an RRSP contribution, as described above.

✓ **CHECK** | **What other provisions on my return are affected by the student's**
IT OUT | **income?** A simple chart, below illustrates them well:

Student's Income Has No Effect on	Student's Income Will Affect These
Line 117 Universal Child Care Benefit	Line 214 Child Care Expenses* Line 303 Amount for Spouse or Common-Law Partner
Line 367 Amount for Children under 18	Line 305 Amount for Eligible Dependant Line 315 Caregiver Amount
Line 364 Public Transit Amount	Line 324 Tuition, Education, and Textbook Amounts transferred
Line 365 Children's Fitness Amount	
Line 370 Children's Art Amount	
Line 313 Adoption Expenses	
Line 318 Disability Amount Transferred	
Line 330 Medical Expenses	
Canada Child Tax Benefit	
GST/HST Credit	
Working Income Tax Benefit	

* For a dependent child from a relationship other than yours and your spouse's.

RESPs. Supporting Individuals should be aware of one other provision that may impact their returns if there is a student in the family: taxable Education Assistance Payments (EAPs).

If the child does not become a student, there are consequences too. When the RESP is collapsed, the Canada Education Savings Grants and Bonds must be repaid to the government (the RESP provider will take care of this step). The contributions to the RESP will be returned to the contributor but any excess (Accumulated Income Payments—these are the earnings generated within the plan) must be reported in income by the contributor. In addition to the normal tax on this income, a special 20% tax will be payable on the Accumulated Income Payments, unless the recipient contributes the funds to his or her RRSP.

Case Study | Accumulated Income Payments

In 2013, Hector collapsed the RESP that he had set up for his only son Jesus who had been killed in a traffic accident. Hector had made contributions of $20,000 to the RESP. The balance in the plan was $27,400 which included $4,000 of Canada Education Savings Grants and $3,400 in accumulated earnings. The RESP provider paid Hector $23,400 and sent the $4,000 in CESGs back to the government. The $20,000 of contributions are not taxable, but Hector must include the $3,400 of Accumulated Income Payments in his income. If he makes an RRSP contribution of at least $3,400 in 2013, he will not be subject to the 20% tax on Accumulated Income Payments. If not, he'll pay tax at his marginal tax rate on the $3,400 plus an additional $680 in tax.

The Bottom Line | Filing a tax return for a student can be complicated, but if completed properly, tax credits can spill over and reduce taxes for supporting individuals, or reduce the graduate's taxes in the future if carry forward provisions are properly managed. Remember too that many provinces offer rebates of tuitions paid against provincial taxes payable if graduates stay in the province to work and raise families. The benefits will keep coming back if you are tax savvy.

26

Medical Expenses

I love this topic! That's because just about everyone I know has an "aha moment" when the topic of tax-deductible medical expenses comes up. We may have skirted around the edges as we have discussed various tax filing profiles so far, but now it's time to get down to business and tell you about the lucrative claims you qualify for when someone becomes sick in the family.

 CHECK IT OUT | **Where are medical expenses claimed?** Medical expenses qualify for a non-refundable credit on Schedule 1. Often your software will have a worksheet for you to enter data on. It may also optimize the claim between family members.

Your total expenses for the immediate family (spouses and dependent children) for *any 12-month period* ending in the year are itemized and claimed on Line 330. This means, that if your biggest medical expenses occurred between June 2012 and May 2013, this is the period you'll claim on your 2013 so long as you did not already claim them on your 2012 return. You'll save the rest of your receipts for 2013 until next year.

Unfortunately, many higher earners can't actually claim medical expenses.

 New for 2013 | The claim for medical expenses is reduced by 3% of the claimant's net income (or the dependant's net income if claiming expenses for other dependants) to a maximum of $2,151. This maximum is reached when net income exceeds $71,700.

Generally that means the spouse with the lower income will get the biggest claim, but it is worth nothing if that spouse is not taxable. In those cases, carry the receipts forward for a possible future claim.

Whose Expenses can be Claimed? Medical expenses paid may be claimed for any of the following people:

- the taxpayer,
- the taxpayer's spouse or common-law partner;
- a minor child or grandchild of the taxpayer or the taxpayer's spouse who depended on the taxpayer for support, and a parent, grandparent, brother, sister, uncle, aunt, niece, or nephew of the taxpayer or the taxpayer's spouse who lived in Canada at any time in the year and depended on the taxpayer for support.

Medical Expenses for Other Dependants. In the case of Other Dependants, those other than your immediate family, the claim is made on Line 331 of the tax return and must be for the same 12 month period as the expenses for the nuclear family. In this case, however, use the dependant's net income in determining the 3% reduction. Claims for dependants other than the immediate family should be made on whichever return provides the most benefit. The following case study illustrates this:

Case Study | Medical Expenses of Other Dependants

Kristina's net income for 2013 was $75,000. Her medical expenses total $12,500. $6,000 were for her son, Drew and $6,500 were for Trevor, her grandfather who lives with her and whose income for the year was $10,000.

Kristina's medical expenses were:

Drew:	$6,000 – $2,151* =	$3,849
Trevor:	$6,500 – ($10,000 x 3%) =	$6,200
Total:		$10,049

* $2,151 because $75,000 x 3% = $2,250 which exceeds $2,151

Claims in the Year of Death. A special rule applies to claiming medical expenses when a taxpayer dies. On the return for the year of death (or the spouse's return for the same year), medical expenses may be claimed for a 24-month period which includes the date of death. This means that expenses paid after death may be included as well as any expenses from the prior year that have not already been claimed.

Allowable Medical Expenses. The following is a list of common medical expenses you may have forgotten to claim. Be sure to adjust prior filed returns if this is to your advantage. Remember, you can go back up to 10 years to recover missed deductions and credits.

Medical Expenses

Medical Practitioners
- a dentist
- a medical doctor
- a medical practitioner
- an optometrist
- a pharmacist
- a psychologist
- a speech-language pathologist
- an osteopath
- a chiropractor
- a naturopath
- a therapeutist or therapist
- a physiotherapist
- a chiropodist (or podiatrist)
- a Christian science practitioner
- certain psychoanalysts
- a psychologist
- a qualified speech-language pathologist or audiologist
- certain occupational therapists
- an acupuncturist
- a dietician
- a dental hygienist
- a nurse including a practical nurse whose full-time occupation is nursing
- a Christian science nurse
- an audiologist

Medical Treatments
- medical and dental services
- attendant or nursing home care
- ambulance fees
- transportation
- travel expenses (see below)
- eyeglasses
- guide dogs
- transplant costs
- alterations to the home for disabled persons (prescribed)
- lip reading or sign language training
- sign language services
- cost of training a person to provide care for an infirm dependant
- cost of deaf-blind intervening services
- reading services provided under a medical practitioner's prescription
- cost of drugs obtained under the Special Access Program
- for medical marihuana or marihuana seeds purchased from Health Canada, or a licensed person under Marihuana Medical Access Regulations (MMAR)
- therapy provided by a medical doctor, psychologist or occupational therapist for a patient who qualifies for the disability amount
- tutoring services for a patient with a learning disability or mental impairment
- drugs prescribed by a medical practitioner (see list above) and recorded by a pharmacist
- lab tests
- private health plan premiums, including group insurance premiums
- Blue Cross premiums including travel insurance costs

Medical Devices

- an artificial limb
- an iron lung
- a rocking bed
- a wheelchair crutches
- a spinal brace
- a brace for a limb
- an ileostomy or a colostomy pad
- a truss for a hernia
- an artificial eye
- a laryngeal speaking aid
- hearing aid
- an artificial kidney machine

For 2012 and subsequent years, the costs of blood coagulation monitors for use by individuals who require anti-coagulation therapy, including associated disposable peripherals such as pricking devices, lancets and test strips if prescribed by a medical practitioner may also be claimed.

Home Modifications as Medical Expenses. These eligible expenses may be quite lucrative, so keep receipts in case of audit.

- *Home Modifications.* Incremental costs of building or modifying a new home for a patient who is physically impaired or lacks normal physical development where those costs are incurred to enable the patient to gain access to, or be functional within, the home. However, the expenditure must not be of a type intended to increase the value of the home or would not typically be incurred by someone who was not impaired.
- *Driveway Alterations.* Costs of alterations to the driveway of a residence of a person with a mobility impairment to facilitate access to a bus.
- *Moving Expenses.* For a disabled person to move to a more suitable dwelling to a maximum of $2,000.
- *Van Adaptations.* The lesser of $5,000 and 20% of the cost of a van that has to be adapted for the transportation of an individual who requires a wheelchair.

Special Needs Persons. The following costs are claimable, provided they are not claimed elsewhere on the tax return:

- incremental cost of gluten-free food products for persons with celiac disease;
- cost of purchasing, operating and maintaining phototherapy equipment for treating psoriasis and other skin disorders;
- cost of real-time captioning, note-taking services, for a person with speech or hearing impairment;
- cost of voice recognition software for persons with a physical impairment;
- beginning in 2004, the cost of talking textbooks used by individuals with a perceptual disability if the expenditure is not claimed as a medical supports deduction;
- cost of operating and maintaining an oxygen concentrator;
- a device that is a Bliss symbol board for use by an individual who has a speech impairment need for which is certified in writing by a medical practitioner;

- a device that is a Braille note-taker for use by a blind individual to allow that individual to take notes, need being certified in writing by a medical practitioner; and
- a device that is a page turner or other devices used by an individual with a severe and prolonged impairment to turn pages of a book or to read print as certified in writing by a medical practitioner.

Medical Travel Costs. The taxpayer may claim travel expenses for the patient and one attendant who must travel 40 km or more to receive medical services not available in their community. If the taxpayer is required to travel more than 80 km from their place of residence, then travel expenses may include hotel and meal costs. Actual receipts can be used for costs of travel including gas, hotel and meals.

Alternatively, or you can claim vehicle expenses using a *simplified method* based on a rate per kilometre. This method does not require receipts to be kept for vehicle expenses, only a record of the number of kilometres driven. If more than one province is involved, the rate is calculated based on the province in which the trip began. An updated list of rates is available early in the New Year from CRA. Most software will have the allowable rates for your province built in.

 The Bottom Line | It pays to hunt down your medical expenses and claim them over the best 12-month period **ending in the tax year**. Baby boomers in particular are at risk of under-reporting medical costs when they care for their aged parents or if their own spouses or siblings become ill. Visit with a tax professional when life events involving the health of a family member occur.

27

Filing for the Sick and Disabled

Did you know that one in five Canadians aged 45+ provides care to seniors living with long-term health problems[5]? Because of the cost of hiring help, the range of services that fall into the gap that family members must fill are extensive. From meal preparation and household chores to time off for appointments with doctors and to deal with financial matters, the time commitment is great and cuts into economic activities for the caregiver, such as employment and self-employment.

In addition, the caregiver may require supports at home as a result: child care for the nuclear family, personal and respite care and resources for specialized nursing care if publicly-provided home care is unavailable or inadequate.

The physical and psychological toll on family caregivers is also huge: up to 75% will develop psychological illnesses; 15 to 32% suffer from depression. These are significant numbers. As our population ages, disability-related caregiving for family members will increase.

In this chapter, we'll discuss the tax supports available on the tax return of the disabled person. In the next chapter, we'll discuss how to claim them on the return of the supporting individual who gives care.

Income Averaging Opportunities. The objective in preparing a tax return for the disabled is first to properly report all the income sources that may come your way, and to keep an eye on tax efficiency. This can be difficult because often, the receipt of income is unpredictable and paid in lump sums.

---

[5] Canadian Study of Health and Aging (CSHA), 1991, 1996, 2001.

Similar to retirement income planning, the opportunity is to layer voluntary income with-drawals from private savings plans while waiting for government sources like CPP Disability amounts, EI, and Workers' Compensation.

Because the adjudication periods for these sources can be long and prone to appeals, the resulting amounts can come in lump sums, which bump up marginal tax rates and affect how much is received for various refundable and non-refundable tax credits.

In addition, some of the amounts previously received from sources like EI, for example, may need to be repaid as income spikes. This can also affect the amounts of credits that can be claimed by supporting individuals, as net income levels of the disabled person will fluctuate.

For all of these reasons, it's usually necessary review the income for a disabled person—not just in one tax year, but over several tax years—to review available credits and average down the taxes payable. You may wish to seek professional help.

Income. The disabled person may need to leave work, temporarily or permanently. Various insurance plans may be available for income replacement, but if they do not produce enough, other investments must be tapped. Following are some of the common income replacement sources that may be available, and how to report them on the tax return.

CPP Disability Pension. After a three-month waiting period, benefits under this plan may be payable up to age 65 if the applicant is permanently disabled. CPP disability pension benefits are taxable and will be reported to you in Box 16 of a T4A(P) slip. Your software will post this amount to Line 114 and Line 152 of your tax return. This is because the benefits are also considered to be earned income for RRSP purposes and this notation will take them into account to enable you to make additional RRSP contributions in future years, which can offset the taxes that may be generated by the benefits.

The payments are made for conditions that are "severe and prolonged."

 CHECK IT OUT | **What is the definition of severe and prolonged?** For CPP Disability Benefit purposes, this refers to a mental or physical disability that regularly restricts the person from doing any type of substantially gainful work. Prolonged means the disability is likely to be long-term and last indefinitely or will likely result in death.

Prorated CPP Premiums. In the year you begin receiving CPP disability benefits, your required CPP premiums will be prorated. Be sure to enter the number of months shown in Box 21 of the T4A(P) slip so your software can complete Form T2204 and determine if you've overpaid CPP.

Retroactive CPP Benefits. You can apply for the benefits retroactively, but only for 11 prior months.

Dependant Benefits. When you qualify for CPP Disability Pension, a Children's Benefit is also available, if the child is your natural or adopted child, or a child in your care and custody, and either under the age of 18 or between 18 and 25 and attending a recognized school or university full time. The child will report that income.

Special averaging will occur on your tax returns if you receive a lump sum that is over $300. CRA will do this automatically for you. When that happens, see a tax pro to ensure other tax deductions or credits—like medical expenses or spousal amounts—require optimization between spouses with the new results.

EI Benefits. You may be entitled to receive benefits from Employment Insurance as a result of your inability to work for up to 15 weeks. These benefits are taxable. They can amount to up to 55% of your average insurable earnings to a dollar maximum. Lower income families can receive up to 80% of the average insurable earnings. However, applying for them involves a qualification process with Service Canada, including health information with a doctor's certificate, as well as detailed employment records. If you are eligible the payments will start in 28 days, after a two-week waiting period.

Complications arise when EI is received in conjunction with other income. For example, any money you receive during the two-week waiting period will be deducted from the benefits you are entitled to receive for the first three weeks, dollar for dollar.

Likewise if you work while receiving EI sickness benefits, or receive commissions, compensation under a work accident plan, group health or group wage loss replacement plan, payments under an accident insurance plan, or retirement income under a public or private plan, the amount you earn will be deducted dollar for dollar.

The good news is that the following types of income noted on the EI benefits website have no impact on EI:

- retroactive salary increases;
- disability benefits;
- survivor or dependent benefits;
- workers' compensation benefits paid under specific regulations;
- additional insurance benefits paid under a private plan that is approved by Service Canada (for example, payments for pain and suffering or medical expenses that you receive from an insurance company after you have been injured in a car accident);
- additional sickness benefits paid by your employer from a supplemental unemployment benefit plan (as long as the income, benefits, and additional amounts combined do not exceed 100% of your weekly earnings);
- sickness or disability payments received under a private wage loss replacement plan.

Self-Employed and EI | Self-employed persons are ineligible for regular EI benefits due to lay-offs or business slow-downs. But they can now elect to receive EI benefits for the following benefits:

- Maternity benefits (15 weeks maximum) are available to birth mothers and cover the period surrounding birth
- Parental/adoptive benefits (35 week maximum) are available to adoptive or biological parents while they are caring for a newborn or newly adopted child, and may be taken by either parent or shared between them
- Sickness benefits (15 weeks maximum) which may be paid to a person who is unable to work because of sickness, injury or quarantine; and
- Compassionate care benefits (6 weeks maximum) which may be paid to persons who have to be away from work temporarily to provide care or support to a family member who is gravely ill with significant risk of death

In order to be eligible for benefits, the individual must register with the Canada Employment Insurance Commission on-line through Service Canada. For the purposes of this EI program, you are considered self-employed if you operate your own business or are employed by a corporation and control more than 40% of the voting shares.

Opt-out. Once registered, you will have 60 days to change your mind. Assuming that you do not collect any EI benefits, you may choose to opt-out at the beginning of any calendar year. If you do receive EI benefits, you are no longer eligible to opt-out of the EI program on self-employed earnings, *ever.* This stipulation remains in effect regardless of your self-employed status or change in self-employment. Once you receive a benefit, you will continue to remain in the program and pay annual premiums.

Income and Premium Requirements. Self-employed persons deciding to "opt-in" will pay the same EI premium as an employee. The business however, will not be required to pay the employer's portion of the EI premium. Premiums will be paid on the individual's personal tax return annually and a minimum self-employed income of $6,000 is required. EI premiums must be paid for one year prior to filing a claim. EI premiums on self-employment income are calculated on Schedule 13.

Repayments of EI and CPP. Because there is often a multi-year process to sort out repayments of those various income sources that overlap in the onerous qualification process and waiting periods. If a repayment is necessary, it is claimed as a deduction on Line 232 Other Deductions, in the year the repayment took place.

Legal Fees. Legal fees paid to object to or appeal a decision under the *Income Tax Act*, the *Unemployment Insurance Act*, the *Employment Insurance Act*, the *Canada Pension Plan Act* or the *Quebec Pension Plan Act* are deducted here, too.

Workers' Compensation. If you receive Workers' Compensation benefits, you will receive a T5007 slip showing the amount received. When you enter the slip, your software will include the amount on Line 144 of your return. The good news is it will also claim a deduction at Line 250. The result of including this amount in income and then deducting it at Line 250 is that the payments are included in your net income but not your taxable income. These payments may then reduce your refundable tax credits and may also reduce any non-refundable tax credits that may be claimed for you.

Wage Loss Replacement Benefits. If you paid all of the premiums for your wage loss replacement plan, then benefits you receive from the plan are not taxable. However, if your employer paid some or all of the premiums, the benefits you will receive will be taxable. You can deduct the premiums you paid from that income before you report the net amount on Line 104.

 Beginning in 2013, you need to enter the total amount you contributed to wage loss replacement plans on line 103.

Example: Connor was injured at work and received benefits from a wage loss replacement plan that was jointly funded by employee and employer premiums. Because Connor's employer paid a portion of the premiums, the benefits are taxable, but Connor can claim a deduction for all of the premiums he paid into the plan that he has not deducted previously.

Severance. If you're leaving your employment due to a disability, you may receive a severance package or job termination payment. See Chapter 19 for details.

RDSP Income. If you have a Registered Disability Saving Plan and are receiving disability assistance payments from the plan, a portion of these payments will be shown in Box 131 of a T4A slip. That amount must be reported and is taxable. When you enter these benefits in your tax software, they will be posted to Line 125 of your return. The beneficiary must start to withdraw funds from the RDSP in the year he or she turns 60.

The portion of your disability assistance payments that represents contributions to the RDSP will not be taxable. In addition, the payments will be excluded from net income for the purposes of calculating an EI or OAS clawback.

 There are a number of changes to RDSPs withdrawals that should be noted before you tap into these plans:

- **Grant and Bond Repayments.** For withdrawals from RDSPs after 2013, the "10-Year Replacement Rule" will be replaced with a "Proportional Repayment Rule". Under the old rule, if any amount is withdrawn from the RDSP any Canada Disability Savings Grants and Bonds (CDSG and CDSB) received in the past ten years had to be repaid. (There is an exception in the cases of a shortened life expectancy). Under the new rule, the repayment amount will be *the lesser of the amount removed x 3* and the amount of the CDSG and CDSB amounts received in the past ten years. You will therefore want to carefully consider making a small withdrawal in these cases.

- **Disability Payments to Increase.** For withdrawals made after 2013, the maximum Lifetime Disability Assistance Payment (LDAP) will be increased to no less than 10% of the fair market value of the assets in the plan at the beginning of the year. Where the maximum amount under the existing LDAP formula exceeds 10% of the asset value, then the maximum is the amount determined under the LDAP formula.
- **Rollovers From Other Plans.** Beginning in 2014, it will be possible to rollover both RESP and RRSPs balances into RDSPs. RESP investments, after Canada Education Savings Grants and Bonds have been repaid may be rolled over to an RDSP so long as the plan holder has sufficient RDSP contribution room. These contributions will not generate Canada Disability Bonds or Grants. Withdrawals of rolled over RESPs will be taxable.
- **Termination of RDSPs When Beneficiary no Longer Disabled.** When an RDSP beneficiary ceases to qualify for the Disability Amount, currently, the RDSP must be terminated immediately. Beginning in 2014, when this happens, the beneficiary may make an election to continue the plan for up to four calendar years after the end of the calendar year in which the beneficiary ceases to be eligible for the Disability Amount. During the election period, no contributions will be permitted and no new CESG and CESB will be paid into the plan. Withdrawals under the Proportional Repayment Rule will be allowed, however.

Current RDSPs which would be required to be terminated before 2014 will not be required to be terminated until the end of 2014.

Critical Illness and Long Term Care Insurance. Premiums paid for private disability or critical illness insurance are not tax deductible, but benefits received are not taxable, they are often paid within a month after the critical illness diagnosis and the money can generally be used for any purpose.

If your life insurance provides for it, a lump sum payment may be available as an advance on the death benefit if you are diagnosed with less than one (or sometimes two) years to live. This is also a good way to receive a tax-free benefit to help pay for the costs of end-of-life care.

Disability Supports Deduction. If you are disabled and incur expenses of an attendant or other disability supports purchased to enable you to earn employment or self-employment income or to pursue education, then you can claim the costs of disability supports on Line 215 so long as the expenses were not reimbursed.

If you are employed or self-employed, your claim is limited to your earned income (employment, net self-employment, taxable scholarships and net research grants).

If you are a student, your claim is limited to the least of:

- $375 for each week you attended school
- Your net income less your earned income
- $15,000

Your combined claim is limited to the amount of your expenses. Unclaimed amounts due to the restrictions above can be claimed as a medical expense on Line 332 may also claim the *Refundable Medical Expense Supplement* on Line 452, discussed below. Your software will make the claim automatically for you.

Real Dollar Value. Because the disability supports deduction reduces both net and taxable income, the dollar value of the deduction depends on the taxpayer's income level. At lower income levels, the value of a deduction is equivalent to a non-refundable credit (income below $43,561 for 2013) but the value is proportionately larger at higher income levels. In addition, the deduction decreases net income and therefore can increase social benefits such as the GSTC and Canada Child Tax Benefit.

Non-Refundable Tax Credits. The disabled individual must first claim certain credits on the tax return; then if not taxable, the amounts can be transferred to a supporting individual.

Disability Amount. If you become disabled, you can claim the disability amount on Line 316 of your return. You'll need to complete a Form T2201A *Disability Tax Credit Application* and have a medical practitioner complete Form T2201B, *Disability Tax Credit Certification by a Qualified Practitioner.* Unless you have a T2201 or T2201B Form already on record with CRA, you'll not be able to use NETFILE to file your return.

If you do not require the full disability amount to reduce your federal taxes to zero, you may transfer the unused portion of the credit to a supporting person. In the case of spouses, that transfer is made on Schedule 2 and on Line 326.

 CHECK IT OUT | **What is the maximum claim for the disability amount?** The maximum claim is $7,697 per adult dependant. As a non-refundable credit, the disability amount reduces the taxpayer's tax bill by $7,697 x 15% = $1,154.55 regardless of income. In addition, each province has a provincial disability amount which varies by province. In Ontario, for example, the dollar value of the provincial disability amount is $390.62 ($7,735 x 5.05%).

Taxpayers with "a severe and prolonged impairment in mental or physical functions" may claim it. Here is what that means:

- A **prolonged impairment** is one that has lasted or is expected to last for a continuous period of at least 12 months.
- A **severe impairment** in physical or mental functions must restrict the patient all or substantially all of the time, which is another way of saying 90% of the time or more.

Examples of Disabilities That Qualify. You will be considered markedly or in some cases significantly restricted if all or substantially all of the time you have difficulty performing one or more of the basic daily living activities listed below, even with the appropriate therapy, medication, and devices:

- speaking
- hearing
- walking
- elimination (bowel or bladder functions)
- feeding
- dressing
- mental functions necessary for everyday life

Life Sustaining Therapy. Those who require life-sustaining therapy will qualify as well, if the therapy is required to support a vital function and the therapy is needed at least **3 times per week**, for an average of at least **14 hours per week**. This includes the daily adjusting of medication and the time spent by a primary caregiver performing and supervising activities for a disabled child. Note: Disability Tax Credits for children will be discussed in the next chapter.

Home and Attendant Care. There are some special rules in making this claim if home or attendant care is involved:

- You may not claim both the costs of nursing home care or full-time attendant care as a medical expense, together with the Disability Amount. One or the other can be claimed but not both.
- Those who pay someone to come into the home to provide care for the sick may claim expenditures up to $10,000 ($20,000 in the year of death) as medical expenses and still claim the Disability Amount.
- Individuals who qualify for the disability amount will also be considered to be infirm for the purposes of the Amount for Eligible Dependants, the Amount for Infirm Dependants, and the Caregiver Amount.

If possible, you should send in the completed T2201A and T2201B forms before filing your return to minimize the delays in sending refunds caused by review of the form. Once the form is accepted by CRA, you may file using NETFILE.

Medical Expenses. Disabled individuals often incur medical expenses that cannot be reimbursed. If the disabled person does not have enough income to claim these, a supporting person may use them:

- *Attendant Care Costs.* Medical expense costs up to $10,000 are allowed without affecting your claim for the disability amount. In other words, you cannot claim the disability amount if you claim more than $10,000 for attendant care costs as a medical expense. Fees for the completion of the *Disability Tax Credit Certification by a Qualified Practitioner* (Form T2201B) are considered to be *medical expenses.*
- *Real Dollar Value.* As a non-refundable credit, claiming attendant care costs as a medical expense reduce your taxes by 15% of the amount claimed. In addition, if there are no other medical expenses, the claim is reduced by 3% of net income (net income of the dependant or net income of the claimant if the claim is for the taxpayer, their spouse, or dependent children).

Case Study | Attendant Care Costs as Medical Expenses

Linda's net income is $21,000. She is eligible for the Disability Amount and has medical expenses totalling $6,000 as well as attendant care expenses of $15,000. Linda relies on her son Ryan for support.

Ryan can claim Linda's medical expenses ($6,000) and by claiming only $10,000 of Linda's attendant care expenses as medical expenses, his claim for medical expenses for Linda is $15,370 ($6,000 + $10,000 – $21,000 x 3%).

See Chapter 24 for a more complete discussion of claiming medical expenses.

Refundable Medical Expense Supplement. Individuals who have at least $3,333 in earned income and have medical expenses may be able to recover some of those medical expenses by claiming the Refundable Medical Expense Supplement.

This supplement equals 25% of the medical expenses claimed to a maximum of $1,141 but is reduced by 5% of net income in excess of $25,279 for 2013.

Real Dollar Value. Because it's refundable, this supplement is worth up to $1,141.

The Bottom Line | When someone in the family becomes disabled, work with both medical and tax advisors to ensure that the tax system provides much needed financial help in these difficult times.

28

Filing for the Care Givers

The biggest concern for caregivers is the maintenance of income sources while they give care to their sick loved ones. This can cause stress, burnout and financial pressure. Your tax return may also be more complicated, but that can be a good thing because you will likely get a bigger tax refund as a result of the circumstances. In this chapter, we'll take a look at getting the biggest returns for caregivers in the family, because they have tapped into available income sources, deductions and tax credits available in these circumstances:

Income. Many employers are accommodating when their employees have to take time off to give care. Speaking to the HR department at work can uncover a host of assistance. However, if you must take a leave without pay, consider the following:

EI Compassionate Care Coverage. Employment Insurance will provide benefits for a maximum of six weeks of compassionate care benefits if your relative is at risk of dying in next 26 weeks. This can be used for psychological or emotional support; arranging for care by a third party or directly providing or participating in the actual care.

To qualify, there must be a 40% or more decrease in income, you must have accumulated 600 insured hours in the last 52 weeks and there is a two-week waiting period. At the time of writing the maximum assistance was $501 per week.

Investment Accounts. You may have to withdraw money to fund the non-working gap period. Taking a tax-free return of capital from one of your non-registered accounts can make sense. The same is true of a TFSA. A less attractive option from a tax viewpoint is to withdraw from a registered account as the amounts will be taxable in the year withdrawn. Use your tax software to do some "what if" scenarios to judge your tax liabilities before making any withdrawals.

Self-Employment. You may have to hire extra staff to cover your workload in your small business. If that results in a loss, you will be able to offset other personal income of the year if your business is unincorporated. Speak to a tax professional to project your income and losses.

Tax Deductions and Credits. Imagine a situation where a single daughter brings her mother into her home to care for her after she has suffered a stroke. The daughter will find that several tax preferences will open up for her:

Child Care Expenses. You may be able to claim child care expenses in an amount up to $10,000 if you must hire care to look after your disabled adult while you work. Complete Form T778 and record the amount on Line 214.

Real Dollar Value. Because child care expenses are a deduction, the real value depends on the claimant's tax bracket. In the lowest bracket, a claim of $10,000 could result in a federal tax reduction of $1,500 with an additional provincial tax reduction that depends on the taxpayer's province of residence. For taxpayers in the highest tax bracket, a $10,000 claim results in a federal tax reduction of $2,900 plus a provincial tax reduction.

Amount for Eligible Dependant. As a single person caring for an infirm dependant in her home, a daughter becomes eligible for this "equivalent to spouse" credit if her mother's income is under $13,078. The amount claimable on Line 305 is $13,078 less the amount of the dependant's net income.

Real Dollar Value. As a non-refundable credit, the amount for an infirm eligible dependant with no income reduces your federal taxes by $1,961.70 (as well as a provincial tax reduction).

Amount for Infirm Adult Over 18. This credit is generally not as lucrative as the Caregiver Amount, because the net income threshold for the dependant is lower. However in this case, the dependant does not have to live with you. You could claim it if you are the supporting individual and the infirm person is living in their own home, hospital or nursing home. Also, another person, perhaps a sibling could also make this claim so long as those making the claim split it between them. The amount of the claim for 2013 is $6,530 less any income of the dependant in excess of $6,548.

Real Dollar Value. As a non-refundable credit, the amount for an infirm adult dependant reduces your federal taxes by $979.50 if your dependant's net income does not exceed $6,548. In addition, there will be a provincial non-refundable tax credit, which depends on the province of residence.

Caregiver Amount. If you provide care for an infirm dependant in your home, you may be eligible to claim the Caregiver Amount if your dependant's net income is less than $21,864.

 For 2013, the maximum claim for the Caregiver Amount is $4,490 if the dependant is not infirm. This definition refers to situations where children look after their parents, age 65 or older, who are not infirm. If the dependant is infirm, the claim is $6,530.

In either case, the claim is reduced by the dependant's net income in excess of $15,334. Your tax software will do this in the background.

Real Dollar Value. As a non-refundable credit, the caregiver amount for an infirm dependant reduces your federal taxes by $979.50 if your dependant's net income does not exceed $15,334. In addition, there will be a provincial non-refundable tax credit, which depends on the province of residence.

Disability Amount. Claim this first on the return of the disabled adult; if not needed, it can then be transferred to a supporting individual, including the spouse. For 2013, the disability amount is $7,697.

For those supporting a disabled minor, this amount is enhanced by an indexed supplement of $4,490 (for 2013). This amount is reduced by amounts claimed under Child Care Expenses on Line 214 and the Disability Supports Deduction on Line 215 in excess of $2,630 (for 2013). Your software will usually calculate this in the background but be sure that all of the information is available. For example, if child care is being claimed by someone else, your software will not know this automatically.

Some provinces also provide additional tax relief for the care of disabled persons.

Real Dollar Value. As a non-refundable credit, the maximum value for a disabled child for whom no child care expenses were claimed is $1,828.05 (plus an additional provincial credit).

Medical Expenses. Caregivers can claim the medical expenses they paid for the people they are supporting. The medical expenses in this case are not based on family net income, or the net income of the individual who is claiming the expenses. Rather it is based on the net income of the disabled person and that generally means a tax reduction will result.

Real Dollar Value. Medical expenses are a non-refundable credit so the value of the claim depends on the total amount of expenses as well as the taxpayer's (or dependant's) net income.

Example: Pierre and Yvette care for and support Pierre's mother, Sophia who lives with them. Sophia's net income is only $5,000 for 2013. Her unreimbursed medical expenses total $9,000. Pierre can claim these medical expenses, reduced by 3% of Sophia's net income ($9,000 − $5,000 x 3% = $8,850 claim).

The Bottom Line | Illness is a life event that has multiple tax consequences in the family, both for the disabled person and their caregivers. It may require an inter-advisory team of financial professionals. Be sure to involve a legal advisor for the completion of the will, the Power of Attorney and a health care directive. A financial advisor can assist with the planning of investments, withdrawals and insurance and a tax advisor with complex and often-missed tax provisions, especially in a year of change.

29

Charitable Donations and the New First-Time Donor's Super Credit

Canadians are charitable people… almost all Canadians (94%) aged 15 and over gave food, goods or a financial contribution to a charitable or non-profit organization. The average annual financial contribution per donor was $446 and the median amount (half the donors gave more and half gave less) was $123. Interestingly, women give slightly more so than men[6].

When you make a financial contribution, and sometimes, a gift in kind, to a charitable cause, the government rewards you too, with a non-refundable tax credit that reduces taxes payable.

 CHECK IT OUT | **How much is the credit for charitable donations?** For those who have donated in the past, it can be close to 50 cents on the dollar, depending on how much you give. First-time donors can get an extra 25% credit for cash donations up to $1,000.

The amount is calculated on Schedule 9 and then posted to Line 349 of Schedule 1. Your software will have a screen to list your donations and calculate the credit, as follows:

1. The first $200 of total gifts is eligible for a credit at the rate equal to the lowest federal tax bracket (15%).
2. The remainder of the gifts is eligible for a credit at the federal tax rate for the highest tax bracket for the year (29%).
3. When provincial taxes are factored in charitable donations over $200 often return close to 50% of amounts donated.

---

[6] Canada Survey of Giving, Volunteering and Participating (CSGVP), 15,482 respondents in 2010 and 21,827 respondents in 2007.

Case Study | Cash Donations by First Time Donors

Siblings Chloe and Janine each donated $500 cash to the United Way in 2013. Chloe donates regularly but Janine has never claimed a charitable donation on her return. Both are single and live in Ontario.

Each is entitled to the following credits:

Federal: 15% x $200 =	$30.00
Federal: 29% x ($500 - $200) =	$87.00
Ontario: 5.05% x $200 =	$10.10
Ontario: 11.16% x ($500 - $200) =	$33.48
Total:	$160.58

In addition, Janine is eligible for the First-Time Donor's Super Credit of 25% x $500 = $125. Her total credit for the $500 donation is $160.58 + $125.00 = $285.58.

Donations may be claimed either by the person who made the gift or by their spouse or common-law partner. Because of the increased tax credit above the $200 threshold, it is often best to group the donations made by the family on one return for a better claim.

First-Time Donor's Super Credit. To qualify for the First-Time Donor's Super Credit (extra 25%), the donation must be in cash and made in the current year. Only the first $1,000 of donations qualify for the credit. A first-time donor is someone who has not claimed a donation credit since 2007. If the donor has a spouse, they do not qualify unless their spouse is also a first-time donor. This credit will be available for tax years 2013 to 2017.

What Can You Give? The allowable claim for the regular donation credit is calculated as follows, based on your qualified gifts which can include cash, publicly traded securities and mutual funds, life insurance policies, personal use property, capital property, depreciable assets, cultural and ecological gifts. Also, be aware that your software will calculate the allowable donations automatically based on your proper data entry:

- First, your donations limit is the least of
  - your total charitable gifts for the year
  - 75% of your net income for the year **plus** 25% of
  - capital gains on gifts
  - reserves from the prior year on gifts of non-qualifying securities
  - recapture on gifts of depreciable property
  - the lesser of net proceeds from gifted depreciable property and the capital cost of that property
  - **minus** any capital gains deduction claimed on gifted property
- Then add 100% of your total cultural gifts and total ecological gifts.

Cultural gifts are gifts of objects that the Canadian Cultural Property Export Review Board has determined meet the criteria set out in the *Cultural Property Export and Import Act*.

Ecological gifts are gifts of land which is certified by the Minister to be ecologically sensitive land, the preservation of which is important to the preservation of Canada's ecological heritage. Such gifts must be made to Canada, a province, a municipality, or a registered charity whose main purpose is the preservation of Canada's environmental heritage. The taxation of the capital gains on such gifts is completely eliminated.

 CHECK IT OUT | **When can I avoid capital gains on transfers of securities to charity?** You can use a 0% capital gains inclusion rate, rather than the normal 50% rate when you transfer qualified securities to your favorite charity, including a private foundation. This can include the following:

- a share, debt obligation or right such as a stock option, listed on a designated stock exchange
- unlisted securities, partnership interests or shares of a private corporation that are donated within 30 days of an exchange for publicly traded securities
- a share of the capital stock of a mutual fund corporation or mutual fund trust
- an interest in a related segregated fund trust
- a prescribed debt obligation
- ecologically sensitive land (including a covenant, an easement, or in the case of land in Quebec, a real servitude) donated to a qualified donee other than a private foundation

What this means is that you can transfer these assets, upon which you have an accrued taxable gain, directly to your favorite charity, avoid paying the tax on the gain and then also receive a charitable donation receipt. If you decide to do so, complete *Form T1170, Capital Gains on Gifts of Certain Capital Property*.

Year End Planning. Consider giving $1,000 in cash to maximize the First-Time Donor's Super Credit, perhaps from selling losing stock. You'll receive a donation receipt. This transaction will also generate a capital loss that will offset other capital gains of the current year, the three prior tax years or any future capital gains. If you also own stock with accrued gains, consider transferring those securities to your favorite charity. You'll avoid the tax on the capital gain and get a charitable donations receipt, too.

There are more complicated rules for more sophisticated investors who want to donate flow-through shares or shares in a private corporation:

Donations of Flow-through Shares. These are shares in an oil and gas exploration company that renounces its eligible exploration, development and project start-up expenses and flows them through to its investors. These flow-through shares are deemed to have a cost base of zero and that results in a capital gain on disposition. For flow-through shares acquired after March 22, 2011, if such an investment is donated to charity, the portion of the capital gain that is exempt from capital gains is calculated as the actual increase in value of the shares over the cost of the shares to the investor. The donor will pay capital gains tax on the lesser of the value of the shares at the time of donation and their original cost.

Donation of Non-Qualifying Securities. A donor will not receive a donation receipt for a donation of a NQS (non-qualifying security, i.e. share in a private corporation) until, within five years of the donation, the shares have been sold for consideration that is not another NQS. In other words, there will be no receipt until the real value of the donation has been realized. This rule will apply to securities disposed of by donees on or after March 22, 2011.

Qualifying Donees. Charitable gifts may be made to the following organizations:

- registered Canadian charities,
- registered Canadian amateur sports associations,
- a Canadian municipality or province, or Canada,
- charities outside Canada to which the Government of Canada has made a donation in the prior 12 months,
- the United Nations and its agencies,
- donations to U.S. charities. Under the Canada-U.S. Tax Convention, Canada is required to give equivalent tax treatment for U.S. charities to the extent that the taxpayer has U.S. source income that is taxed in Canada. Thus, the donations claim limit is *75% of U.S. source income* for U.S. charities that do not otherwise qualify.

 New for 2013 | A charity outside Canada if the organization applies to be a "qualified donee" and works to provide disaster relief or urgent humanitarian aid or provides services in the national interest of Canada.

Qualifying Donation Receipts. The amounts donated to registered Canadian charities must be supported by receipts that have official registration numbers. This means if you have a donation receipt that does not have the charity's registration number, you don't have valid documentation to back up your donation. Charities may issue interim receipts without their registration number and issue one receipt for all your donations in the year with the registration number on that receipt.

However, gifts made through employment are supported by an entry on the taxpayer's T4 *Statement of Remuneration Paid (slip)* rather than an official receipt. Cultural gifts must be certified by the Cultural Review Board as to their Fair Market Value and gifts of ecologically sensitive land must be certified by the Minister of the Environment.

Stay Away from Charity Schemers | If you participate in an abusive charitable donations tax shelter, you're opening yourself up to a sure audit. These schemes generate tax savings that far exceed their cost—buy low, donate high schemes, gifting trust arrangements and leveraged cash donations are listed by CRA as abusive. Starting in the 2013 tax year, CRA will be allowed to collect up to 50% of the taxes they think are owing as a result of your participation in the scheme, even if you decide to file a Notice of Objection. They are betting on the fact that the donation is not legitimate and you'll have to prove otherwise.

Donation of Options. The donation of an option to acquire a property is allowed and, in the past, a receipt has been issued immediately when you make the donation. New rules will delay the receipt until the option has been exercised. As well, the donation receipt will be issued for the difference between any amount paid for the property and/or option by the donee (the advantage) and the Fair Market Value of the property at the time the option is granted. As is the case with all donations, if the advantage exceeds 80% of the FMV then it is not considered a gift and there will be no receipt. These rules have applied to options granted on or after March 22, 2011.

Timelines for Claiming Charitable Donations. Gifts made by you or your spouse in the current year or in any of the immediately preceding five years can be claimed on this year's return so long as those donations have not already been claimed.

Carry Forwards for Donations. If it's not to your advantage to claim the donation credit this year, you can even elect not to claim your donations and carry the unclaimed gifts forward for *five years*. This would be advantageous if you are not taxable or where claiming the total gifts would create a non-refundable credit in excess of your taxable income.

The Bottom Line | Recent charitable donation schemes and scams have added hardship for well-meaning donors. There are specific rules regarding the valuation of various gifts and in addition, if someone offers to sell you a big charitable donation receipt for a fraction of its value, beware: this is fraud and it is against the law to purchase a receipt for these purposes. Stay on the right side of tax law when it comes to making charitable donations for a well-rewarded community experience.

30

Attribution Rules

A discussion about family tax filing cannot be complete without addressing what the Attribution Rules are. These rules deny you the opportunity to split income in the family when you transfer assets to your spouse or minor children. If you do this, any earnings from the transferred property are "attributed" back to you, which means, you report the income. Consider the following case study:

Case Study | Planning for the Attribution Rules

John transfers $75,000 to his wife Sue to invest in the stock market. John has a very high income and wants Sue to be able to report future capital gains. Unfortunately, John will have to report those gains because of the Attribution Rules.

Now, let's say John transfers $75,000 to his 15-year-old son. This money earns interest, dividends and on disposition a capital gain. In this case, John must report the interest and dividends until his son turns 18. However, his son may at any time sell the shares and the resulting gain is taxed to his son.

May is 79, very ill and has an adult daughter. May wants to put her daughter's name on her bank accounts so she can look after her affairs if she becomes incapacitated. May, however, will continue to report the income from those accounts, even though her daughter's name appears on the account and the T5 slip.

Confused? Many people are. Here are the rules:

Property Transferred Between Spouses is Subject to Attribution. If one spouse transfers property to the other spouse for investment purposes, resulting income from the investment is taxed in the hands of the transferor. Exceptions include:

- *Tax-Free Savings Account Contributions.* Although the attribution rules apply to contributions to a TFSA, the earnings within the TFSA are not taxable so no earnings are attributed back to the transferor. Thus the higher-income spouse may provide funds to the lower-income spouse for contributions to their TFSA with no income tax consequences. Parents may also provide funds to their children for contributions to their TFSAs (children must be 18 or over to contribute to a TFSA).

  Example: Terri earned $45,000 in 2013 while her husband Uri was a full-time student with no taxable income. Terri gave Uri $5,500 to contribute to his TFSA. So long as the funds remain in the TFSA, no taxes are payable on the earnings either by Uri or by Terri.

- *Registered Disability Savings Plan (RDSP) Contributions.* Earnings on contributions to an RDSP are not taxed while the funds remain in the plan. Once they are withdrawn, the earnings are taxable to the plan beneficiary and are not attributed back to the contributor.

- *Spousal RRSP Contributions.* Contributions to a spousal RRSP, including the earnings on those contributions become income of the spouse three years after the last contribution is made to a spousal RRSP. If the funds are withdrawn from the spousal RRSP in the same year as the last contribution or in either of the following two calendar years, then a portion of the withdrawals will taxable to the contributor. The calculation of the allocation is done using Form T2205 *Amounts from a Spouse or Common-law Partner RRSP or RRIF to Include in Income.*

  Example: Quentin contributed $5,000 to a spousal RRSP for Rosie in 2010 and 2011. In 2013, Rosie took $6,000 out of the plan. Because of the 2011 contribution, $5,000 of the amount withdrawn must be added to Quentin's income in 2013. The remaining $1,000 is Rosie's income.

- *Non-Registered Investment Accounts.* Income resulting from transactions in which bona fide "inter-spousal" loans are drawn up to transfer the capital and, where interest is charged at the prescribed rate or more and is actually paid to the lender at least once a year during the year or within 30 days after the year end.

  Example: William earns $150,000 annually while his common-law partner Jackie is an aspiring writer with annual earnings of $15,000. Because William is in the highest tax bracket and Jackie is in the lowest, William would like to have the earnings on his $500,000 investment portfolio taxed in Jackie's hands. To do this, in January they drew up a loan agreement for $500,000 with interest payable at 1% (the prescribed rate at the time of the loan). Jackie then used the loan proceeds to purchase William's investment portfolio. So long as Jackie pays the interest each year by 30 days after the end of the year, the earnings on the investment portfolio are not attributed back to William. Note that the $5,000 interest on the loan is income to William and Jackie can claim the expense as a carrying charge.

- *Profits Resulting From Investments in a Business.* Only income from property is subject to the attribution rules; business income is not subject to these rules. Thus one spouse may give the other funds to start a business and, so long as they are not a partner in the business, the business income is taxed only to the business owner.

Example: Anne gave her husband, Bruno, $25,000 to start a business in 2010. In 2013, the business made a profit of $20,000. The $20,000 income is Bruno's income and is not attributed back to Anne even though she provided the funds to start the business.

- *Transfers Resulting From Marriage Breakdown.* The Attribution Rules do not apply to assets transferred as a result of a marriage breakdown (e.g. assets transferred as part of the separation or divorce agreement). Also the attribution rules no longer apply to assets transferred between spouses once they are no longer spouses.

Example: While they were married, Carl gave Dianne money to invest. In 2013, Carl and Dianne were divorced. Any income earned on those investments prior to the divorce is attributed back to Carl. However, any income earned after the divorce is taxable to Dianne.

- *Income on Property After it is Inherited.* Income earned on assets transferred at death is income of the beneficiary. Attribution does not apply to the deceased taxpayer.

Property Transferred to Minor Children. Income in the form of dividends and interest will be attributed back to the transferor, however capital gains will be taxed in the hands of the minor.

Example: Each year Evan gave 100 shares in The Walt Disney Company to his grandson David. While David is under age 18, all of the dividends earned on those shares are attributed back to Evan. However, when David turned 16, he sold the shares to buy a car. The capital gain on the sale is David's income and not attributed back to Evan.

Kiddie Tax. A "tax on split income," will be applied if minors receive dividends from private corporations owned by their parents. This "kiddie tax" also applies to income paid to minors from a trust or partnership, and cancels the advantage of income splitting.

Example: When Frank set up his corporation, he issues shares to himself, his wife and his three children. Originally he thought that he could pay $8,500 in dividends to each of his children on a tax-free basis each year. His advisor explained to him that if he paid dividends to his minor children from his corporation then these dividends would be taxed at the highest marginal rate (43.3% in his province) so he decided not to pay dividends to the children until they turn 18.

Other exceptions to the Attribution Rules on transfers of capital to minors include:

- **Contributions to RRSPs and RESPs.** When parents make contributions to an RESP, the earnings are not taxed while in the plan and they become income of the children if they become students. Likewise, when parents give their children money to make RRSP contributions based on that child's earned income, the earnings are not taxable while the funds remain in the RRSP and are taxable to the child when they are removed from the plan.

  Example: Greg gave his daughter Amanda (who is a full-time student) $6,000 to contribute to her RRSP. Amanda had sufficient earned income based on her summer jobs. By taking the RRSP deduction, Amanda did not need to deduct so much of her Tuition, Education, and Textbook Amount and was able to transfer it back to Greg. The earnings within the RRSP remain untaxed until Amanda removes them from her RRSP. At that time, they are taxed to her.

- **CCTB and UCCB.** Any income earned on the investment of Canada Child Tax Benefits or Universal Child Care Benefits in an account held in trust for the child.

  Example: Each month Irene takes her Canada Child Tax Benefit and Universal Child Care Benefit cheques and deposits them into an account for her only son Jacob. So long as the only amounts deposited to that account are from the CCTB and UCCB payments, the income earned in the account is Jacob's income (and consequently is not taxed).

- Employment income actually earned by a child working in a parent's business—so long as amounts paid to a child are reasonable and the work is actually done by the child, those earnings are income of the child and deductible as a business expense to the business.

  Example: Ken operates a small business. He pays his daughter Kim $100 per week to clean the office on Sundays. Kim's earnings are taxable to her (and deductible as a business expense to Ken's business).

Property Transferred to Adult Children. There are no restrictions on the type of property that can be transferred to adult children, and all resulting income will be taxed in their hands except if the tax department believes the main reason for the loan was to reduce or avoid taxes by including the income on the adult child's return.

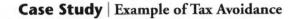

Case Study | Example of Tax Avoidance

Lisa is in a high tax bracket but her son Jeffrey is in the lowest tax bracket. Jeffrey dropped out of college and currently lives at home in his parent's basement. With no income, Lisa and her husband provide Jeffrey with spending money while he figures out what he wants to do with his life.

Lisa decided it would be a good idea to temporarily transfer to Jeffrey the portion of her stock portfolio that is paying dividends. Jeffrey could then use the dividends for spending money and Lisa would not have to provide it. The net result of this transfer is that the taxable dividends that were once reported on Lisa's return would now be reported on Jeffrey's return, one could expect that the CRA would see this as a tax avoidance maneuver and attribute the dividend income back to Lisa.

The Attribution Rules will not apply if:

- Amounts transferred are used for non-taxable investments: in a TFSA for example, principal residence, in the costs of education, car purchases, and so on;
- Contributions are made to the child's RRSP, RESP, or RDSP[7];
- A bona fide investment loan is drawn up, with interest actually paid at least once a year within 30 days after year-end, similar to inter-spousal loans; or
- Transferred funds are used to start the child's business.

Q & A | Understanding the Attribution Rules

The following are other common questions families may have about the economic activities they have with one another. See if you can answer the questions:

Q. How are amounts in joint accounts reported?

A. Income earned in joint accounts must be reported by the person who earned the capital in the account. Where more than one person contributed capital earned in their own right, then the income in the account must be allocated based on the capital provided by each contributor.

Q. How do I report income from a rental property we jointly own as spouses?

A. Income from a rental is income from property so the Attribution Rules apply and require that the rental income be reported by the person (or persons) that provided the capital to acquire the rental property—this would be the down

---

[7] Registered Retirement Savings Plan, Registered Education Savings Plan or Registered Disability Savings Plan.

payment if the rental income is used to make the mortgage payments. Where both spouses contributed capital, the rental income should be allocated to them according to the capital provided by each.

Q. **I lent my spouse money for a business she runs out of our home. Who reports the income?**

A. Business income is not income from property so the Attribution Rules do not apply. Any income earned by the business is income of the owner of the business. So, unless you drew up a partnership agreement with your spouse, then the income earned in the business is her income.

The Bottom Line | Families have a tremendous opportunity to combine their time and money to build family wealth. Taxes are a major wealth eroder, so whenever a legitimate opportunity arises to split income or transfer assets to lower earners who then have the opportunity to report income, apply losses or report future capital gains, the family will win financially by increasing its net worth. Don't hesitate to speak to a financial advisory team to help you understand this better, even if you continue to do your own tax returns.

31

Relationship Breakdown

According to Statistics Canada, there are approximately 71,000 divorces in Canada each year. Over 40% of marriages will end up in divorce, which is less than the U.S. divorce rate at 46% and the Swedes, which have the highest rate at 55%. There are all kinds of reasons for divorce: communications breakdowns, infidelity, a midlife crisis, abuse and financial issues.

Those financial problems can be exasperated when there is trouble with the taxman, and there often is, unfortunately, because people who separate don't understand the rules for reporting income, assets and expenses. This is worse if the couple isn't communicating.

A couple need not be legally or formally separated for their tax status to change. A couple is considered separated if they cease co-habitation for a period of at least 90 days.

Software Tips. When a couple separates, each person will be taxed as an individual and income and assets will be separated. Your software should ask you the date that your marital status changed if it changed in the year. If you are separated or divorced at the end of the year, enter that as your marital status and your software should take care of making claims on that basis. However keep in mind what you learned in the last chapter when deciding what income to report on your return. Remember, attribution ends with the relationship.

Let's discuss how various income sources, deductions and credits are handled when a couple separates:

Support Payments. The recipient of taxable child or spousal support payments must report those amounts as income and pay the tax.

CHECK **When do I have to pay tax on Spousal and Child Support**
IT OUT **Payments?** The rules differ for each, as explained below.

Support for Spouses. Payments made to a spouse or common-law partner are taxable to the recipient and deductible by the payor. In the year of separation or divorce, however, the payer may claim either the deduction for support or the spousal amount, but not both. The only way for the recipient to avoid this tax status is to receive a lump sum, in which case the payment is neither deductible nor taxable.

Making Instalment Remittances. The spouse who receives the taxable amount will often be unprepared for the tax consequences when a large balance due is due on April 30. In addition he or she may need to pay quarterly instalment payments on this income in the year after it is first paid and reported. This should be discussed before the separation or divorce papers are finalized to ensure the net tax result intended is actually paid and received.

Support for Children. For all agreements or court orders after May 1997, child support payments are not taxable to the recipient or deductible by the payor. For income tax purposes, any support stipulated in an agreement or court order is deemed to be child support if it is not identified as spousal support.

Complications can arise when support payments are in arrears. All arrears payments are deemed to be child support payments until child support is up to date. Subsequent payments are considered to be spousal support payments that are taxable to the recipient and deductible to the payor.

Example: Martin lost his job during the tax year and was not able to keep up with his required support payments. He was required to pay $500 per month in spousal support and $1,000 per month in child support. For the year, he paid $15,000. For income tax purposes, this is deemed to be $12,000 child support (the required amount) and $3,000 spousal support. Martin may deduct only $3,000 of the $15,000 paid and his ex-wife is only required to report $3,000 as income from spousal support.

Separating Assets. Income attribution ends when there is a separation providing that the couple continues to live apart. Therefore the new owner of the property after a relationship breakdown is responsible for all tax consequences on the earnings and capital appreciation (or depreciation) of the property. The cost at which the assets are transferred is also important, because it determines what numbers you will use to calculate future gains and losses from taxable investments or income from registered investments, as described below:

Spousal RRSPs. Spousal RRSP contributions will no longer be allowed. Withdrawals from spousal or common-law partner RRSPs made by the annuitant are generally reportable by the contributing spouse if any RRSP contribution has been made in the current year or the previous two years. However, this rule is waived for separated/divorced couples.

Example: In 2012 Hans made a $10,000 spousal RRSP contribution. In June 2013, his wife Heidi left him and did not return. Had Heidi removed funds from the RRSP prior to the separation, the income would have been reportable by Hans. However, if she withdrew funds from the RRSP after the separation, those funds are considered to be her funds and Hans does not have to include them in his income.

RRSP Accumulations. Funds that have accumulated in RRSPs may be rolled over on a tax-free basis to the ex-spouse when the parties are living apart and if the payments follow a written separation agreement, court order, decree or judgment. The transfer must be made directly between the RRSP plans of the two spouses and one spouse cannot be disqualified because of age (over age 71). The same rules for tax-free transfer of funds apply to RRIF accumulations. Form T2220 is used to authorize the transfers between the plans.

TFSA Accumulations. These can also be split on a tax-free basis. The funds from one party's TFSA may be transferred tax free to the other party's TFSA. This will have no effect on the contribution room of either of the parties.

Principal Residence. After separation, CRA recognizes two family units, and therefore it is possible for each to own one tax-exempt principal residence.

Other Property. The transfer of depreciable property (those upon which Capital Cost Allowance can be claimed) takes place at the undepreciated capital cost of the property. As a result, no recapture, terminal loss, or capital gain takes place on the transfer.

For other capital property, the transfer takes place at the Adjusted Cost Base of the assets, so again, there is a tax-free rollover.

Case Study | Planning For the Transfer of Property on Divorce

Rachael owned two rental properties but in her divorce settlement, one of the properties was transferred to her ex-husband Daniel. The rental property consists of two assets: the building (which is a depreciable capital asset) and the land that is not depreciable.

Per the assessment at the time of purchase, the land was worth $100,000 and the building $120,000. At the time of transfer, the land was worth $130,000 and building was worth $140,000. Rachael had claimed CCA on the building so its UCC was reduced to $110,000.

The land is transferred to Daniel at is original cost ($100,000) so Rachael has no capital gains tax to pay on the transfer. Daniel's cost base is $100,000 so he already has an accrued capital gain of $30,000.

The building is transferred to Daniel at $110,000 so Rachael has no recapture or capital gain to report as a result of the transfer. Daniel is deemed to have acquired the building for $120,000 and to have already claimed $10,000 in CCA.

Choosing FMV. By special election, assets may be transferred at their Fair Market Value. This could result in significant tax savings if, for example, the transferor had unused capital losses to apply to gains on the transferred property. See Part 4.

Deductions. Three deductions need to be addressed regarding separation or divorce:

Line 214 Child Care Expenses. Child Care Expenses must normally be claimed by the lower-income spouse but may be claimed by the higher-income spouse during a period where the taxpayer was separated from the other supporting person due to a breakdown in their relationship for a period of at least 90 days as long as they were reconciled within the first 60 days after the taxation year.

If the taxpayers were not reconciled within 60 days after the taxation year, then each spouse may claim any child care expenses they paid during the year with no adjustment for child care expenses claimed by the other taxpayer.

Example: Susan and Ron separated in September 2012. They both work and so had Child Care Expenses for their son for the full year. If they reconcile before March 1, 2013, then the spouse with the lower net income (Susan in this case) must claim the child care expenses less the $175 per week that Ron may claim for the period of separation. If they do not reconcile by March 1, 2013, Ron may claim whatever child care expenses he incurred and Susan may claim the expenses she incurred.

Line 220 Support Payments. These will be deductible in the following cases, and qualify for RRSP earned income purposes.

The payments must be periodic spousal support payments made pursuant to a written agreement or court order are deductible and only if the spouses remain living apart and payments are made directly to the spouse or to a third party for maintenance of the spouse. Note the following:

- Lump sum payments in lieu of periodic spousal support payments are not deductible (or taxable) as mentioned above. However, a lump sum payment to pay deductible periodic payments that are in arrears is deductible.

- Child support payments are not deductible (or taxable) unless they are made pursuant to a written agreement or court order dated prior to May 1997 which has not been altered since that date.

Form T1198 Qualifying Lump Sum Payments. Certain lump sum payments made after 1994 will qualify for income averaging; lump sums from spousal or taxable child support payments will qualify if the amount exceeds $3,000. The calculation is done by CRA when the form is submitted.

Line 232 Legal fees on separation or divorce. Legal fees to obtain a divorce or separation agreement are normally not deductible. However, CRA considers legal costs incurred to obtain support relating specifically to the care of children (not the spouse) under the *Divorce Act* or under provincial legislation, as well as the costs incurred to obtain an increase in support or make child support non-taxable, to be deductible.

Tax Credits on Separation or Divorce. Refundable and non-refundable tax credits will be allocated based on individual net income levels, and certain social benefits can be split as described below.

Universal Child Care Benefit. In the case of joint custody, each parent can apply to receive equal shares of this income the month following the month of marital status change by filing Form RC65.

Child May Report UCCB. A single parent may choose to claim any UCCB received as the income for the child for whom the Amount for an Eligible Dependant was claimed rather than as his or her own income. This is generally beneficial if the parent's income level is above the lowest tax bracket.

Example: Megan is a single mom with two children under age six. She received $2,400 UCCB income in 2013. Her taxable income is $45,000 so she is in the second tax bracket. If she includes the UCCB in her income, she'll pay $528 federal tax on the income (plus provincial tax). She is claiming Kyle as an eligible dependant. Her claim for him is $11,038, which results in a federal credit of $1,655.70.

If she elects to include the UCCB in Kyle's income, her federal taxes are reduced by the $528 she would have paid and her claim for Kyle is reduced by $2,400, which results in a reduction of $360 in her federal credit for him. The net result is a federal tax saving of $168. She also saves on her provincial taxes by making this election.

Federal Refundable Tax Credits. The Canada Child Tax Benefit (CCTB) and Goods and Services/Harmonized Sales Tax Credit (GSTC) are calculated based on net family income from the prior tax year.

When a family breakdown occurs, CRA should be immediately notified so that the calculation of the credits for the next CCTB or GSTC payment may be made without including the estranged spouse or common-law partner's net income. Notify CRA no later than the month following your change in marital status if you become divorced. If you become separated, the separation is not recognized if you reconcile within 90 days so do not notify CRA until the 90 days have elapsed. In the case of joint custody, each parent has the right to receive half these amounts.

Otherwise, the government assumes that the eligible CCTB recipient is the female parent. However, "prescribed factors" will be considered in determining what constitutes care and upbringing and who is fulfilling that responsibility.

For example, if after the breakdown of a conjugal relationship, the single parent and child returns to live with his or her parents (the child's grandparents), the single parent will still be presumed to be the supporting individual unless he or she is under 18 years old. In that case, the grandparents may claim the Canada Child Tax Benefit for both their child and grandchild.

Provincial Tax Credits. Many provinces have tax reductions or refundable credits that are based on family net income. In most cases, in the year of separation, it is not necessary to include the estranged spouse or common-law partner's income in the family income calculation and normally no credits or reductions on behalf of the estranged spouse or common-law partner will be allowed. Each partner will claim the credits or reductions to which he or she is entitled.

Non-Refundable Tax Credits. Here are the general rules on who claims in sole or joint custody cases:

- *Spousal Amount*—The spousal amount may not be claimed when a couple is separated or divorced except in the year of separation where no claim is made for spousal support.
- *Age Amount and Transfers*—No transfers are allowed between spouses if they are separated or divorced at the end of the year.
- *Amount for an Eligible Dependant*—A single parent may claim an amount for an eligible dependant if they support that child in their own home at some time during the year. No claim may be made for a child by a taxpayer who is required to make support payments for that child. In the case of joint custody, if both parents qualify to claim the amount for an eligible dependant, they must agree who will make the claim—it cannot be split between them.
- *Amount for Children Under Age 18*—In the case of sole custody, the parent who has custody may claim the amount for the child. In the case of joint custody, only the parent who qualifies to claim the amount for an eligible dependant for the child may make this claim. The claim may not be split. No claim may be made by a taxpayer who is required to make support payments for the child unless both parents are required to make support payments, then only the one who claims the amount for an eligible dependant may make this claim.

- *Public Transit, Fitness and Arts Amounts*—These amounts may be claimed by either spouse so long as the same expense is not claimed twice and the total claim is not more than the maximum allowed for the child.
- *Caregiver Amount*—The Caregiver Amount may be claimed by more than one individual so long as the combined claim does not exceed the maximum allowable claim for the dependant. However, if anyone claimed an amount for an eligible dependant for that dependant, no one else may claim the caregiver amount for the same dependant.
- *Disability Amount Transferred from a Dependant*—The transferred disability amount may be claimed by more than one taxpayer so long as they agree on how much will be claimed by each and the total claim does not exceed the maximum allowed.
- *Medical Expenses*—Medical expenses for a child may be split between parents so long as the same expense is not claimed twice. Medical expenses may not be claimed for your spouse or common-law partner after separation or divorce.

 The Bottom Line | Separation and divorce is expensive and complicated. Filing a tax return to the best benefit if the family unit is harder, too. Make sure you get the right results to minimize the financial impact. Consider consulting with a tax pro if you are unsure. Use your tax software to do "what if" calculations to better understand your tax filing options.

32

When to See a Pro

It's a good idea to seek professional help any time there is a birth, death, marriage, divorce or new common-law relationship in the family. While each member of the family is taxed as an individual, tax benefits are often received as one household. Because economic decisions are made as a unit, powerful opportunities exist to build capital over time. With the right documentation in place, families can split income, pay salaries to one another, and sometimes transfer tax credits as well as assets.

While tax software automatically "optimizes" some of those opportunities, new life or financial events warrant checking in with a professional tax advisor. This is particularly important as well, when couples separate. A checklist of questions might include the following:

☐ When are we considered to be a couple for tax purposes?
☐ We broke up for 3 months during the year—are we still considered to be spouses?
☐ When do we need to combine our incomes for tax purposes?
☐ When will my individual net income level affect my spouse's claim for me?
☐ At what age can we split income from our employer-sponsored pension plans? The CPP? What about our RRSP accumulations—can we split those too?
☐ Can my spouse pay me a salary to help with office administration if he or she is a commissioned sales employee? A self-employed consultant?
☐ Can our investment income be transferred from one spouse to the other for a more advantageous tax results? Who reports the investment income from our joint accounts?
☐ How many personal residences can we own on a tax exempt basis?
☐ Does a spousal RRSP make sense for a common-law couple?
☐ Will I have to give up my TFSA if we split up?
☐ Who should claim the child care expenses? The moving expenses? The safety deposit box?

Be aware that you can transfer the following non-refundable tax credits to your spouse:

- *Age Amount*—if you have reached the age of 65 in the year;
- *Amount for Minor Children*—check this out if you've had a new baby;
- *Disability Amount*—lucrative, if someone has a severe health restriction;
- *Pension Income Amount*—check it out if periodic pension receipts started or if an election was made to split pension income; and
- *Tuition, Education, Textbook Amount*—a great benefit if one of you is at post-secondary school this year, and your income is too low to use these amounts.

The following can also be claimed by either or shared between you:

- *Amount for Infirm Adult Dependants*—if you care for a disabled adult;
- *Caregiver Amount*—this is claimed only if care is provided in your home;
- *Child Art and Fitness Amounts*—these credits will offset expensive costs of extra-curricular activities taken on by minors outside of the school system;
- *Adoption Amount*—many expenses are eligible starting when applications are made to the court system;
- *Public Transit Amount*—monthly travel is more affordable because of the tax credits;
- *Home Buyer's Tax Credit*—get some advice before you buy a home to make sure you tap into all your tax advantages;
- *Medical Expenses*—generally claimed by person with lowest net income, this credit is often missed by families—even your private health care premiums can be claimed; and
- *Charitable Donations*—generally grouped to exceed $200 on one return—remember this year a new First-Time Donor's Super Credit may apply but only if neither of you have claimed a donations credit over the past 5 years.

If you are unsure about your rights to any of these provisions, a couple of hours with a tax pro can really help to save money and time when you do your taxes in the future.

PART 4

Reporting Investment Income

There is evidence that we do not save enough money in Canada. According to a survey by the Canadian Payroll Association in September 2013, almost half of Canadians put away only 5% or even less of their paycheques, and 42% of employees would be in financial difficulty if their pay was delayed even by a week. The last thing savers need is for taxes to erode away those precious savings. Therefore it matters where you invest your savings, particularly if you are saving in a non-registered account, because different investment income sources are taxed in different ways.

In this section, we will be discussing how to develop a strategy for your investment activities so that you can build capital that will be taxed advantageously at disposition as well as buy homes, and rental properties to round out your family net worth. One of the great advantages of the tax-astute investor is that both income and savings can grow faster because you'll keep more in your own accounts.

The good news is that household net worth in Canada topped $400,000 in 2013… chances are, you are well positioned to build on your increasing net worth, with tax efficiency. You may simply need to tweak your order of investing and be vigilant about expensive and non-deductible debt, like credit card debt. Let's get started with a synopsis of what you'll learn about filing tax returns for investors.

 What's New

We are in a relatively low tax environment in Canada at the moment. Over the past several years, corporate income tax rates have decreased in order for us to be more competitive in a global economy. This has affected tax reporting by individual investors who have earned dividends. The current gross-up for "eligible dividends" is 38%, meaning you'll have to report $138 for each $100 dividend income you receive. You will receive a federal and provincial dividend tax credit in return, to reduce taxes payable. For small business dividends the gross-up is 25% but there are changes on the horizon for the reporting of dividends from Canadian Controlled Private Corporations (CCPC) starting in 2014.

Hard Copy

Gathering up documentation for investors can involve not just the various T-slips, but a thorough search for the cost base information on assets you have disposed of this year. This can be more difficult if you acquired them years ago. You may also need appraisals of Fair Market Value on others, particularly if you acquired these assets as an inheritance or family transfer. Special rules are extended to those who transfer financial assets to their favorite charities. Wise investors will start their document retrieval tasks early and save important valuation information in their Permanent tax files.

Software Tips

Your tax software will do an excellent job of posting most information found on T3 or T5 slips to their proper destinations. However, beware of tricky entries. For example, for foreign income, you'll need to ensure that the foreign tax credits are claimed.

If you have capital dispositions, the dispositions must be entered in the appropriate section of Schedule 3 so the software can apply the correct rules for that type of disposition, especially when applying losses. If you have capital gains reserves, a capital gains deduction, principal residence designation or rental property, be sure you understand where to find the required forms and how they work in your software. We'll help you with this part.

Tax Sleuthing

The most common deductions and credits relating to investment income are listed below; they are also often missed.

- Carrying charges, including your safety deposit box for the last time in 2013, investment counsel fees and interest paid on money borrowed to invest.

- All reasonable expenses of earning rental income including mortgage interest, property taxes, advertising, and routine maintenance costs. Improvements like the cost of a new roof are often misclassified and can cause audit problems.

Tax Pro Alert

Consider consulting a tax pro if you have any of the following transactions this year:

- purchase or sale of a rental property, debt forgiveness, mortgage foreclosure (rental or business) or repossession of business assets;
- capital gains election or capital gains deduction; or
- conversion of rental or business property to personal use or vice versa.

33

Doing it Right: Reporting Strategies for Investments

Tax efficient investing is the cornerstone of a comprehensive wealth management strategy, which should focus on the accumulation, growth, preservation and transition of wealth with sustainable purchasing power; that is, after taxes and inflation. Many financial events can take place over a longer investment period; exposing a portfolio to performance risk. Mitigating tax risk, therefore, can significantly preserve the value of an investment portfolio over time. But here too, it's important to have a strategy. This begins with understanding which types of savings accounts you should invest in and when. You will learn more about this here, as well as the tax rules for reporting income from your investments, and any gain and/or losses that result, when you dispose of your assets.

 What's New? | The way Canadians invest has been impacted by the introduction of several new savings options… the TFSA (Tax-Free Savings Account) and the PRPP (Pooled Retirement Pension Plans) for example. To understand which investment deposit comes first for your family, consider the tax efficiency of your actions. That is, how will your investment be impacted by taxes?

The Impact of Tax on Investments. Your investment choices will be impacted by tax in three basic ways:

- **Sources of Investment.** Whole "pre-tax" dollars will grow faster than smaller "after-tax" dollars… so the objective is to start here and determine how can you qualify to invest "whole dollars?"
- **Source of Income.** The growth (or income) from the investments can be structured to be either tax free (ideal), tax deferred (which means eventually you'll report income on your tax return and pay tax on it) or taxed annually, which is the least ideal.

- **Tax Consequences on Withdrawal or Disposition.** You will want to choose investment vehicles carefully to produce the tax outcomes you want within your overall wealth management plan. Upon withdrawal of income and/or principal, understand what will happen on your tax return, and when. Remember, that upon disposition, income-producing assets and pension savings may be subject to tax in whole, in part, or not at all, depending on circumstances.

Understanding the impact of taxation when you invest, as your money grows and when you withdraw or sell, should help you to choose investment vehicles, in the right order. For example:

1. **RRSPs, PRPPs, and RPPs.** These investments are of top priority if you meet eligibility criteria, because they create new dollars when you invest. That is, taxes previously withheld are refunded at current marginal tax rates. In addition, because the deductions for these contributions reduce your net income, it is possible that you may qualify for larger refundable and non-refundable tax credits, too. You can then use your bigger refund to invest in one of the next two categories below; a great way to leverage your resources. This makes your invested capital "whole".

2. **RESPs and RDSPs.** Dollars on which taxes have already been paid are invested in these accounts – that is, there is no deduction for your contribution. But these investments qualify for matching grants and in some cases, bonds, from government. This can add to investment growth significantly because these savings enhancements are deposited up front, when you make your contributions. Even better: earnings on both your contribution and the government's grow on a tax-deferred basis in these accounts, creating a real tax shelter.

3. **TFSAs.** "After-tax" dollars are again invested here. There is no deduction when you make the contribution. But, earnings grow without taxation, and are not taxed on withdrawal, and include no government incentives.

4. **Non-Registered Accounts/Revenue Properties.** When your money (before or after tax) is invested in a non-registered account or a rental property; the "income from property" that is generated—interest, dividends, rents, royalties—is added to your taxes annually. The increase in value of these income-producing assets is subject to tax when there is a disposition, generating a capital gain or loss which is taxed at a preferred rate.

The reporting of income earned in the first two categories of registered accounts, usually happens on withdrawal. The deferred taxation on earnings accelerates quickly, because of the investment's uninterrupted growth. That deferral strategy provides a great hedge against inflation, particularly if rates of return exceed inflation rates. But you'll need to plan withdrawals carefully in the future. Try to avoid taking lump sums into income which will spike up your marginal tax rates. Instead, try to "average in" your taxable income over time. The TFSA is, of course, your ticket to tax freedom in the future.

Please see Part 5 for a discussion of the withdrawal of registered retirement income, Part 2 for savings rules in RPP and RRSP/PRPP accounts, and Part 3 for investments in TFSAs, RESPs and RDSPs.

Focus on Non-Registered Accounts. The reporting of income in non-registered accounts—the fourth category—happens along the way. Bear in mind that dofferent income sources may be taxed differently.

Two specific types of income from property invested in non-registered accounts next—interest and dividends—which are reported on Schedule 4. We will also cover income from Limited Partnerships. Income from the disposition of property is reported on Schedule 3, is the subject of our next chapter.

Income from Property

Definitions. Income from property includes any income earned from investment in your non-registered accounts which produce interest, dividends, rent or royalties. This is passive income, which differs from active income that is earned through employment or self-employment.

Income from property also differs from the capital gain or loss which may occur on the disposition of an asset. That's important because it affects where and how to report the earnings and also expenses like interest costs. Income from property is also treated differently than capital gains and losses under the Attribution Rules.

Schedule 4 Statement of Investment Income is used to report amounts from taxable dividends, interest and other investment income, net partnership income, and the carrying charges that have been incurred to earn that income.

 CHECK IT OUT | **How are investment earning reported on Schedule 4?** The slips you receive can include a T3 slip from investments held in a trust, a T5 slip when the source is a corporation, a T5013 slip from an investment in a limited partnership, or a T5008 slip for securities transactions. In some cases, this income will be self-reported.

T-Slip Entry. When entering amounts from your T-slips, it's important for you to compare all the data on your hard copy with the results on your return, which will be added together when there are multiple slips. It's easy to forget a slip or miss a box so double-checking is important. The following are line links to possible deductions and credits. Carrying charges will be discussed later, but you will find out more about the dividend tax credit, which is used to reduce taxes payable, in this chapter.

Schedule 4 & Related Income Lines	Possible Deductions on Schedule 4	Possible Credits
120 Taxable amount of dividends from T3 or T5 slips	**221** Carrying charges like interest or investment counsel fees	**Schedule 1:** **405** Foreign Tax Credit
121 Interest and other investment income from T5 slips	**221** Carrying charges like safety deposit box fees	**425** Dividend Tax Credit
Income Lines	**Possible Deductions**	**Possible Credits/Taxes**
122 Net partnership income on Form T5013	**251** Limited partnership losses of other years	**424** Possible Tax on Split Income for Minors
127 Taxable capital gains on Schedule 3 from T3 or T5 slips	**253** Net capital losses of other years **254** Capital gains deduction	**349** Donations Credit on Schedule 9

For most people, reporting investments in non-registered accounts is simple: just enter the data from various T-slips—that's it! The tax software does most of the rest of the calculations, with little human intervention required.

Reporting Traps. There are three to take note of:

No T-Slips. An issue facing investors in recent times is the very low rates of return these investments have garnered. A $10,000 deposit earning half of one per cent, for example, will only have earned $50 for the year. Financial institutions need only issue a slip if the earnings are $50 or more. So, investors must self-report interest on deposits under this. Be sure to dig out your bank books or statements, as well as your *Notice of Assessment* or Reassessment to find any interest paid to you from CRA, too. The amounts should be entered into Schedule 4 and from there they will be posted by your software to Line 121.

Joint Accounts. Report the interest earned in the same ratio as the principal was deposited into the accounts, based on who earned that capital in his or her own right.

Example: Debra, who normally stays home and raises the children, deposited all of the money that she inherited from her father in a joint account with her husband. In this case, 100% of the earnings are reported by Debra. If her husband, Jason, who earns all the other income for the family, deposited 100% of savings in another joint account, he reports 100% of the earnings from that account. A third account holds their gain on the sale of their principal residence last year; to which they each contributed one half of the cash gifts they received from their wedding. In this case, each spouse reports 50% of the interest earnings.

Kiddie Tax? In some cases, when reporting dividends received in the hands of minors or some limited partnership income, there may be a possible Tax on Split Income on the minor's return. You may require some professional guidance here. Be sure to review Attribution Rules in Part 3 as well.

Line 120 Taxable Amount of Dividends

Dividends are earned as a result of an investment by an individual in a corporation, that is incorporated and resident in Canada throughout a period that began at any time after June 18, 1971. Dividends are the after-tax distribution of earnings by a company.

When dividend amounts are reported on the income tax return of the individual shareholder, the actual dividends received are "grossed up" so the taxpayer reports an amount higher than that received. Offsetting this *grossed-up amount* is a "*dividend tax credit*" (DTC), which is computed on *Schedule 1 Detailed Tax Calculation* as a reduction of federal taxes payable. A provincial credit is also calculated on the tax calculation schedule for your province of residence. The objective with these calculations is to integrate the corporate and personal tax systems to avoid double taxation.

The amount of the gross-up and DTC will depend on whether the corporation is a public or private company and, as a result, there are two specific terms for the dividends earned:

- *Other Than Eligible or "Ineligible" Dividends.* These are dividends by *Canadian Controlled Private Corporations (CCPCs)*, whose income was within the Small Business Deduction (SBD) and therefore subject to a lower rate of corporate tax. The SBD is $500,000 federally and in most provinces. For ineligible dividends, the taxable amount is 125% of the actual dividends with an offsetting dividend tax credit of 13.33% of that taxable amount.

 New for 2014 Reporting of ineligible dividends will change in 2014, as follows: the gross-up will be reduced from 25% to 18% and the Dividend Tax Credit will be reduced from 13.33% to 11% of the taxable amount. For most taxpayers this will mean a slight increase in the taxes paid on such dividends.

- *Eligible Dividends.* Eligible dividends are those paid after 2005 by Canadian resident public corporations and also *CCPCs*, where the income from which the dividend is paid has been subject to tax at the "general" corporate rate because it exceeded the Small Business Deduction. For 2013, the taxable amount for eligible dividends is 138% of the actual dividends with an offsetting dividend tax credit of 15.02% of that taxable amount.

Each province also has a provincial Dividend Tax Credit to offset provincial taxes on the grossed-up dividends. Good news: the tax software will calculate all of this accurately for you, if you enter the data from the slips carefully. When you earn dividends, there are several planning issues.

Grossed-up Dividends and Net Income. The increased gross-up may be problematic for taxpayers who are in a clawback zone for non-refundable tax credits, refundable tax credits, or the OAS or EI Benefits. It may reduce or eliminate these provisions, and so you'll want to plan your investment income sources with this in mind. An RRSP contribution will also reduce net income to protect your benefits.

Example: Tyler earns $40,000 employment income as well as $5,000 eligible dividend income. Because of the dividend gross-up, his net income is $46,900. Also because of the dividend tax credit, Tyler's payable taxes on his investment income are $886 less than had he earned the $5,000 as interest income. Tyler has three children, and because of the $1,900 dividend gross-up increases his net income, his family's Canada Child Tax Benefit is reduced by $76 and their GST Credit is reduced by $95.

A $1,900 RRSP contribution would restore these refundable credits while retaining the tax benefits of the dividend income.

Dividends are Otherwise Tax Efficient. Canadian dividends can produce very tax-efficient results because they are subject to lower marginal tax rates than ordinary income sources like interest or pensions. To illustrate, the marginal tax rates for 2013 for the province of BC, appears below:

Marginal Tax Rates on Investment Income Sources

Taxable Income Range in 2013	Ordinary Income	Capital Gains	Ineligible Dividends (SBC)	Eligible Dividends
Up to $10,276	0%	0%	0%	0%
$10,277 to $11,038	5.06%	2.53%	2.07%	-6.82%
$11,039 to $37,568	20.06%	10.03%	4.16%	-6.84%
$37,569 to $43,561	22.70%	11.35%	7.46%	-3.20%
$43,562 to $75,138	29.70%	14.85%	16.21%	6.46%
$75,139 to $86,268	32.50%	16.25%	19.71%	10.32%
$86,269 to $87,123	34.29%	17.15%	21.95%	12.79%
$87,124 to $104,754	38.29%	19.15%	26.95%	18.31%
$104,755 to $135,054	40.70%	20.35%	29.96%	21.64%
Over $135,054	43.70%	21.85%	33.71%	25.78%

Negative Tax Rates. Where income is in the lowest tax bracket, the dividend tax credit may in fact, exceed the tax levied on the grossed-up dividends. This may result in a "negative marginal tax rate" on dividend income. What this means is that the dividend tax credit will help to offset taxes owing on other types of income earned in the year, and that makes dividends very tax efficient.

Spousal Income Transfer is Possible. The Attribution Rules generally require the spouse who earned and invested the capital that generated the dividends be the one to report the dividend income. However, if the lower-income spouse has dividends but cannot benefit from the dividend tax credit because his or her income is too low, the higher-income spouse may report the dividends. However, that higher-income spouse can only report the dividends *if the claim for the spousal amount is created or increased* by removing the dividends from the lower-income spouse's income. Software will generally not make this transfer automatically.

Example: Ryan earns $55,000 from employment. His wife Ashley's only income is $3,000 from eligible dividends on shares she inherited from her grandfather. If Ashley reports the dividends, her net income will be $4,140 reducing Ryan's claim for her to $6,898. Ashley is not taxable so she cannot benefit from the dividend tax credit. If Ryan elects to include the dividend income on his return, he will have to pay $444 taxes on the income, but the additional claim for Ashley will reduce Ryan's taxes by $830. The net result of the election is a tax savings of $386.

Minimum Tax Possible. Taxpayers who receive a large part of their income by way of eligible dividends may find themselves subject to *Alternative Minimum Tax,* if the dividend tax credit entirely eliminates tax payable. This calculation is made automatically by your tax software on Form T691 and it's a long complicated form. However, if you had to pay minimum tax, the carry-over functions in your software will record this for you and that's important, because any minimum tax paid this year, will be used to offset regular taxes payable in the following seven years until used up. But if you continue to earn a large part of your income from dividends, you may continue to be subject to minimum tax which you may never be able to recover.

Example: In 2012, Clyde's only income was $70,000 from eligible dividends. Normally, after the dividend tax credit, his federal taxes would have been $2,578 but, because Clyde is subject to minimum tax, his federal taxes for 2012 were $2,877. The extra $299 Clyde had to pay may be used to reduce his federal taxes in 2013 so long as he is not subject to minimum tax again in 2013.

Other Dividends. Other types of dividends may confuse you and, if so, do speak to a professional about the source documents you may have received from your investment firm. Here is a short list of some unique circumstances:

Capital Dividends. These are dividends paid out of the Capital Dividend Account (CDA) of a private corporation and they reflect the 50% tax exempt portion of capital gains earned by the corporation on the disposition of capital property, capital dividends received from other corporations or life insurance policy proceeds, for example. These distributions are not taxable. The corporation must file Form T2054 on the day the dividend becomes payable or on the first day any part of such a dividend is paid, whichever is earlier. As the recipient of a capital dividend, you will not receive a T-slip because the income is not taxable to you.

Capital Gains Dividends. These dividends are received from mutual fund companies and reported on a T5 slip and on *Schedule 3 Capital Gains and Losses,* because they reflect capital gains realized in the fund rather than dividends. These "dividends" are eligible for a 50% income inclusion rather than the gross-up and dividend tax credit. Capital gains dividends will be reported in box 18 of your T5 slip.

Example: Amber's T5 slip shows $550 of capital gains dividends (Box 18). When she keys this into her tax software, it gets posted to Line 174 of Schedule 3 and $275 is then posted to Line 127 of her return as a capital gain.

Deemed Dividend. When a corporation reorganizes, shareholders may be deemed to have received a dividend, and a T5 will be issued. This can occur, for example, where a share is redeemed or cancelled. Where the dividend is deemed to have been paid by a Canadian corporation, it is subject to the normal gross-up and dividend tax credit rules.

Example: Brandon held 1,000 CIBC Series 32 preferred shares that were redeemed in the tax year. He received $26 per share that was allocated by CIBC as $25 per share proceeds and $1 per share deemed dividend. Brandon received a T5 slip showing the $1,000 actual dividend ($1,380 taxable) that is eligible for the dividend tax credit. The remaining $25,000 is considered proceeds of disposition of the redeemed shares and is used to calculate his capital gain for the year.

Dividend Reinvestment Programs. When a corporation reinvests the dividends in shares of the corporation rather than paying a cash dividend, the amount of the dividend is included in income in the tax year the cash dividend would have been paid. The cost base of the asset is then increased by the amount of the reinvestment. This is a popular method used by mutual funds and segregated funds.

Example: Lauren owned 1,000 common shares of CIBC that were in a dividend reinvestment plan. The cost of the shares was $75,000. During the tax year, the stocks paid $376 in eligible dividends that were reported to Lauren on a T5 slip. She did not receive the money but instead received five additional shares. She must report the $376 ($518.88 taxable) dividends on her tax return. By the end of the year, she owned 1,005 shares with a cost base of $75,376).

Income Bonds and Debentures. These instruments may be issued with terms up to five years by corporations in financial difficulty and under the control of a receiver or trustee in bankruptcy. A return on an income bond is paid only if there is a profit on the operations, in which case the amount paid or received is considered to be a dividend. In the year that the income is paid, a T5 slip will be issued with the deemed dividend shown in Boxes 24, 25, and 26.

Foreign Dividends. Foreign dividends do not qualify for the gross up and dividend tax credit that Canadian dividends do. Rather, the actual amounts are reported in Canadian funds when received.

If the dividends were subject to withholding taxes in the foreign country, the Canadian resident will qualify to claim a *foreign tax credit*, which offsets taxes on Schedule 1 *Detailed Tax Calculation*. This will be calculated automatically by your tax software if you record the amounts in the right boxes on the data entry screen. However, there are three possible provisions that will be involved in making sure as much of that foreign withholding tax as possible is offset to avoid double taxation: the *Federal Foreign Tax Credit* (Form T2209), the *Provincial Foreign Tax Credit* (Form T2036 for all provinces but Quebec, which has its own calculations and forms) and, if an unabsorbed balance of tax still remains, a deduction is claimed on Line 232 *Other Deductions*. Where your effective tax rate is less than the foreign tax rate, you may claim the taxes that are not credited as a deduction instead.

If you can't claim them in the current year, you may carry forward unabsorbed foreign taxes paid on business income for a period of 10 years; but, unfortunately, there is no carry forward provision on non-business income.

Non-Residents Receiving Canadian Dividends. Non-residents must pay tax on the income earned in Canada either through *withholding taxes* on passive income sources such as investments, pensions and management fees.

When a Canadian corporation issues dividends to a non-resident, it is necessary to withhold taxes and issue an NR4 Slip. This is all the tax the non-resident will need to pay and there is no need to file a tax return, unless there are other sources specifically subject to tax.

Tax Treaties. The amount of withholding tax is determined by the tax treaty in force between Canada and the foreign country. At the time of writing there were 90 tax treaties in force, ten signed but not yet in force and another nine under negotiation.

In general the withholding tax rate is 15% for non-residents of countries with whom we have a tax treaty, and 25% for those resident in non-treaty countries.

 CRA is now requiring a certificate of residency from each shareholder in order to apply withholding taxes properly, with re-certification required every third year, as well as Form *NR301—Declaration of Eligibility for Benefits Under a Tax Treaty For A Non-Resident Taxpayer*.

These rules will impact tax planning for family businesses where family members travel or work abroad as non-residents. A more tax-efficient method of distribution of family wealth may be required in planning for those people. Failure to remit can attract penalties of up to 10%; 20% for repeat omissions.

Patronage Dividends (Allocations). Patronage dividends or allocations are received from cooperative corporations and reported on a T4A slip in Box 030. If you are operating a business, such as a farm, add the portion of the amount to income that represents a rebate on expenditures for business purposes. If you are a consumer, the amounts represent a discount off your personal purchases and are not taxable. You may be asked to show the breakdown of taxable and non-taxable patronage allocations on your tax software screen.

Example: Farmer Ben buys groceries and fuel at the local co-operative. At the end of the year he received a T4A representing his patronage dividend in the amount of $950. He notes that $100 tax was also withheld, which would show up as a credit on Line 437 of his tax return. His farm books show that 50% of expenditures at the Co-op related to groceries (personal use), with the balance to fuel (farm use). The portion of the patronage dividend that relates to fuel purchases is taxable ($450) because it represents a reduction in the amount paid (and already deducted) for fuel costs.

Stock Dividends. These dividends are paid by the corporation by issuing of additional stock of that corporation, rather than cash. They can also be known as "dividends in kind." For tax purposes they are treated the same way as an ordinary dividend. You will report the grossed-up amount (as shown on your T5 slip) on your tax return and claim the dividend tax credit if the amounts are issued by either a public Canadian corporation or a Canadian Controlled Private Corporation. The actual amount of the dividend is deemed to be the cost of the new shares.

Stock Splits. There are no immediate tax consequences on a stock split. This occurs when there is an increase in the number of outstanding shares of a company's stock but the percentage of ownership remains the same. No T-slip will be received. Most commonly investors would experience a 2-for-1 split, in which case one share owned becomes two, which will affect the cost base of the shares. The tax consequences are later recorded on the sale or loss of the securities. Please see the next chapter.

U.S. Investment Accounts. Financial transactions between Canada and the U.S., with whom we have a tax treaty, can be complicated and expensive. Canadian residents holding investments in U.S. securities may have tax consequences in both countries; dividends earned on U.S. securities, for example, are taxed in the U.S. first through withholding taxes and then in Canada. Portfolio gains on U.S. securities held by Canadians will be taxed in Canada. You can get relief from double taxation through a foreign tax credit in Canada to offset federal and provincial taxes. Unabsorbed foreign taxes from non-business investments cannot be carried forward although they can be deducted if you have Canadian taxes to pay.

 Don't forget, you may be required to report your foreign investment income, cost of assets held, and accounts held at any time of the year on Form T1135 *Foreign Income Verification Statement*, if your "specified" foreign properties have a cumulative cost of $100,000 or more. This is not required if you have received a T3 or T5 Slip from that investment source, however. Check with your investment advisor if you hold foreign securities.

U.S. Citizens Residing in Canada. U.S. citizens living in Canada must pay tax in the US on world income no matter where they live, so filing a 1040 tax return no later than June 15 is required. Investors face a minimum penalty of $10,000 for failing to report details of their foreign financial accounts, including those in Canada. Starting in 2014, Canadian financial institutions will be required to disclose financial information to the IRS about funds held for U.S. citizens. You will be asked if you are a U.S. citizen, where you were born, and whether either of your parents are U.S. citizens for these purposes.

Reporting Interest and Other Investment Income

Interest income results from an investment in a "debt obligation." That is, you loan capital to a financial institution, company or another person, and in return for the use of your money, you are paid interest at a certain percentage. That interest can be paid to you periodically—once a month, once or twice a year, and so on—depending on the terms in your contract. Or the interest may be automatically reinvested and left to compound.

Examples of interest-bearing investments are Guaranteed Investment Certificates (GICs), Canada Savings Bonds (CSBs), Treasury Bills or T-Bills, strip bonds or income bonds, or debentures, which link interest paid to a corporation's profits or cash flow. Indexed debt obligations can be linked to inflation, too. Government of Canada Real Return Bonds are an example of this.

Interest Reporting Methods. Most tax filers will receive a T3 or T5 slip on which interest is reported. That data is then entered on the appropriate screen in your tax software.

Behind the scenes, however, know that some investments will report interest on a calendar-year basis (January to December); alternatively, on a bond year basis as in the case of Canada Savings Bonds, October 31 to November 1. Therefore, the anniversary date of an interest-bearing investment is important: accrued interest will have to be reported one year from its date of issue less a day, the anniversary of that date in each subsequent year, or the day of disposition.

Compounding vs. Simple Interest. An investment compounds when earnings are reinvested so that you can earn interest on those earnings as well as the principal. For compounding investments acquired after 1989, annual reporting is required. All interest that accrues in the year ending on the anniversary date must be reported, even though you may not have received the money.

Simple Interest Received. Interest is considered earned for tax purposes when it is received or receivable by the taxpayer. This can be cash or by cheque, as a credit to your bank account, in kind in lieu of cash, or when a new term deposit certificate is issued for interest earned on a matured certificate. Matured bond interest is considered to have been received when the bond is cashed, sold, given in payment of a debt, or another form of negotiated payments.

Interest Accrued. As indicated above, interest must be reported on your tax return each year it continues to accrue even if it is not paid or payable. For example, if you have a five-year investment that pays interest only when it matures at the end of the five-year period, you'll still receive a T-slip and you'll have to report the interest that accrues each year. In the final year when you actually receive the interest, you'll only have to report the difference between the amount received and the amount already reported.

Other Interest-Bearing Investments. Interest earned on corporate or government bonds is reported according to the rules above. If your bond is purchased at a discount to maturity, the interest amount reported in the year of acquisition will increase your adjusted cost base when you sell the bond on the open market. This is discussed in the next chapter.

Other Interest. Sometimes parents will lend money to kids to buy their first home or corporations will lend money to employees to buy stocks in the company. Here is how to handle the interest paid:

- *Mortgages.* You must report the interest on the mortgage you hold for another, including your child, as "other investment income" on your tax return. Don't report the principal in the blended payment—just the interest.
- *Employer-Provided Loans.* In this case a taxable benefit may be reported in employment income in Box 14 of the T4 slip to account for the difference in interest rates between the low rate and the prescribed rate of interest. The prescribed rate was 1% for most of 2013 and has been for several years. For the last quarter it was 2%. If your employer provided you with an interest-free loan when the prescribed rate is 1%, then your taxable benefit will be the interest that you would have paid had the loan been at the 1% prescribed rate. This amount is included in income (as shown in Box 14) and this is important, because, if you used the loan proceeds to earn investment income, that amount can be used as a carrying charge as interest paid to earn investment income.

Limited Partnership Income

Some investors like the opportunity to participate in tax shelters known as limited partnerships. Because the partnership does not pay taxes itself but passes on a portion of its income, losses and credits to its partners, partnerships offer an attractive opportunity for immediate tax savings based on losses that are shared amongst the partners.

A limited partner is an inactive member of a partnership whose liability in respect of the partnership interest is, as the name implies, limited by law. In general terms, investors in a limited partnership will be responsible for reporting a portion of the taxable activities. For example, a partnership must calculate its net income for the fiscal year as it were a separate "person." All partners must then include in their income a portion of the partnership's net income for the year.

Limited partnership income is generally reported to the investor on Form *T5013 Statement of Partnership Income* and transferred to the tax return on Line 122 or as Rent or other investment income depending on the nature of the business operated by the partnership.

Limited Partnership Losses. Unfortunately, this is where things get tricky. Losses that exceed the partner's *"at-risk amount"* cannot be used to reduce income from other sources.

That means that unless you have income from the limited partnership, your losses will not be deductible beyond the amount that you invested in the partnership. Limited partnership losses may not be carried back, either, but may be carried forward indefinitely to be applied against future income from the limited partnership that gave rise to the loss. Limited partnership losses of other years are deducted on Line 251. The partner's at-risk amount is shown in Box 22-1 or 22-2 of the T5013 *Statement of Partnership Income* slip.

Investors often do not understand the tax reporting and are angered that they can't write off all the losses immediately. For that reason, ask your investment advisor to run you through all the tax consequences before you invest.

Labour-Sponsored Funds. Investments in a Labour-Sponsored Investment Fund (LSIF) will generate a non-refundable credit which is claimed on Line 414 of Schedule 1. In addition, a provincial credit may be available for your province.

Federally registered LSIFs qualify for federal tax credits of 15% of cost of original acquisition of shares to a maximum of $5,000 or a maximum credit of $750 each year. The investment can be made up to 60 days following the end of the year and create a credit claimable in the year. The provincial credit rate varies by province.

Eligible investments will be reported on Form T5006 *Statement of Registered Labour-Sponsored Venture Capital Corporation Class A Shares.*

The federal credit is being phased out beginning in 2015.

 The Bottom Line | Many investors are fleeing to the safety of guaranteed, interest-bearing investments at a time when the yield is not great. Should interest rates go up in the future, they may be locked into a term at low rates or worse, lose on the sale of a bond in the open market because no one wants a low return investment. That's why you need to do some careful tax planning.

34

Reporting Gains and Losses

The reporting of capital gains and losses—the sale or other disposition of your assets—may be a bit mind-boggling for you. Many taxpayers just see these terms on their T-slips, enter them into their software and something happens behind the scenes to make it all work out, it seems.

But, if you can get past the tax jargon—and we'll help you here—you'll find that understanding how to use the many tax advantages in reporting accrued gains and losses, when they occur, will make managing your capital assets interesting because it can also make you very wealthy over time. So isn't that just the right motivation to dive in and learn more about reporting dispositions on of capital assets on Schedule 3 of your tax return?

 CHECK IT OUT | **How is a capital gain or loss generated?** A capital property is usually acquired for investment purposes (securities such as stocks, bonds or mutual fund units) or for business purposes to earn income (land, building, equipment). When you dispose of it, you may occur a capital gain or loss, if its value has changed.

A **capital gain** or loss can occur if you have disposed of, or are "deemed" to have disposed of a capital property. For many taxpayers, however, the capital gains on their investments in mutual fund corporations and trusts will be reported on a T5 or T3 slip respectively, so reporting is simple. In other cases, it will be necessary to gather documentation from your investment advisor to properly compute the gain or loss.

How is a Capital Gain Calculated? A capital gain will occur, and you will need to report this on your tax return, when a capital property is sold or "deemed" to be sold for more than its adjusted cost base and the outlays and expenses you have incurred to dispose of the property. If you dispose of the asset for less than its cost base, there is a capital loss. We'll define those terms in more depth later. A capital gain is basically the following:

Proceeds of Disposition – Adjusted Cost Base – Outlays and Expenses = Capital Gain (or Loss)

Capital Gains Inclusion Rate. One half of this capital gain is included in your taxable income. The income inclusion rate, in other words, is 50%. (That income inclusion rate has changed over the years. A short history appears at the end of this chapter, in case you need to go back to the information for assets held over time.)

Example: An investor buys a share for $50 and sells it for $75 (with no outlays or expenses). The capital gain in this case is $25 ($75 – $50 = $25). The amount added to income and subject to tax is 50% of this or $12.50.

Proceeds of Disposition. This part of the equation can simply mean the selling price. However, in some cases, there is a "*deemed disposition.*" In that case, a *Fair Market Value (FMV)* must be determined because there is no actual sale.

✓ **CHECK** | **When do you have a "deemed disposition" for tax purposes?**
IT OUT | A deemed disposition occurs when:

- One asset is exchanged for another;
- Assets are given as gifts;
- The property is stolen, destroyed, expropriated or damaged;
- Shares held by the taxpayer are converted, redeemed or cancelled;
- An option to acquire or dispose of property expires;
- A debt owed to the taxpayer is settled or cancelled;
- Property is transferred to a trust;
- The owner of the property emigrates from Canada, becoming non-resident;
- The owner changes the use of the asset from business to personal (and vice versa); or
- The owner dies (the disposition is considered to have taken place immediately prior to death).

Fair Market Valuation. In the dispositions above, the FMV is determined as the price a stranger (unrelated to the taxpayer) would pay for an asset on the open market. To get that value, it's important to see appraisals or listings of similar assets sold recently on the open market.

Valuation Days. Due to the history of the taxation of capital gains in Canada, numerous valuation days for various assets may also be used as proceeds of disposition. For example, capital gains were not taxable at all prior to 1972, so valuation was required for all assets owned at that time. At the end of this chapter is a history to be used in your calculations as various assets are disposed of.

 CHECK IT OUT | **What is adjusted cost base (ACB)?** Simply put, this is the value of your property that is not subject to tax on disposition. It's what you paid for it or its value at the time you acquired it, if you received it as a result of a deemed disposition. The cost to the taxpayer acquiring the asset is equal to the proceeds of disposition of the party who disposed of it. Some exceptions apply to this rule. More on that later.

Outlays and Expenses. The costs of disposing of a capital property may be used to reduce a capital gain or increase a loss, as the case may be. Examples are:

- advertising costs,
- brokerage fees,
- commissions,
- costs incurred to improve the property,
- finder's fees,
- professional fees: legal, surveyor's, appraisals, and
- transfer taxes.

Example: Marissa acquired a rental property she wanted to fix up and sell. The real estate cost $250,000. She replaced the roof and upgraded the carpets for a total of $10,000. The roof and carpets were improvements, which she added to her cost base, bringing it up to $260,000. She sold the property within two months for $325,000 and incurred expenses of $25,000 on the sale. Her capital gain was $40,000 ($325,000 − $260,000 − $25,000).

Capital Losses. Capital losses are important. They can offset capital gains of the year, the prior three years or any future year.

Example: Marissa funded her real estate improvements by selling one of her investments. She had purchased the shares for $12,000 and at the time of sale, they were worth $11,500. She paid brokerage fees of $125 on the trade. Her loss was calculated as follows:

Proceeds of Disposition	$11,500
Adjusted Cost Base	($12,000)
Outlays and Expenses	($ 125)
Capital Loss	($ 625)

This loss will be used to offset the capital gains of the year, $40,000 in this case. Marissa's net capital gain, therefore is $40,000 less $625 = $39,375 and the taxable gain is 50% of this or $19,687.50.

Many investors think that because they have no capital gains this year to absorb losses, as Marissa did, that the capital loss they incurred is worthless. This is not so.

Capital Loss Carry Back. Marissa's brother, Mark, was not so lucky this year. He lost $30,000 in the stock market. He had no other capital gains this year, but last year he had a great year; he made $40,000 in the stock market. He can now reach back and recover some of the taxes he paid last year with a loss carry back. He would use Form *T1A Request for Loss Carry Back* to do so.

Capital losses can be carried back to offset capital gains in the previous three years or, at Mark's option, he could have carried those losses forward, for use against future capital gains. The carry over options (back or forward) do not need to be made in any particular order.

In Mark's case, his other income of the year was $65,000 from employment. He paid $13,365 in taxes on his total income. The loss carry back created a refund of $4,672 and so was very worthwhile. Mark contributed that extra money to his TFSA.

Adjusting Prior Filed Returns to Claim Losses. If you have missed claiming a capital loss anytime in the past 10 years, consider making an adjustment to those prior-filed returns.

Classification of Property. There are special rules for the classification of certain capital properties that are important in understanding how to claim losses. A very special tax break, the Capital Gains Deduction is also available on the disposition of certain investments.

Capital property does not include inventory of a business or insurance policies, with the exception of units in segregated fund trusts.

There are some special classifications of property where the loss application rules are restricted or varied. These are discussed next.

 CHECK IT OUT | **What are the classifications of capital property?** You won't get a convenient T-slip for some of the capital dispositions you may make for the assets you own. Let's discuss those in three profiles: dispositions by individuals, investors, and business owners.

Individuals

What are the tax consequences when you sell your home, a personal-use property, for a loss or make a bundle on grandma's antique silver goblets, a listed personal-use property? Here are the rules.

Personal-Use Properties. The gains and losses on the sale of a personal-use property, which includes all items used for personal use, such as homes, cars, boats and furniture, must be reported as they are subject to the "$1,000 Rule." That is, the Proceeds of Disposition and Adjusted Cost Base of personal-use property are deemed to be no less than $1,000 for the purposes of computing any gain or loss. This eliminates reporting small transactions. Losses on personal-use properties are not deductible, however.

Example: Peter put a lot of money into his cabin at the lake. He bought it for $50,000 and then put in a deck and an addition for another $50,000. He did not use it as a rental property and after a year, he had to sell it for only $80,000 as he took a job in another city. His $20,000 loss, unfortunately, is not deductible.

Listed Personal Properties. These possessions usually don't depreciate in value. They can include artwork, jewelry, rare books or stamp and coin collections. Again the $1,000 Rule applies, however, in this case, losses can be deducted but only against other listed personal property gains of the year. If there are none, you can apply unabsorbed losses by carrying them back three years or forward seven years but only against gains on listed personal property.

Investors

Investors may need to record capital dispositions for three types of assets:

- Publicly traded shares, mutual fund units, other shares;
- Bonds, debentures and promissory notes; and
- Real estate, such as vacant land or a revenue property.

Publicly Traded Shares, Mutual Funds and Other Shares. For many tax filers, the reporting of capital transactions for mutual or segregated funds is easy: simply enter the amounts from the T-slips into your software data sheet and they will all appear on Lines 174 and 176 of Schedule 3. The software will keep track of any unabsorbed capital losses as well. These transactions reflect trading within managed accounts and the resulting capital gains and other income that has flowed through to the investor.

However, when you sell or otherwise dispose of the securities or mutual fund units themselves, you'll need to report that disposition separately. That involves finding your statements for the cost of acquisition and any additions (reinvested amounts in the case of mutual or segregated funds) as well as outlays and expenses (brokerage fees) to properly compute the Adjusted Cost Base (ACB). This can be tricky in some cases, as described below:

Identical Property. Shares in the same class of the same corporation or units in a specific mutual fund are known as "identical properties." Each share or unit is the same as the others and you can't tell one from another. When a taxpayer trades a portion of a group of identical properties, the taxpayer must calculate an *average cost* of all properties in the group to determine the adjusted cost base (ACB) of the property sold and report the capital gain or loss. Simply stated, each time there is a purchase, add the adjusted cost base of all the shares or mutual units in the group and divide by the total number of shares or units held.

Example: On January 1, Sarah purchased 1,000 shares of QRS Corp. for $12,000. On March 15, she purchased another 1,000 shares in the same corporation for $8,000. Then she disposes of 1,000 shares on July 15, for $11,000. There are no other transactions in the year and for these purposes, no outlays or expenses. The capital gain to be reported is calculated as follows:

- The average cost of the share is: ($12,000 + $8,000) / 2,000 = $10 per share.
- The Adjusted Cost Base of the shares she sold is $10/share x 1,000 shares or $10,000.
- The Capital Gain is $11,000 – $10,000 or $1,000.
- This is reported on Schedule 3.
- Half of this is added to total income.

Mutual Fund Exchanges and Switches. In the year you acquire a mutual fund, you will usually receive a full annual distribution, even if you invested late in the year. These amounts will generally be reinvested for you and you'll need to keep track of this to increase your cost base. If you exchange an investment in one fund for another (e.g. you switch from an equity fund into a balanced fund), a taxable disposition is considered to have occurred. However, there are no tax consequences when you switch from one class or series of funds to another, provided the investment is in corporate class funds.

Example: During the tax year, Justin purchased 1,000 units of ABC Equity Fund for $8,547. He received a T5 slip showing allocated earnings of $174.50 which was not paid to Justin but were used to acquire 21.86 more units in the fund. In July, Justin decided he would transfer his investment to ABC Balanced Fund. The ABC Equity Fund units were selling at $8.05 per unit at the time of the sale and the ABC Balanced Fund units were selling at $7.45 per unit so Justin's 1,021.86 Equity units were exchanged for 1,104.16 units in the Balanced Fund. There were no transaction fees associated with this transfer.

As a result of this transaction, Justin has a capital loss, calculated as follows:

Capital Gain or Loss =	Proceeds of Disposition – Adjusted Cost Base – Outlays
Proceeds =	1,021.86 units @ $8.05 per unit = $8,225.97
ACB =	$8,547.00 + $174.50 = $8,721.50
Outlays =	$0.00
Gain or Loss =	$8,225.97 – $8,721.50 – $0.00 = $495.53 Loss

Justin can use this loss to decrease any other capital gains in 2013. If his losses exceed his gains in the year, he can carry the loss back to reduce capital gains reported in 2012, 2011, or 2010. If the losses are not applied to gains in those years, he can carry the loss forward and apply it against gains in future years.

Corporate Class Funds. Corporate class funds are mutual fund corporations with multiple share classes—each of which constitutes a different fund. Corporate class mutual funds have been a tax efficient investment vehicle, particularly right for a family in which each member has maximized contributions to registered plans. The primary advantage, within a non-registered account, is that investors can switch between mutual funds within the same corporation without triggering a capital gain. In addition, because all expenses and non-capital losses are allocated against income across all share classes within the corporate structure, taxable distributions can be reduced. Finally, because those taxable distributions are paid as eligible dividends or capital gains dividends, they are taxed more advantageously than ordinary income or interest would be within a non-registered account.

Reporting for corporate class funds differs from other mutual funds as follows:

- Any distributions or allocations are reported at tax time on a T5 slip rather than a T3 Slip.
- The corporation itself manages its distributions, share redemptions and capital gains and losses across all funds in the corporation to minimize taxes.
- T-series corporate class funds can offer a regular tax efficient income stream by blending a return of capital with distributions. After you've removed your principal, there will be future capital gains tax consequences because the adjusted cost base has changed. However, at that time the investor may be able to offset capital gains with losses of the current or prior years.

 Budget Changes Reduce Tax Benefits | The March 21, 2013 federal budget targeted tax arrangements that reduce taxes by converting, through the use of derivative contracts, the returns on an investment from ordinary income (100% taxable) to capital gains (50% taxable). The series of events leading to the result was appropriately called "Character Conversion Transactions". The Budget announced measures to ensure ordinary income transactions in these arrangements will be taxed as such—with a 100% rather than 50% income inclusion. In some cases, an adjustment will be required to the cost base of the property. Such arrangements were commonly used by corporate class funds to reduce taxable distributions to the unit holders. Professional advice should be sought. However, not all corporate class funds will be subject to the new treatment.

Segregated Funds. These are mutual funds wrapped up with a life insurance policy to provide a death benefit as well as a guarantee of principal. The money is held in trust and income is distributed to the beneficiaries and then generally immediately reinvested, much like mutual fund distributions. Income allocations do not affect the value of the segregated fund, unlike mutual funds. In addition, capital losses can be flowed through to the segregated fund holder to offset other capital gains.

Insurance segregated funds differ from mutual funds primarily in that they offer maturity and death guarantees on the capital invested and specifically, reset guarantees—the ability to lock in market gains. This is usually 75% to 100% of the amount invested, which will be returned to the taxpayer on death or maturity. Depending on the insurer, a reset can be initiated by the investor two to four times per year. The guaranteed period on maturity is usually 10 years after the policy is purchased, or after the reset. There are no tax consequences at the time the accrued gains in the investment are locked in by way of reset.

Guarantee at Maturity. If the value of the fund has increased over the reset amount, the disposition is reported as a normal capital gain.

Example: Ariel purchased 500 units in a segregated fund for $5,450. During the tax year, she sold her 624 units (the number had increased over the years due to reinvestment of income allocations) for $9,048. The ACB of her units was $8,161. Her last reset was at $14 per unit. Since her proceeds amount to $14.50 per unit, the guarantee was not invoked. She has a capital gain on disposition of $9,048 – $8,161 = $887 assuming no expenses of disposition.

If, at maturity, the value of the fund has dropped, the insurer must top up the fund by contributing additional assets to bring the value up to the guaranteed amount. When it is sold at maturity, the difference between the adjusted cost base (which will include all allocations of income over time) and the proceeds received to the guaranteed amount will be accounted for. This is how to report this on Schedule 3:

Example: If the value of Ariel's investment (previous example) was only $13 per unit, the guarantee would have been invoked and Ariel's proceeds would be $14 per unit x 624 units = $8,736 and she would still have a capital gain but for $8,736 – $8,161 = $575 in spite of the fact that the actual value of the units was less than her ACB.

Guarantee at Death. The policyholder is deemed to have disposed of the contract at its FMV at death. If the value of the assets in the fund increases, the gain will be a capital gain to the policyholder when the policy matures or to his estate if the policy owner dies. The example below demonstrates how to report this on Schedule 3.

Example: Mark had purchased 1,000 units in ABC segregated fund for $8,450 which, through income allocations had increased to 1,247 units at the time of his death during the tax year. The ACB of the units was $10,600 at the time of his death. At that time the value of the fund units was $9.05 per unit. On Mark's final return, a capital gain of $685.35 must be reported in Part 3 of Schedule 3:

Proceeds of disposition:	$9.05/unit x 1,247 units = $11,285.35
Adjusted cost base:	$10,600.00
Outlays and expenses:	$0.00
Capital gain:	$11,285.35 – $10,600.00 – $0.00 = $685.35.

If the value of the assets in the fund decreases, the taxpayer is deemed to have acquired additional notional units in the fund, so no gain is incurred even though the taxpayer receives more than the value of the notional units. A capital loss may occur if the guaranteed value is less than 100% of the investment. See the following example.

Example: When Ester died, she owned 1,500 units in DEF segregated fund. The ACB of her units was $7.49 per unit. She had a guarantee at death of $10 per unit but the unit value at that time was $9.00 per unit.

Ester's estate will receive $15,000 (1,500 units x $10.00 per unit guaranteed value). Technically this is accomplished by allocating more units to Ester at $9 per unit to ensure the $15,000 guarantee is met. However, on Schedule 3 of Ester's final return the gain is calculated in the normal manner:

Proceeds of disposition: $15,000
Adjusted cost base: 1,500 units x $7.49/unit = $11,235
Capital gain: $15,000 – $11,235 = $3,765.

Income Trusts. If you have investments in income trusts, these investments now pay income to investors in the form of dividends. In some cases, these investments pay a *Return of Capital*, which must be tracked in order to properly reflect a declining adjusted cost base, as described below.

Return of Capital. In some cases, most commonly with mutual funds, distributions are made to investors that represent a portion of the original investment rather than earnings. Because the return of capital does not represent earnings, these distributions are not taxable when received. You'll find them reported Box 52 of a T3 slip or in a footnote on a T5 slip. Since these are not taxable distributions, you will not find an entry field for them in your tax software.

However, since some of your investment was returned to you, *the adjusted cost base of the units is decreased by the amount returned.* You'll need to take that into account when reporting any capital gain or loss when the units are disposed of.

Gifts. Where property is acquired by gift or bequest, the cost to the recipient of the property is deemed to be its FMV at the time of the gift. An exception is a gift to a spouse where a tax-free rollover can take place. FMV may be elected, however if FMV consideration is paid in cash or through a spousal loan.

Example: Henry and Elizabeth purchased their cottage many years ago and, because of health issues are no longer able to use it. The cottage was worth $200,000 in 2013 when they decided to pass it on to their son Michael. The ACB of the cottage was $120,000. The fees associated with the transfer were $5,000.

Although Henry and Elizabeth received no proceeds from the transfer, they must report a capital gain on the disposition to Michael.

Gain = Proceeds (FMV deemed proceeds) – ACB – Outlays
Gain = $200,000 – $120,000 – $5,000 = $75,000.

This gain will be reported on each owner's tax return on the basis of his/her ownership interest in the property. Michael's ACB is deemed to be $200,000.

Immigration. When a taxpayer immigrates to Canada, the taxpayer is deemed by to have acquired the capital properties owned at that time at a cost equal to the fair market value of the property at the time of immigration. This becomes the cost base of those assets for the purposes of reporting future capital gains.

Example: When Myron immigrated to Canada in 2010, he brought with him a piece of artwork that was valued at $10,000 CDN. Myron had purchased the artwork some years earlier for the equivalent of $3,000 CDN. When he sold the artwork during this tax year for $12,000, he had to report a capital gain of $2,000 ($12,000 – $10,000) on his Canadian return. The gain that accrued prior to Myron immigrating is not taxed in Canada.

Real Estate. Lots of people like to dabble in real estate when markets are hot. The issue for tax filing purposes is whether you held the property for personal use, as a passive investment or whether you are in fact in the business of buying and selling real estate.

When real estate is held for investment purposes, any income it earns will be "*income from property,*" generally in the form of *rent*. Upon disposition of the property, any increase in value will usually be taxed as a capital gain. However, if you are continuously flipping your properties, it's possible you're in business.

 CHECK IT OUT | **When are you considered to be in the business of buying and selling real estate?** The *Income Tax Act* does not prescribe when gains from the sale of real estate will be considered income rather than capital. In making such determinations, the courts have considered factors such as:

- the taxpayer's intention with respect to the real estate at the time of its purchase;
- feasibility of the taxpayer's intention;
- geographical location and zoned use of the real estate acquired;
- extent to which the intention was carried out by the taxpayer;
- evidence that the taxpayer's intention changed after purchase of the real estate;
- the nature of the business, profession, calling or trade of the taxpayer and associates;
- the extent to which borrowed money was used to finance the real estate acquisition and the terms of the financing, if any, arranged;
- the length of time throughout which the real estate was held by the taxpayer;
- the existence of persons other than the taxpayer who share interests in the real estate;

- the nature of the occupation of the other persons who share interest as well as their stated intentions and courses of conduct;
- factors which motivated the sale of the real estate; and
- evidence that the taxpayer and/or associates had dealt extensively in real estate.

The more closely a taxpayer's business or occupation is related to real estate transactions, the more likely it is that any gain realized by the taxpayer from such a transaction will be considered to be business income (report on a business statement—100% income inclusion) rather than a capital gain (report on Schedule 3 as a capital gain—50% income inclusion).

In addition, it's not necessary for you to buy and sell properties. If CRA considers the transaction to be an *Adventure or Concern in the Nature of Trade*, even a one-time transaction can be considered to be a business transaction. The result? Again, you must report business profits (100% taxable) as opposed to a capital gain (50% taxable.)

Generally, when the intention of the taxpayer is to earn income from the sale of real estate, based on these factors, the income is included in income from business. When the asset is held for investment purposes (i.e. to earn income from property—interest or rent is earned—the gain on sale is capital in nature).

Vacant Land. Special rules apply to vacant land. If it's held for speculation; that is there is no potential for income from the property, a capital gain or loss will eventually occur. Interest, land transfer taxes and property taxes cannot be deducted along the way, either. You must be able to show the potential for rental income to deduct interest and property taxes, but if there is no potential for income, the expenses cannot be deducted. However, so long as the land is not held for personal use, interest and property taxes may be added to the adjusted cost base of the land reducing the capital gain on disposition.

Vacant land that is capital property used by its owner for the purpose of gaining or producing income from the sale of lots, will be considered to have been converted to *inventory* at the earlier of:

- the time when the owner starts making improvements with a view to selling it; and
- the time of making application for approval of a plan to subdivide the land into lots for sale, in order to develop a subdivision.

The subdivision of farmland or inherited land in order to sell it will not, of itself, constitute a conversion to inventory and so capital gains treatment should be preserved in these cases.

Options on Real Estate. Where an arm's length lease-option agreement exists, reasonable rental paid prior to the exercise of the purchase option by the lessee is considered to be rental expense to the lessee and income to the lessor. This is true even where a rebate or discount on the purchase price for a portion of the previous rentals paid is given at the time the option to purchase is exercised.

Upon exercise of the purchase option, the option price for the property, less adjustments for previous rentals paid, if any, will be considered the cost of property to the lessee purchaser.

Example: Susan operates a proprietorship. She wanted to purchase a storefront for her business but was unable to provide the required down payment for financing so she entered into a lease option agreement to purchase a property. Under the agreement, she paid $1,000 per month for five years and at the end of the lease could purchase the building for $150,000. As the $1,000 per month was reasonable rent on the building, she was able to deduct the payments as rent. If she purchases the property for $150,000 at the end of the lease, her ACB will be the $150,000 paid (plus any additional expenses of acquisition).

Selling Land and Building. When land and building are held to earn income (either business income or rental income) then the building is a depreciable property (see below). Because special rules apply to depreciable property, the land and building are considered to be separate assets and the ACB must be established for each at the time of purchase. Likewise, proceeds of disposition must be allocated to the land and building according to their value.

In the simplest case, where no CCA (Capital Cost Allowance—the tax equivalent of depreciation) has been claimed and the value of the property increases, the result of the allocation is simply to split the capital gain into two parts. However, where CCA has been claimed, the value of the property decreases, or the value of the land increases and the value of the building decreases, then the rules become more complicated. You may want to seek professional assistance if you sold real estate that was held for investment or business use.

Case Study | Planning to Sell a Rental Property

Dexter purchased a rental property in 2010 for $250,000. Per the appraisal, the building was worth $100,000 and the land worth $150,000. In order to reduce his rental income to zero each year, Dexter claimed a total of $5,000 CCA as a deduction. In this tax year, Dexter sold the property for $275,000. Per an appraisal done at the time of the sale, the $170,000 of the proceeds were allocated to the land and $105,000 to the building. Outlays and expenses totalled $18,000 which were allocated on the same basis as the proceeds ($11,127 to the land and $6,873 to the building).

The capital gain on the land (as shown on Dexter's Schedule 3) is $170,000 – $150,000 – $11,127 = $8,873.

Because the net proceeds for the building ($105,000 – $6,873) are more than the depreciated value ($100,000 – $5,000 CCA), Dexter has over-claimed depreciation and he must add back the excess (recapture) of $3,127 into income.

Business Owners

Small business owners may dispose of three types of properties on their personal tax returns: depreciable property and eligible capital property in the case of unincorporated businesses as well as qualifying shares of a small business corporation. Best to see a professional for help in disposing of depreciable property, eligible capital property, and Qualified SBC Shares.

Significant Dates in Capital Gains Taxation and Valuation Days

- Prior to 1972: Capital gains were not taxable in Canada
- December 22, 1971: Valuation day for Canadian publicly traded securities
- December 31, 1971: Valuation day for all other capital property
- January 1, 1972: Capital gains inclusion rate is **50%**; two tax-exempt principal residences allowed per household comprised of a legally married couple
- December 31, 1981: Valuation day for family homes—one tax exempt principal residence allowed per household comprised of a legally married couple
- January 1, 1985: Capital gains deduction is introduced
- January 1, 1987: Capital gains deduction is capped at $100,000, but the Super Exemption of $500,000 is introduced for qualifying farms and small business corporations
- January 1, 1988: Capital gains inclusion rate increases to **66⅔%**
- January 1, 1990: Capital gain inclusion rate increases to **75%**
- January 1, 1993: One tax-exempt principal residence per common-law couple of the opposite sex
- February 22, 1994: Capital Gains Election date, which occurred on the elimination of the $100,000 Capital Gains Deduction
- January 1, 1998: Same sex couples could *elect* conjugal status with the result that only one tax exempt residence is allowed per couple
- February 27, 2000: Capital gains inclusion rate drops to **66⅔%**
- October 18, 2000: Capital gains inclusion rate drops to **50%**
- January 1, 2001: Same sex couples are now limited to one tax exempt residence per conjugal relationship (no election)
- May 1, 2006: Qualified fishing property allowed for CGD purposes
- March 18, 2007: Capital Gains Exemption increases to **$750,000**
- January 1, 2014: Capital Gains Exemption increases to **$800,000**

 The Bottom Line | The buying and selling of assets can help you build your family's wealth. You'll want to control the timing of those transactions for the best tax consequences. Make sure you keep a current list of valuations handy. Also, a personal net worth statement filed in your safety deposit box every year will make life much easier for your executors, who must compute gains or losses on your final return due to a deemed disposition.

35

Personal Residences

Did you just buy your first home? Inherit a second home when your grandmother passed away? Are you wondering about the taxes on the big increase in value on your family cottage? What about the rental income you get for that spare room downstairs? Is the gain on your principal residence taxable when you sell it? These are common questions about one of the most significant assets Canadians have—their principal residence.

 CHECK IT OUT | **What's a principal residence?** It's a residence that you (or a member of your family) ordinarily inhabit in the year and designate as your principal residence. When you sell it, gains in value are completely tax free, in most cases. A principal residence can be any of these:

- a house, cottage, condo, duplex, apartment;
- a trailer that is "ordinarily inhabited" by a taxpayer or some family member at some time during the year.

Except where the principal residence is a share in a co-operative housing corporation, the principal residence includes the land immediately subjacent to the housing unit and up to one-half hectare of adjacent property that contributes to the use of the housing unit as a residence.

If the lot size exceeds one-half hectare, it may be included in the principal residence if it can be shown to be necessary for the use of the housing unit. This is most commonly the case when the farm home is sold. Additional land required because of the location of the home may also be eligible for the exemption but land and buildings used principally for the operation of the farm will not qualify.

One Per Household. The principal residence is an important concept because each household (defined as an adult taxpayer and/or that person's spouse) may choose one property as a principal residence for each year that it is owned and avoid a capital gain when that property is sold. But what happens if you own both a home and a cottage? Which one would you choose?

One Property Only. This is the simplest scenario. If the family owned only one property and lived in it in every year while they owned it, there will be no taxable capital gain on the property. But do you have to report this sale? Technically, the *Income Tax Act* requires that a taxpayer file a "*principal residence designation*" for the year in which the property is sold using Form T2091 *Designation of a Property as a Principal Residence by an Individual (Other Than a Personal Trust)*, however, administratively CRA doesn't require this. No reporting is required when you sell a property that was your principal residence for the entire time it was owned.

No Losses. Recall that a principal residence is considered to be "*personal-use property,*" and so any loss on disposition is deemed by to be nil. No reporting required here either.

No Capital Cost Allowance. There's a special rule and a trap for software users whenever a statement for rental or business income from a home-based business is prepared. Often tax software will automatically calculate capital cost allowance on the building in the background. You will want to override this to preserve that exempt status for any of your personal residences. That's very important because the claiming of *CCA* on any of your residences, even if only a small portion of the home is used in a home-based business, will compromise your tax exemption on that part of the home.

More Than One Residence. Where a family owns more than one property and both properties are used by the family at some time during the year, the calculation may become slightly more difficult. Back in the day, (for periods including 1971 to 1981) each spouse could declare one of the properties as their principal residence, which allowed a family to shelter gains from tax on a home and a cottage for example.

But starting in 1982, only one property per year can be designated as a principal residence for the family. This means that any accrued capital gain on one of the properties (that is not designated as a principal residence) will be ultimately subject to tax when sold.

This is where Form T2091 *Designation of a Property as a Principal Residence by an Individual (Other Than a Personal Trust)* comes in. This form may not be available in your tax software so check that out. If it's not there, print it out from the CRA website.

Form T2091 is used to calculate the exempt portion of a capital gain on a principal residence. Here's how it's done:

1. *Calculate the gain.* The capital gain on the property is first calculated, using regular rules for capital gains and losses.

2. *Calculate the exempt part of the gain.* Once this has been done, the exempt portion is then subtracted from the capital gain. The exempt portion of the gain is calculated as follows:

$$\text{Total gain} \times \frac{\text{(Number of years designated as Principal Residence + 1)}}{\text{Number of years the property was owned}}$$

Note the "+ 1." Because the numerator in the exemption formula adds 1 to the number of years that a property is designated as a principal residence, it is only necessary to designate a property for one year less than the total number of years it was owned to exempt the entire gain. This is because two residences will be owned in the year that the taxpayer moves from residence to another.

Case Study | Planning Sale of Home and Cottage

Phil and Sylvia have owned their home in the city for 20 years and their cottage at the lake for 10 years in that 20-year period. The cottage was sold for a substantial sum last year—$500,000—despite the fact that they only paid $150,000 for it. They did not report it for tax purposes, because they designated it as their tax-exempt residence for the entire ownership period.

This year they are thinking of selling their home, which cost them $225,000. They think they can get a price of $650,000. Will any part of the gain be tax exempt?

The answer is yes. That's because there was a period of time before they owned the cottage in which the exemption would qualify. Phil and Sylvia would have to complete Form T2091 to take this into account.

The calculations would look like this:

1. The capital gain on the city home is $425,000 (= $650,000 less $225,000).

2. Tax-exempt portion: Designate the city home as principal residence for 10 years, as only 10 years of the ownership period included the cottage.

To calculate the exempt portion, the number of years the house is designated as the principal residence plus 1 (10 + 1 = 11) is divided by the total number of years the house was owned (20 years).

The exempt portion of the gain: (11/20 x 425,000) = $233,750.

The taxable portion of the gain: $425,000 – 233,750 = $191,250, and 50% of this is taxable on Schedule 3 ($95,625).

Capital Gains Election. The taxable capital gain is further reduced by any capital gains election made to use up the $100,000 Capital Gains Deduction on February 22, 1994. Look for *Form T664 Capital Gains Election* from the 1994 return to find the amount of the election. Where the capital gains election was made on the property being designated, use Form T2091(IND)-WS *Principal Residence Worksheet* in addition to T2091. Warning: This is complicated. Best to have a tax professional help.

Change in Use of a Principal Residence. When a taxpayer starts using a principal residence for income-producing purposes (for example, as a rental, or for a home office) you'll need to take care of the following details to prepare for a future capital gain:

- *The Fair Market Value (FMV)* of the property is required as it is considered to have been disposed of at this amount and then immediately reacquired at the same amount.
- *Personal to Business Use.* The gain resulting, if any, would be nil if the home was used in each year before this as a principal residence. However, if the taxpayer owns another residence that has appreciated more in value, you'll want to value this property on change of use, as you will report a taxable disposition.
- *Business Use to Personal Use.* If the property is converted back to be used as a principal residence only in the future, the same FMV assessment must be done as there is another deemed disposition and reacquisition of the property to account for. Tax consequences are then assessed, possibly resulting in a capital gain or loss. Note that a loss would be allowed only on the land (the building is depreciable property) because during this period, the property was not personal-use property.

Administratively, CRA will ignore these dispositions (so the property remains exempt under the principal residence rules) if the following criteria are met:

- No structural changes are made to the property to accommodate the change;
- No CCA is claimed on the property; and
- The business use of the property is ancilliary to the personal use of the property (i.e. no more than 40% of the property is used for rental or business purposes).

Elections. *Two special elections can help you avoid the tax consequences above.*

Deferral to Actual Disposition (S. 45(2) Election). When a principal residence is converted from personal use to income-producing use, an election may be made to ignore the deemed disposition normally required to be reported under the change of use rules above. You can instead choose to defer any capital gain/loss until the time of actual disposition, or at any time you choose to rescind the election.

Example: During the tax year, Liam decided to make renovations and convert his basement into a rental apartment. Normally this would mean that he had disposed of part of his principal residence and acquired a rental property. However, Liam may elect to defer the recognition of the disposition until he actually sells the property.

Moving and Renting. In addition, you can choose to designate the property as a personal residence for up to four years after moving out of the house; longer if your employer requires you to relocate to a temporary residence that is at least 40 kilometres away. If you move back to your original home before the end of the calendar year in which employment is terminated, you'll avoid any capital gain.

This election is made by attaching a letter to the tax return, noting that an election is being made under S. 45(2). The election should be signed, and a description of the property should be attached. If you're filing your return electronically, send the election letter to CRA by mail. But do observe these rules:

- Capital Cost Allowance (CCA) must not be claimed.
- No other property can be designated a principal residence at the same time.
- You must have been a resident or must be deemed to be resident of Canada.
- Any rental income earned on the property while you were absent is to be reported in the normal manner (see next chapter).

Rental to Personal Residence (S. 45(3) Election). It is also possible to make a special election when a taxpayer converts a rental property to a principal residence. In that case, there is a deemed disposition at fair market value, but the capital gain is deferred to be reported on the actual disposition of the property. *This is only allowable, however, if no capital cost allowance was claimed on the property since 1984.* Follow the same election procedures as described above.

No Attribution. You may wish to purchase a home for your 19-year-old son and daughter so they can have their own tax-exempt principal residence. There is no attribution because the child is an adult and there will be no tax avoidance on the subsequent tax-exempt sale. So that's a good move.

 The Bottom Line | Your home is your castle. The principal residence exemption makes it a tax exempt one if you follow proper procedures on change of use or when you have more than one personal residence. It's important to update your property values so that you can make sound decisions about the taxes you may need to pay when that great offer to sell comes along. Also remember to look for evidence of a 1994 Capital Gains Election so you don't understate your adjusted cost base on the taxable residence.

36

Rental Property

Do you collect rent? Would you like to rent out your basement suite? Newly single and thinking about taking in a university student? If so, you will want to get your documentation ready for a change in your tax filing.

Your tax software will do a great job helping you calculate the numbers you enter, but you'll need to keep your rental agreement on file, as well as back up for retrieval at tax time: income record, expenses and your valuation of the property when you changed its use from personal rental.

Look for *Form T776 Statement of Rental Income*. You can use this as a printed checklist behind which to attach your receipts.

✓ **CHECK IT OUT** | **How do you report rental income?** Here are some basic rules:
- *Use a Calendar Year.* Income and expenses will be reported on a calendar year basis. *Accrual accounting* (report income when receivable and expenses when payable) is supposed to be used but administratively CRA will accept cash basis accounting for most individuals so long as the cash income reporting does not differ significantly from the accrual basis.
- *Report Gross Rental Income.* Do open a separate bank account for your rental income and expense transactions.
- *Charge Rent at FMV.* You may not be able to write off losses if you can't justify that you are charging rent at fair market value. Take newspaper clippings and other proof of rentals in the area and add to your permanent records so you can make a case for what you are charging, especially if you're renting to a related person.

- *Income Reporting.* Advance payments of rent can be included in income according to the years they relate to. Lease cancellation payments received are also included in rental income.
- *Expense Reporting.* To deduct operating expenses from rental income, there must be a reasonable expectation of profit on an annual basis. Fully deductible operating expenses include maintenance, repairs, supplies, interest, and taxes. Partially deductible expenses could include the business portion of auto expenses and meal and entertainment expenses incurred. But this is where many tax filers make mistakes. Take note of these traps:
  - **Trap #1** Maintenance and repairs are 100% deductible, but improvements over the original condition or that extend the useful life of the asset are added to cost base because they are capital in nature. Put those expenses on the Capital Cost Allowance (CCA) statements instead. But don't claim CCA if you're renting part of your principal residence.
  - **Trap #2** Land is not a depreciable asset. Separate the cost of the land from the cost of the buildings for the purpose of your CCA statement.
  - **Trap #3** The deduction for CCA is always taken at your option so if your assets, particularly the building, are appreciating in value rather than depreciating, you may wish to forego the claim to avoid Recapture in income later.
  - **Trap #4** CCA deductions cannot be used to create or increase a rental loss. This rule is applied to all rental properties you may have together. Thus, if you have more than one property, CCA may be claimed to create a loss on one property so long as you do not have a rental loss on all properties combined.
  - **Trap #5** Don't claim auto expenses for visits to collect rents if you own only one rental property. However, if you personally do the maintenance and repairs for a nearby property, and use your car to carry the tools to do so, the claim will be allowed.
  - **Trap #6** Don't deduct any personal living expenses.
  - **Trap #7** Family member rentals may be exempt. If you are renting to your youngest son, Charlie, for the cost of the groceries, there is no expectation of profit. Don't expect to be able to deduct a rental loss against other income, but in this case, unless there is a demonstrable profit motive, you don't need to report the income, either.

✓ **CHECK IT OUT** | **Are there more deductible rental expenses?** Aside from the above, common deductible operating expenses include:

- *Advertising*—Amounts paid to advertise the availability of the rental property.
- *Condominium Fees*—Applicable to the period when the rental condo was available.
- *Insurance*—If the insurance is prepaid for future years, claim only the portion that applies to the rental year, unless you are using cash basis accounting.

- *Landscaping*—Deduct in the year paid.
- *Lease Cancellation Payments By Landlord*—Deduct these amounts over the term of the lease, including renewal periods. In the case of dispositions at arm's length, a final amount may be deducted, but based on the current capital gains inclusion rate (50%). The full amount of the lease cancellation payment may be deducted on a sale if the building was considered to be inventory rather than capital property.
- *Legal, Accounting and Other Professional Fees*—Note the following:
  - Legal fees to prepare leases or to collect rent are deductible.
  - Legal fees to acquire the property are added to cost base.
  - Legal fees on the sale of the property are outlays and expenses which will reduce any capital gain on the sale.
  - Accounting fees to prepare statements, keep books, or prepare the tax return are deductible.
- *Maintenance and Repairs*—Costs of regular maintenance and minor repairs are deductible. For major repairs, it must be determined if the cost is a current expense (restoration) or capital in nature (improvement).
- *Management and Administration Fees*—If you pay a third party to manage or otherwise look after some aspect of the property, the amount paid is deductible. Note that if a caretaker is given a suite in an apartment block as compensation for caretaking, a T4 slip must be issued to report the fair market value of the rent as employment income.
- *Mortgage Interest*—Interest on a mortgage to purchase the property plus any interest on additional loans to improve the rental property may be deducted, provided you can show there is a reasonable expectation of profit from the revenue property. Note the following.
  - If an additional mortgage is taken out against the equity in the property and the proceeds are used for some other purpose, the mortgage interest is not deductible as a rental expense, but may be deductible as a carrying charge if the proceeds were used to earn investment income.
  - Other charges relating to the acquisition of a mortgage (banking fees, for example) are not deductible in the year paid, but can be amortized over a five-year period starting at the time they were incurred.
  - If the interest costs relate to the acquisition of depreciable property, you may elect to add the interest to the capital cost of the asset rather than deduct it in the year paid. This will be beneficial if, for example, the property generates a rental loss and you cannot use that loss to reduce your taxes owing.
- *Office and Other Supplies*—Office and other supplies used up in earning rental income are deductible as are home office expenses in situations where you use the office to keep books or serve tenants.
- *Property Taxes*—These are deductible.

- *Renovations for the Disabled*—Costs incurred to make the rental property accessible to individuals with a mobility impairment may be fully deducted.
- *Utilities*—If costs are paid by the landlord and not reimbursed by the tenant, they will be deductible. Costs charged to tenants are deductible if amounts collected are included in rental income.

Multiple Owners. When two or more taxpayers jointly own a revenue property, it is necessary to determine whether they own the property as co-owners or as partners in a partnership. If a partnership exists, all the partners are subject to the same CCA claim. Then a partnership allocation of net profits is made. If a co-ownership exists, each owner can claim CCA individually on his/her share of the capital costs.

 The Bottom Line | Rental properties can increase wealth in two ways: by providing cash flow to pay for the mortgage and building net worth with an increase in value of your investment. However, revenue properties are often audited, so be sure you stay out of the traps identified.

37

Deducting Carrying Charges

The costs of earning income from property (other than rental), commonly called carrying charges, are deductible on Schedule 4 and Line 221 of the tax return. They reduce all other income of the year and so are very lucrative. Yet, so many people miss making the proper claims, at significant expense now, or potentially, when audited later.

For example, likely the most missed tax deduction is the *safety deposit box*... few people remember to claim it at tax time. A small but mighty carrying charge, over a 10-year adjustment period it can amount to several hundred dollars in your pocket, so if you missed it, make the adjustment.

 A change is coming to the deduction of the safety deposit box: starting in 2014, the safety deposit box will no longer be tax deductible!

✓ **CHECK** | **What other carrying charges can be deducted on Schedule 4?**
IT OUT | Following is a checklist of commonly missed items.

Accounting Fees. These are claimable if they relate to business income or investments. In the case of investors, the fees pertaining to the income tax schedule for investments count, unless you otherwise hire an accountant to help with accounting for your wealth management or business activities.

Canada Savings Bond Payroll Deductions. The difference between the face value of the CSB you bought at work and the total you paid is a deductible carrying charge.

Example: Monthly deduction of $35 x 12 = $420
                   Face value of bond   <u>$400</u>
                   Carrying charge $ 20

Employer-Provided Loans. The interest benefit from a low- or non-interest-bearing loan is deductible if you use the money to buy investments including the employer's stock. Look to your T4 slip for the amount in Box 36.

Exploration and Development Expenses. A separate line is devoted on the return for the expenses of investment in petroleum, natural gas or mining ventures. Form T1229 *Statement of Resource Expenses and Depletion Allowance* must be completed and the total from Part III posted to Line 124. These expenses will be allocated to investors in petroleum, natural gas or mining ventures. The amounts allocated to you will be shown on a T5 slip, a T101 slip, or a T5013 slip. Enter the box numbers and your software will post to the T1229 form and make the claim on Line 124.

Interest on Investment Loans—Traceable Use. Are you using your operating line to buy the kids a big screen TV and also to fund your investment activities? This may not be a good idea. It's important to keep your borrowings separate and traceable if you want to write off the interest costs as a carrying charge. The onus is on you to establish that the borrowed funds are being used for the purposes of earning income from a business (claim on business statement) or from property (claim on Schedule 4) or from for your rental (claim on your rental statement T776).

Borrowing for Exempt or Registered Funds. No interest is deductible if the loan is made to acquire property which produces exempt income or to acquire an interest in a life insurance policy, RRSP, PRPP, RESP, RDSP or TFSA. An exception is borrowing to top up past service contributions to an RPP. The interest paid on money borrowed to make a past service RPP contribution may be deducted as part of the RPP contribution (on Line 207).

Borrowing to Buy Stocks. For interest to be deductible, the investment must have the potential to produce "income from property." If the investment does not carry a stated interest or dividend rate, which might be the case with some common shares or mutual funds, the interest costs on an investment loan may not be deductible. CRA will generally allow interest costs on funds borrowed to buy common shares to be deductible if there is a possibility of receiving dividends, whether or not they are actually received, but each case may be assessed individually upon audit.

Diminished Asset Values. If the source of income for which you borrowed no longer exists or has substantially diminished because the investment has lost significant value, you may continue to write off the interest on the loan as if the underlying asset still existed. The amount considered "not to be lost" must however be traceable to the loan you are paying off. If you dispose of the asset at a loss, you may continue to write off the interest costs so long as the proceeds were used to pay down the loan amount.

If the property was acquired by a creditor for a reduction in debt owing, this reduction in debt is subtracted from the amount of the loan on which you can make an interest deduction.

Investment Counsel Fees. Fees paid to a financial, investment or wealth advisor or advisory firm, other than commissions, are claimable if they are paid for advice on buying or selling securities or for the administration of those assets, if this is the principal business of this individual or firm. Note that fees paid to a person related to you are only deductible to the extent that they are reasonable based on the amount of work done and the time spent in doing it.

Fees paid to stockbrokers are not deductible for these purposes unless the broker also provides investment portfolio management and administration services for which a separate fee is charged. Also not deductible are fees paid for newspaper, newsletter or magazine subscriptions or fees paid to a trustee of an RRSP or TFSA.

Life Insurance Policy Loans. If you borrow against your cash value in your life insurance policy to then invest the money, you can claim the interest paid as a carrying charge. If the interest is not repaid but rather deducted from the value of the insurance, you'll need to complete Form *T2210 Verification of Life Insurance Policy Loan Interest.*

Student Loan Interest. Claim this as a non-refundable tax credit on Line 319.

 The Bottom Line | If you have borrowed to invest, or paid investment counsel fees, and keep your records in a safety deposit box, chances are you'll have a deduction against all other income as a carrying charge on Line 221. This deduction will reduce net income, thereby increasing your tax credits as well as reducing your taxes payable.

38

When to See a Pro

Just as family tax return preparation is most effective when all the returns are prepared at the same time, structuring investments to provide tax efficient income and capital to each member of the family, now and in the future, can help you build significant wealth. A tax professional can assist throughout the year to choose investments that meet the risk management objectives of each family member, so that the right tax results are achieved during tax season. Consider seeing a professional in the following cases:

1. **To vary income sources from investments.** Income diversification is an important component of a tax efficient investment strategy. Logically, families might arrange to have income sources subject to 100% income inclusion—like interest—taxed in the hands of lowest income earners, like minors, for example. They may also want to earn more income by generating capital gains. At top marginal tax rates, capital gains are taxed at 21.85% in B.C., 19.5% in Alberta and 24.76% in Ontario, half the rates for ordinary income applied to interest.

2. **To split income between family members.** Income splitting moves assets and income from tax exposure at higher marginal tax rates to lower marginal tax rates, resulting in potentially significantly more after-tax dollars for the family. But, to set up family income splitting opportunities between high income earners and their minor children, spouses and other adults, taxpayers must legally circumvent the Attribution Rules.

3. **To discuss six tax tactics** in a tax efficient investment strategy:
   - *Minimize tax* by using investments that provide tax exempt income (TFSA for example).
   - *Defer tax* by investing in a registered account such as an RRSP, or choose investments such as corporate class funds in a non-registered account.

- *Earn tax preferred income*; that is, income that is only partially included in income or taxed at more advantageous tax rates (Canadian dividends or capital gains for example).
- *Time receipt of fully taxable income* carefully; that is, time it to blend well, if possible, with other income sources, keeping an eye on the avoidance of social benefit or tax credit clawback zones and which federal and provincial tax brackets taxable income will fall into.
- *Blend income and capital* for tax preferred cash flow. Choosing T-class funds with Return of Capital (ROC) for example, may be a good solution.
- *Manage non-financial assets like vacant land, farms, personal residences and rental properties.* The tax consequences can be complex so see a pro before acquisition and disposition.

4. **To plan to sell or transfer assets in lifetime and at death.** What are the accrued values in your financial and non-financial assets? How will you get that valuation for all your assets? Will some of them be rolling over to your spouse or children when you die? What are the tax consequences, if any? Do you need additional life insurance to pay the taxes? Where is the safety deposit box where the ownership documents reside? What is the cost of that box?

5. **To leverage value in assets.** Should you be borrowing against the value of your assets to increase your wealth? Will the interest be tax deductible? What happens to that tax deductibility status if the value of the assets diminish?

6. **To maximize the use of the Capital Gains Deduction** by each shareholder in a family business.

PART 5

Pensioners—Where the Action is!

Did you know that an increasing number of people in Canada are centenarians—in fact, the rate of growth for those who reach 100 is the second highest of all age groups in Canada—after those who turn 60-64.

This could be worrisome, financially speaking, given recent pension savings trends from Statistics Canada, based on the 2011 year. While about 6 million people contributed just under $35 Billion to their RRSPs in Canada, that represents only 24% of eligible contributors and only 5% of what could have been contributed: $773 billion. In total, close to 23 million Canadians have about $685 Billion in unused RRSP contribution room, and the median RRSP contribution in Canada is just under $3,000.

At that rate, in the absence of other income sources, your total retirement nest egg over a 35 year working life from your private savings would amount to only $105,000 before investment returns… if you retire at 60 and live to 100, obviously it's not enough.

Fortunately, seniors can tap into public pension benefits from the CPP if they contributed to the plan, and in most cases, to the universal Old Age Security. However the OAS has recently been postponed by two years to age 67 starting in 2023. If that affects you, you need to start saving a little more now.

Taxes erode pension benefits—except if you're smart enough to save for your retirement in a TFSA—so you will need to plan for the tax bite, as well as the inflation erosion that comes with time. Therefore, this section is as much for younger taxpayers as it is for seniors.

What's New

The age of eligibility for Old Age Security (OAS) and Guaranteed Income Supplements (GIS) will be gradually increased to 67 from 65, starting in April 2023, with full implementation by January 2029. Also, as of July 2013, you can elect to defer taking your OAS income for up to five years to build a bigger pension for later. OAS income will get clawed back when net income exceeds $70,954 in 2013. So plan your income streams to come in under this number, if possible.

Hard Copy

Newly retired? It's possible you will need to make quarterly tax instalment remittances for the first time as your income profile changes from employed to pensioner. That means your relationship with CRA will change: you'll get new notices reminding you to pay, regularly. Also, collecting receipts for new costs, like medical expenditures, can become more daunting, as they increase with age. This may all happen as you travel more, so organizing yourself around new tax compliance will become more important. You may also be a Power of Attorney or Executor for others, which means you'll be in charge of their hard copy, too.

Software Tips

While reporting pension income sources on the tax return is easy—just enter the numbers off the slips in your software program—and there can be lots of them: The T4(OAS), the T4A(P) for CPP Benefits, the T4(A) for private periodic pensions, T4RSP for RRSP withdrawals, the T4RIF for Registered Retirement Income Fund withdrawals. But look for software that "optimizes" pension income splitting opportunities between spouses, which can save you thousands of dollars each year.

Tax Sleuthing

The devil is in the details for pensioners. They will claim different tax credits— the Age Amount, for example, or the Family Caregiver Amount and/or Disability amount if someone in the family is infirm or disabled. Statistically, as people age, they give more to charity, they look after others in their home, and they gain access to new tax credits like the Amount for Eligible Dependant, the Caregiver Amount and, of course, medical expenses. Seniors who go back to school will find new rewards in the claiming of non-refundable tax credits for their tuition, education, and textbook amounts, too.

Tax Pro Alert

Capital preservation counts when you start tapping into your savings in retirement. You want that money to last, so you need to manage risks: market fluctuations, tax and fee erosion. This is about paying the least taxes on each income source and withdrawing only the capital you need to minimize tax instalments. See a tax pro before withdrawing large amounts from your accounts or transferring assets… you'll want to avoid a tax spike because you have entered a higher tax bracket, or the clawback zone for OAS.

39

OAS Pension Reforms

People can retire at any age, but it is increasingly rare for people to simply go from earning income from employment or self-employment directly to withdrawing income from investments and other sources including pensions. After the financial crisis, and as a result of changing demographics, most people will continue to work well into their 60s and possibly 70s, if they can maintain their health.

Close to five million Canadians are reporting Old Age Security (OAS) income today, and over six million tax filers are reporting Canada Pension Plan (CPP) benefits. But recent pension reforms are providing important new planning opportunities that started in 2012. This has been bewildering to some, who confuse the "universal" OAS benefits (everyone who is age 65 may qualify for OAS so long as they've been resident in Canada 10 years) with benefit payments from the CPP, which come from contributions by the individual and their employer throughout a working life.

You need to know the difference: one plan is contributory (CPP), the other is universal (OAS) but the amounts you'll receive monthly will depend on when you choose to start receiving the money. In the case of the OAS, what your income level is makes a difference, too. In this chapter, we'll help you understand the OAS better and how to report your income from it.

How Much is the OAS Pension? OAS amounts are paid monthly but they are adjusted for inflation every quarter. At the time of writing, the monthly benefit was just under $545 and the annual OAS pension for the full year was $6,579.06 for the year.

Consider that the average life expectancy in Canada at age 60 is 87.3 years for men and 89.4 years for women. Assuming retirement at age 65 when OAS becomes payable, men will receive OAS for an average of 22.3 years and women for an average of 24.4 years. Therefore, OAS is worth, on average, $146,000 for men and $160,000 for women. For an average couple, that means $306,000. You want to make sure you tap into most of that.

The OAS income is taxable, reported on a T4 (OAS) slip and on Line 113 of your tax return. However, it is offset by the Age Amount—a non-refundable tax credit found on Line 301 of Schedule 1.

 CHECK IT OUT | **What is the Age Amount?** The Age Amount is a non-refundable tax credit found on Line 301 of Schedule 1 of the federal tax return. (Provincial amounts may vary). The federal amount is $6,854 in 2013 and is phased out when net income on Line 236 exceeds $34,562, by 15% for every dollar over this. If your income exceeds $80,255, your age amount will be zero. Your tax software will automatically calculate this for you:

Example: Rupert is 66. His net income in 2013 was $65,000. His federal age amount will be: $6,854 – [($65,000 – $34,562) x 15%] = $2,288.30. In real dollar terms, this saves him $350.54, assuming he lives in Ontario (where his provincial age amount was only $144.70 because his income is so high).

Age Amount Transfers. If you have a spouse who has a low income, you'll be able to transfer the Age Amount to your return, doubling up your tax benefits. Your tax software will do this for you automatically on Schedule 2 and Line 326. That could save you over $1,000.

Example: Eunice's income is $15,000, consisting of OAS and RRIF (Registered Retirement Income Fund) benefits. Her husband Gerald's income is $45,000, including CPP, OAS and RRIF income. Because Eunice does not need her full Age Amount to reduce her taxes to zero, she can transfer the unused amount ($4,892) to Gerald. This saves Gerald $734 federally, plus $35 provincially (assuming they live in Ontario).

Why do you need to know this? You're often in control of the timing of new taxable income sources. If, for example, your income is largely comprised of dividends from your small business corporation, remember they will be "grossed up" for tax purposes, and this gross up will increase your net income, the number used to determine the amount of both your Age Credit and the OAS you get to keep. You may wish to plan to earn interest or capital gains from your investments, instead.

Example: Helen is 68. If she earned $50,000 in interest income (in addition to $6,579 OAS and $10,890 CPP) her net income would be $67,469 so her federal Age Amount would be $6,854 – [($67,469 – $34,562) x 15%] = $1,917.95.

If, instead of the interest, she earned $50,000 in dividends from public corporations, her net income would be $86,469 (it's much higher because the $50,000 is grossed up by 138% to $69,000). She would not qualify for an Age Amount now and her taxes would rise by $6,726, mostly because she is now in the clawback zone for Old Age Security.

Clawbacks. Some of your OAS must be returned via the tax return if net income is over $70,954. If you receive a full year of OAS, it is completely repayable when net income reaches $114, 815. You'll want to manage your income levels, if you can, to avoid the clawback zone.

Software Tips. Your tax software takes care of all the clawback calculations for you, but you still need to be aware of them because this *Social Benefits Repayment* is a tax that can be avoided if you structure your income properly. There are also a lot of entries, which may confuse you. First, you will find the calculation of the clawback is entered on Line 235 as a deduction, which reduces net income. The actual repayment is entered on Line 422 and is added to your federal and provincial taxes payable on Line 435.

Worse, any repayment you make on your tax return this year will reduce the OAS monthly benefit you will qualify to receive in July. Finally, the reduction in your OAS will be shown on your T4A(OAS) as a "recovery tax," which is entered on Line 437 Income Tax Deducted.

Case Study | Planning to Maximize OAS and Minimize Instalment Payments

Joanne is a single, senior manager who makes $85,000 from her employment. She will continue to work well into the future even though she turned 65 last December. This year she is unsure how much OAS she will retain after taking into account withdrawals from her RRSPs and earnings in her non-registered savings accounts. She also wants to stay invested. She would prefer to minimize the amount of quarterly instalment taxes she must pay. Here is how it stands for Joanne:

If Joanne continues to earn $85,000 salary plus $6,579 OAS in 2013, she'll have to repay $3,094 of the OAS, leaving her with a net amount of $3,485 on which she would pay an additional $1,513 in income taxes (assuming she lives in Ontario). This is an equivalent tax rate of more than 70% on her OAS income.

To avoid the clawback, Joanne would have to arrange her affairs so her net income is less than $70,954. If she wishes to continue earning $85,000 salary then she could reduce her net income by making an RRSP contribution of $14,046 (she is earning $15,300 of contribution room each year).

OAS Pension Benefit Deferral Reforms. As of July 2013, OAS recipients can elect to defer taking their OAS pension for up to five years. This would provide for a larger pension then.

However, keep in mind that those five years will represent 22% of the life expectancy of a male after 65 and 20.5% of the life expectancy of a female. Therefore, for the average man, the bump in the OAS needs to be at least 28.9% to make up for the lost earnings in postponement. For the average woman, the bump needs to be at least 25.8 %. The maximum OAS deferral of five years will result in a 36% increase in benefits received at that time so you will normally benefit from deferral if you live beyond your 79th birthday. Our average male who would receive $146,000 from OAS if he started at age 65 would receive $150,000 if he deferred starting to age 70 (assuming he lived to age 84.3).

For high-income earners who are subject to the OAS clawback, the deferral will have no current year loss of income and could increase future cash flows. Nothing to lose in choosing the postponement.

For those who have already started to receive their Old Age Security, you must make the decision to defer within 6 months of your start date. After this, you can't change your mind and decide to defer your pension. But if you have already started receiving your OAS and, in the first six months, you change your mind and decide to defer starting until a later date, you will have to send back any OAS you've already received. For high-income earners who would have that income clawed back anyway, the repayment is equivalent to the OAS clawback. For those who have not yet applied for their OAS pension, simply defer application until you are ready to receive your pension.

Planning with Other Income Sources. The postponement might also work to your advantage to reduce taxes on other income, particularly if you are single and can't split income with a spouse. By creating this *"untaxed retirement income room"* you could generate tax on other sources, such as RRSP or RRIF savings, that would otherwise attract higher tax rates if OAS were taken at the same time, or at death.

Example: Barbara will turn 65 in June 2014. She is a widow with $500,000 in her RRSP that was transferred to her when her husband passed away. Her income from her husband's pension, CPP survivor benefit and investment income will total $90,000 in 2014. If she begins receiving OAS in July, she'll have to repay all of it so she should elect to defer the pension.

Since Barbara is currently in the 26% federal bracket and her income at death will be in the highest bracket, she might consider removing some funds from her RRSP to pay taxes now at a lower rate than she would if the funds remain in her RRSP when she dies. The funds could be put into a TFSA so the earnings outside the RRSP are not taxed. Or, they could be invested in some other non-registered investment.

OAS Age Eligibility Deferral Reforms. If you are currently in your mid 50s, you should take note that your OAS Pension may begin later—age 67 instead of age 65—starting in 2023. This amounts to a potential loss of over $13,000 in current dollars. These changes will be phased in as follows shown below.

- If you are born on or after Feb. 1, 1962, you will be eligible for OAS at 67; and
- If you are born between April 1, 1958, and Jan. 31, 1962, your OAS will start between 65 and 67.

If you are a low-income earner, the ages at which the *Guaranteed Income Supplement (GIS)* Allowance and the Allowance for the Survivor are provided will also gradually increase from 60 and 64 today to 62 and 66 starting in April 2023. This change will not affect anyone who is age 55 or older as of March 31, 2013.

Low-income earners. Low-income pensioners may receive the GIS as noted above. The Supplement is included in total income and net income, but is deducted in computing taxable income. In other words, it will reduce any tax preference—such as refundable and non-refundable tax credits that are based on net income, while it does not itself attract tax.

 The Bottom Line | When planning for retirement, recent pension reforms require some strategizing. To maximize the OAS pension benefit, which can amount to well over $300,000 for a senior couple, you'll need to keep your eye on the income sources you are earning, the level of income each one of you is earning and the clawback zones for the Age Amount and the OAS itself because this will make a difference to your cash flow all year long. If you do this well, you're in a better position to preserve other savings, which you'll need if you live to a ripe old age!

40

The New Canada Pension Plan Benefits

The Canada Pension Plan (CPP) is paid to Canadian residents who have contributed to the plan through employment or self-employment. The amount of the CPP pension depends on the level of contributions made and the number of years on contributions. The maximum amount is just over $12,000 a year or over $1,000 a month.

Normally recipients begin receiving the CPP retirement pension when they reach age 65 but they may apply for an early (reduced) pension once they reach age 60. They may also defer starting CPP and receive an enhanced pension beginning at any age up to age 70.

Prior to 2012 it was possible to apply for early CPP benefits at age 60, but you had to stop working or significantly reduce the hours you worked. This is no longer necessary, but now there are changes in how you contribute at work, when you also receive CPP retirement benefits:

- *For CPP recipients under the age of 65*, contributions are **required** (by both the employee and the employer) even if they are receiving the CPP retirement pension;
- *For CPP recipients age 65 to 69*, contributions are optional but if an employee does not opt out of contributing, then their employer will also be required to contribute. Employers will automatically deduct CPP contributions for these employees unless the employee submits Form CPT30 *Election to Stop Contributing to the Canada Pension Plan, or Revocation of a Prior Election*; and
- *For CPP recipients over the age of 69*: You are no longer allowed to contribute to the CPP.

The additional contributions made while you are working will increase the amount of CPP pension possibly above the "maximum" pension payable. See Post Retirement Benefits later in this chapter.

Reporting CPP on the T1. CPP retirement benefits are reported on a T4(A)P Slip and it's important to show how many months of the year you received your CPP benefits, because in some cases, the premiums are prorated, which reduces your required contribution.

 CHECK IT OUT | **Are my CPP premiums prorated when I start to draw benefits from my CPP?** If you're over age 64 when you begin receiving your CPP retirement pension and you opt not to continue contributing, your required contributions will depend on the month that you begin receiving your pension. The calculation of the required contribution will be made by your software on Form T2204.

Example: Lawrence began receiving his CPP retirement pension in July 2013 when he turned 65 and opted not to continue to contribute. His required CPP contributions for this tax year will be prorated so he will make one-half of the contributions he would have had to pay had he not opted out of making additional contributions.

Splitting CPP Income. If your spouse is at least age 60, it may be advantageous to apply for an assignment of benefits. That splits the CPP credits earned during the marriage by one or both spouses equally between the two and can save tax dollars, particularly if one spouse's income is significantly higher than the other's. Do the returns in your software both ways to be sure whether or not to apply. An application to split CPP benefits must be made through Service Canada.

Example: Robert receives $10,000 in CPP retirement benefits. His wife of 40 years, Mary, did not contribute to CPP so she is not entitled to any CPP benefits. The couple did not make any RRSP contributions and neither is eligible for an employer pension. Luckily, Robert did accumulate significant non-registered investments. His investment income is $50,000 annually. Mary's only income is $6,579 in OAS.

For 2013, the couple's tax bill is $12,162. The couple is eligible to apply to split Robert's CPP pension equally between them giving each $5,000 per year. If they had split the CPP, their tax bill would have been reduced to $11,429, saving them $733 in income taxes each year.

Other CPP Benefits

- *Disability Benefits*—These are reported in Box 16 of the T4A(P) slip and are posted to both Line 152 and Line 114 of the return. No CPP contributions are required once a taxpayer begins receiving a CPP disability benefit. In addition, these benefits are considered to be "earned income" for RRSP purpose.
- *Disabled Contributor Child Benefit*—Children of taxpayers who receive a CPP disability pension are eligible to receive a child benefit if they are under age 18 or

are under age 25 and are attending school at a recognized financial institution on a full-time basis. This child benefit is reported in Box 17 of the T4A(P) slip and is posted to Line 114 on the return for the child.

- *Survivor's Benefits*—When a taxpayer who has contributed to CPP dies, his spouse may be eligible for a survivor pension. The amount of that pension depends on a number of factors:
  - Age of the survivor at the time of death
  - Amount of pension to which the deceased was entitled
  - Whether the deceased was disabled
  - Current age of the survivor
  - Whether or not the survivor is receiving a CPP retirement pension

  The survivor pension is reported in Box 15 of the T4A(P) slip and is posted to Line 114 of the survivor's return.

- *Deceased Contributor Child Benefit*—Children of taxpayers who contributed to the CPP may be eligible to receive a child benefit if they are under age 18, or are under age 25 and are attending school at a recognized financial institution on a full-time basis. This child benefit is reported in Box 17 of the T4A(P) slip and is posted to Line 114 on the return for the child. This could affect non-refundable tax credit claims for your child.

- *Combined Retirement and Survivor Benefit*—When the recipient of a CPP survivor's benefit begins receiving their own CPP disability or retirement benefit the amount of the survivor benefit may be reduced *because the maximum CPP pension that can be received is limited.*

Knowing this may have an impact on whether you elect to continue to contribute to the CPP while working after age 65. It may be better to save the equivalent of the CPP premiums in a TFSA, which will provide for a survivor's benefit. For 2013, the maximum CPP retirement pension (or combined retirement and survivor pension) is $1,012.50 per month. The maximum disability pension (or combined disability pension and survivor pension) is $1,212.90 per month). The maximum annual premium is $2,356.20 if income exceeds $51,100.

- *CPP Death Benefit*—When a CPP contributor dies, a one-time death benefit is paid to the deceased's estate. The maximum CPP death benefit is $2,500 but this amount is reduced if the deceased was not entitled to a retirement pension of at least $416 per month. The death benefit is income of the recipient (or the deceased estate). It is not income of the deceased. The amount is reported in Box 18 of a T4A(P) slip and is posted to Line 114 of the recipient's return.

Special averaging for lump sum benefits. Lump sums received in retrospect are averaged by CRA over the period of years in which the benefits should have been paid. This is done after you file your tax return, and an additional refund may result.

Starting Your Pension Early or Late. An adjustment to your "regular" CPP benefits will occur if you choose to start your benefits either before or after the normal age 65 start date. The adjustment is 0.54% for each month before the taxpayer's 65th birthday and 0.70% for each month after the taxpayer's 65th birthday (for pensions starting in 2013). The pension may be decreased as much as 32.4% for those who opt to receive their pension at age 60 or increased by as much as 42% for those who opt to receive their pension at age 70.

- The augmentation for late pension take-up was increased to 0.7% per month, over the period 2011 to 2013.
- Over the period 2012 to 2016, the reduction for early pension take-up is being increased from 0.50% to 0.6% per month.

Example: Paul will turn 60 in 2014. Per his CPP Statement of Contributions, he will be eligible for a CPP retirement pension of $950 when he turns 65. If Paul decides to start the CPP retirement pension early at age 60, his pension entitlement will be reduced by 0.56% per month x 60 months or 33.6% to $630.80 per month.

If, instead, he opts to defer receiving her CPP retirement pension until he turns 70 in 2024, his pension will be increased by 0.7% x 60 months or 42% to $1,349 per month.

Quebec. Quebec has gone forward earlier, with plans of their own to bolster the pension benefits system with similar plans. Quebec Pension Plan (QPP) contributions will also rise to encourage workers to stay at work longer.

Post-Retirement Benefit (PRB). If you contribute to CPP after you begin receiving your retirement pension, the additional premiums will earn you an additional pension amount, called your Post-Retirement Benefit. You will begin to receive the additional pension in the year after you make the contribution. For those who earned the maximum CPP insurable earnings in 2012 ($50,100), the PRB earned was $25.31 per month effective for January 2013. The lower your level of earnings, the lower your PRB.

The Bottom Line | Deciding when to take your CPP retirement benefit requires planning under the new reforms which are designed to encourage you to work longer and defer taking your benefits. Use your tax software to do "what if" scenarios to plan the layering of private pension sources if you defer the CPP. Or check out the CPP Income Calculator at www.knowledgebureau.com/calculators for help with this decision.

41

Benefits From
Private Pensions

You've been saving all your life for this time: the golden years of retirement. Yet for some actually taking the money out seems wrong. For others, doing it without paying attention to the tax erosion can prematurely wipe out too much capital. That's why you need to carefully plan and report your private pension sources.

Private pension income can come from a couple of different sources. Commonly, those who participated in an employer-sponsored Registered Pension Plan (RPP) will receive a periodic monthly pension on retirement. Other employees may have been members of a Deferred Profit Sharing Plan (DPSP). Still others, who may not have had the opportunity to participate or who were largely self-employed, may have accumulated their own tax-assisted retirement saving through a Registered Retirement Savings Plan (RRSP). New on the horizon is the Pooled Retirement Pension Plan (PRPP) that provides pension savings opportunities for those who work for small employers. See Part 2 for an explanation of the contribution rules and recent changes to these and other private pension plans.

Retirement is not always voluntary, however. Retirement planning may, in fact, begin there for you. Here's what you need to know, if you receive a retiring allowance or severance:

Retiring Allowances. Retirement often begins with a termination from employment. Employees who retire after long service may receive a retiring allowance. For some this is the largest lump sum of money they will receive in their lifetime so it needs to be carefully managed. Retiring allowances are also sometimes paid in instalments over a period of years.

A retiring allowance is taxable and is reported on Line 130. Simply key in the amounts shown on your T4A slip and the software will post them automatically. The amounts received may qualify for an RRSP rollover—that is, they can be contributed to an RRSP over and above the normal RRSP contribution room, thereby deferring taxation.

Amounts that qualify for transfer to an RRSP are reported as "eligible" on the T4A (Box 026). Amounts that do not qualify are reported as "non-eligible" (T4A Box 027). These rules were discussed under RPP contributions in Part 2.

Do work to minimize tax on this income distribution. If you are going to receive it late in the year, for example, ask whether your employer will consider paying it in two lump sums: part in the current year and the balance in the new year. That will help you defer the tax to another tax year and also, could save you several percentage points in your marginal tax rate. Or if you have unused RRSP contribution room, consider contributing as much of your severance as possible to fill up that room, so that the offsetting tax deduction can reduce your taxes on the severance.

Case Study | Splitting Severance

Tom, who is 58 and single, earns $65,000 at his job at the local manufacturing plant where he has been a supervisor for 10 years. He received a layoff notice from his employer on November 15. He is has decided to take an early retirement and to begin receiving a periodic pension ($4,000 per month) from the company-sponsored pension plan. His employer will also pay him a severance package of $50,000. Tom has asked that this be paid to him half on December 1 and half on January 2. Using his tax software he has computed this will save him thousands of dollars:

Had Tom received both his salary and the full severance in one year, his taxable income would have been $115,000 in the year of retirement and $48,000 in the next year. This would have resulted in tax bills of $32,951 and $8,218 in the two years. The total tax bill would be $41,169.

By splitting the severance into two $25,000 amounts his income in the year of retirement would be $90,000 and $73,000 in the following year. This would result in tax bills of $22,098 and $16,348 respectively. The strategy reduces his tax bill from $41,169 to $38,446 saving them $2,723.

Alternatively, Tom could contribute the $50,000 severance to his RRSP as he has enough unused contribution room. That would wipe out his taxes on the severance this year and allow him to bring that income into the next tax year, when his marginal tax rates are lower. This strategy could save Tom about $1,880 in taxes (or more if he spreads out the withdrawals).

Pre-Retirement Counselling. Employer-provided pre-retirement counselling is considered to be a tax-free benefit, so taxpayers should be sure to take advantage of this before leaving their employment.

Starting Your Pension Benefits. When you start receiving a periodic pension from your employer-sponsored pension plan (an RPP or PRPP) or from savings in your RRSP, you will need to bring the full amount of the pension benefit into income. There may be an offsetting non-refundable tax credit, the $2,000 pension income amount, but for RRSP/RRIF pensions this will depend on your age in some case and/or whether the amounts are received as a result of your spouse's death. Age will also affect the tax deferral opportunities you have within your registered plans.

Professional help is a good idea before you make your retirement income plans, as a tax efficient solution around the integration of public and private pensions and investment funds throughout the retirement period can make tens of thousands of dollars of difference to you. Following are some tips.

Pension Income Splitting. If you have a spouse with a lower income than you, you may be able to elect to split your qualifying pension income by filing Form 1032 *Joint Election to Split Pension Income.* This will be discussed in more detail in the next chapter.

Do You Have to Remit Taxes Quarterly? Make sure your tax withholdings from this pension are adequate, if you are uncomfortable with making quarterly instalment remittances yourself. Otherwise, if you have the choice, you may wish to take and use the gross pension, saving money for your quarterly tax instalments as required.

Note that if the balance due on your return is $3,000 or more for two out of three years, you'll be required to make instalments quarterly. Each instalment will be one-quarter of that balance. You'll get a reminder from the tax department outlining the details once your return is assessed. If you find that your balance due exceeds $3,000 this year, you should adjust your withholding so that it doesn't happen a second time.

Also, if you're making instalments and your income decreases, be sure to adjust your instalments downward as well. Your tax software can help you choose the alternative instalment payment options. You don't necessarily have to follow CRA's billing method. But do know that if your alternative instalment payment schedule is deficient, you'll be charged interest.

Pension Income Reporting from T-Slips. When it comes to filing your tax return, once your benefits have started, the tax reporting process is quite easy, because much of it is on T-slips, described below. Foreign pension income sources, however, are usually self-reported.

T4A—The T4A slip is used to report income from a Registered Pension Plan—a pension generally set up by an employer or a union or a PRPP—a Pooled Retirement Pension Plan. Periodic payments from these pensions (Box 016) are eligible for the $2,000 pension income amount and pension income splitting between spouses (see next chapter). Lump sum payments (Box 018) will be posted to Line 130 and are not eligible for the pension income amount or pension income splitting.

T4RSP—Amounts withdrawn from your RRSP will be reported on a T4RSP slip. Annuity payments (Box 16) from a matured RRSP are eligible for the pension income amount and for pension income splitting but only if you are over age 65 or if they are received as a result of the death of a former spouse. Most RRSP withdrawals (except HBP and LLP withdrawals) will be reported on Line 129 of your return and are not eligible for the pension income amount or pension income splitting regardless of your age.

T4RIF—Amounts withdrawn from your RRIF will be reported on a T4RIF slip. Amounts withdrawn from your RRIF are eligible for the pension income amount and pension income splitting if you are over 65 or if they are received as a result of the death of a former spouse. RRIF withdrawals that are eligible for the pension income amount and pension income splitting will be reported on Line 115 of your return and amounts that are not will be reported on Line 130.

Others—You may also receive a T3 slip eligible (Box 31) or lump sum (Box 22) pension benefits or a T4A RCA slip if you're a member of a Retirement Compensation Arrangement. Eligible pension amounts reported in Box 31 of a T3 slip are posted to Line 115 and are eligible for the pension income amount and pension income splitting. Lump sum payments and Retirement Compensation Arrangements (RCA) income are reported on Line 130.

Generating a Pension from an RRSP. It can be sad to see people live frugally for many years in their late 50's and 60's, fearing they will run out of money during their golden years. The big unknown, of course, is how long we will live and whether long-term care to ensure the dignity we desire will be a part of the final stages of life. However, often it is the taxman who gets the biggest piece of the pie if couples don't plan effectively. RRSP accumulations are a common example. They can be withdrawn before or after maturity with varying tax results.

Age Eligibility. Before the end of the year in which the taxpayer turns 71, RRSP accumulations must be either cashed out in full (not generally a good idea), transferred to a Registered Retirement Income Plan (RRIF) or used to purchase an annuity, so periodic taxable pension payments can begin. Taxpayers may no longer contribute to an RRSP after the end of the year in which they turn 71, unless they have unused RRSP contribution room and a spouse who is age-eligible—under 72, in which case a spousal RRSP contribution can be made.

Example: Edward is 72 so he is no longer eligible to make contributions to his own RRSP. However, he has unused RRSP contribution room and his wife Edith is only 69, he can make a spousal RRSP contribution using his own contribution room and taking a deduction for that contribution.

RRSP Withdrawals Before Maturity. Individuals can make withdrawals at any time and in any amount but in the year that they do the full amount of principal and earnings will be added to their income. Your lump sum withdrawals will be reported in Box 22 of your T4RSP slip along with the required income tax withholding in Box 30. Your software will post the amount from Box 22 to Line 129 and claim a credit for the withholding tax on Line 437.

RRSP Withdrawals After Maturity. Once your RRSP has matured, it will pay you a pension which will be shown in Box 16 of your T4RSP slip. Your software will post this to Line 129 and, if you're over age 64 the software will claim the pension income amount on Line 314. If you're over age 64, this pension will also be eligible for pension income splitting using Form T1032.

 CHECK IT OUT | **How do I report RRSP withdrawals on my return with tax efficiency?** RRSP withdrawals are reported on a T4RSP slip and on Line 115 or on 129 in the following instances:

- pensions paid out of a matured RRSP (Box 16) will be posted to Line 115 and, if you're over 64, will trigger the pension income amount on Line 314 and are eligible for pension income splitting; and
- lump-sum payments withdrawn from your RRSP (whether before or after maturity and no matter what your age) are reported on Line 129 and are not eligible for the pension income amount or pension income splitting.

Spousal RRSPs. Unless the taxpayer has equalized RRSP contributions with a spousal RRSP throughout the accumulation period, it is not possible to split RRSP retirement income until the taxpayer is 65 (when the RRSP income becomes eligible for the pension income amount). Withdrawals must be reported as income by the plan annuitant.

In the case of a spousal RRSP, the withdrawals are taxed in the hands of the "annuitant spouse," that is, the spouse whose name is on the account rather than the contributing spouse, if three years have passed from the last contribution to a spousal plan.

Example: Jerry made spousal RRSP contributions of $6,000 for his wife Frances in 2010 and again in 2011. If Frances removes $5,000 from her spousal RRSP in 2013, Jerry will have to report the income because it was not left in the plan for three years. If she waits until 2014, the income will be reported on her return.

Where the annuitant spouse transfers the RRSP savings to his or her own RRIF, the minimum payments required under the plan will be taxed in his or her hands. But any amounts over this will be taxed in the hands of the contributor spouse until the restriction period has passed.

Example: If Frances (previous example) had transferred her spousal RRSP to a RRIF and then withdrew the same $5,000, a portion of the withdrawal will be taxed in her hands and the remainder in Jerry's. If the full balance in the RRIF was $12,000 (Jerry's contributions) and Frances was 60 years old at the time of the withdrawal, then she would be required to withdraw $12,000 x 1/(90-60) = $400. The $400 minimum withdrawal is her income and the excess withdrawal ($4,600) is reported on Jerry's return.

Pension Income Splitting and the Spousal RRSP. Seniors with eligible pension income and a spouse or common-law partner may elect annually to split up to 50% of pension income on their income tax returns, as discussed above and in the next Chapter. In the case of an RRSP, you must wait to be age 65 or receive the amounts as the result of a spouse's death. See below for details.

If your plan is to retire earlier, withdrawing from a Spousal RRSP first may be a good idea. Before you withdraw, do some "what if scenarios" in your tax software to anticipate how much tax will be payable. Also bear in mind you could be setting your spouse up to pay quarterly tax instalment amounts. How can you avoid this? By ensuring that taxes owing at the end of the year are not over $3,000.

Surviving Spouses. When you die, the full amount of your RRSP accumulations is included in income on the final return and taxed, but it is possible to transfer (or "roll over") any RRSP accumulations on a tax-free basis to an RRSP, RRIF for your spouse or an RRSP or RDSP for a surviving financially dependent child, according to the rules below.

Rollovers to Spouses—Deadlines and Forms. At death, RRSP accumulations may be rolled over on a tax-free basis to the surviving spouse's RRSP or RRIF. For an *unmatured* RRSP (that is, periodic pension payments are not being paid from the RRSP), the value of the RRSP will be reported in Box 18 of the T4RSP slip in the name of the surviving spouse if the spouse is a named beneficiary. If there is no beneficiary named, the amount will be shown in Box 28 of the T4RSP slip issued to the estate.

If the RRSP is unmatured and the surviving spouse is not the named beneficiary, but receives the funds from the estate, then the deceased's legal representative and the surviving spouse may jointly elect, using Form T2019 *Death of an RRSP Annuitant – Refund of Premiums for 20__,* to include part or all of the Box 28 amount in the surviving spouse's income. Any or all of that amount may be rolled over into the survivor's RRSP, RRIF or a life annuity. A deduction may be claimed by the survivor on Line 208 for the amount transferred to an RRSP. Use Line 232 for the amounts transferred to a RRIF or used to purchase a qualifying annuity. *The transfer or annuity purchase must be completed by 60 days after the end of the taxation year in which the RRSP funds are received.*

For a matured RRSP (RRSP is paying a periodic pension), the amount will be shown in Box 28 or the T4RSP. The slip will be issued to the spouse if that person is the named beneficiary or to the estate if the spouse is not.

If the surviving spouse is a named beneficiary, and the amount is rolled over to the survivor's RRSP by December 31 of the year following death, the RRSP income will not be included in the deceased income for the year of death. It must be included in the surviving spouse's income for the year the transfer is made. An offsetting deduction is then claimed for the RRSP contribution. Note: *The transfer must be completed by 60 days after the end of the taxation year in which the RRSP funds are received.*

Financially Dependent Children. When RRSP accumulations are left to a financially dependent child (someone who earns less than the Basic Personal Amount), two rules apply:

- *For children who are not disabled*, RRSP accumulations must be used to buy a term annuity to age 18.
  - *If the child is a named beneficiary*, the T4RSP slip will be issued in the name of the child and must be reported in income at line 129. If funds are used to purchase a qualifying annuity, a deduction for that amount may be claimed at line 232. The annuity purchase must be completed by 60 days after the end of the taxation year in which the RRSP funds are received.
  - *If the child is not a named beneficiary*, a T4RSP slip will be issued to the estate. If the child is a beneficiary of the estate, then the deceased legal representative and the child (or their legal representative) may elect, using Form T2019 *Death of an RRSP Annuitant – Refund of Premiums for 20__*, to include part or all of the Box 28 amount in the child's income. Any or all of that amount may be used to purchase a qualifying annuity. If funds are used to purchase a qualifying annuity, a deduction for that amount may be claimed at line 232. The annuity purchase must be completed by 60 days after the end of the taxation year in which the RRSP funds are received.
- *For infirm children*, accumulations can be transferred to their own RRSPs, RRIFs or RDSPs, or to a life annuity thereby further deferring taxes. For an infirm child, the same rules apply as for a surviving spouse (see above) for rollovers to the child's RRSP, RRIF or to a life annuity.

Rollovers to RDSPs. If the rollover is made to the child's RDSP, the rollover amount (maximum $200,000) will have to be reported on the deceased's return (Line 129) and a deduction for the rollover is taken at Line 232. In addition, the amount must be reported on Line 129 of the dependant's return and the amount of the transfer deducted at Line 232. Form RC4625, *Rollover to a Registered Disability Savings Plan (RDSP) Under Paragraph 60(m)*, must be attached to the returns of both the deceased and the child. If using NETFILE, keep the completed form in your files in case CRA asks for it. Note that when funds are rolled over into the child's RDSP, the transfer is not eligible for the Registered Disability Saving Grant.

Average Income Down over Time. It can make sense to "average down" the taxes you will pay on the RRSP accumulations over a longer period of time, especially if you are in a lower tax bracket when you choose to do this than you will be in the year you die.

When the second survivor passes on, all remaining accumulations in the RRSP must be added to income and will be taxed at the marginal tax rate of the final survivor. For these reasons it's very important to plan to "average down" the tax on your RRSP accumulations over a longer period of time. This is sometimes referred to as an RRSP meltdown strategy. If you are not going to spend the money, simply reinvest it—perhaps to your TFSA, which will produce tax-exempt income in the future.

Example: Margaret is a 73-year-old widow. She has $750,000 in her RRIF. Her taxable income in 2013 was $52,000, including her required RRIF withdrawal, so her marginal tax rate is 32% (she lives in Alberta). When Margaret dies, the remaining balance in her RRIF will be added to her income putting her into the highest possible tax bracket of 39%. By withdrawing enough out of her RRIF each year to bring her income to just below the OAS clawback threshold, she can have that income taxed at her current marginal rate (32%) rather than 39% when she dies. Even if she lives to use up her RRIF funds, this method will not increase her taxes paid on these funds or the earnings from them.

Foreign Pension Income. Self-reported pension sources can include amounts received from foreign pension sources. Depending on the terms of the tax treaty between Canada and the country in question, some or all of that income may be deductible, as illustrated by the examples below.

- *German Social Security.* Social security pensions from Germany are added into pension income on Line 115, and will qualify for the $2,000 *Pension Income Amount* and pension income splitting but, in addition, this income will qualify for a partially offsetting deduction on Line 256. What you qualify for can be complicated, however.

  In the year that you begin to receive your social security pension from Germany, the exempt percentage is set. For those whose pension started in 2013, the exempt portion is 34% (you'll pay tax on 66%). For 2012, the exempt portion was 36%. That same percentage applies to the pension received in the following year. For subsequent years, the exempt amount is the amount (in Euro) that was exempt in the second year of receipt (the first year you received pension for the entire year). All foreign income sources must be reported in Canadian funds so the amount received, as well as the exempt amount must be converted from Euro to Canadian dollars before reporting the income or claiming the deduction for the exempt portion.

  As these pensions are only partially taxable in Canada, there may also be a requirement that you file a German tax return as well. Consult a tax professional regarding these filing obligations if you receive a social security pension from Germany.

- *U.S. Social Security* income is recorded in full at Line 115, qualifies for the $2,000 Pension Income Amount but also for a 15% deduction on Line 256 Other Deductions. (15% rate in effect from 1996 to date). For seniors who began receiving U.S. Social security before 1996, the deduction is 50% of the amount received. The taxable portion of U.S. Social Security is eligible for pension income splitting. Again report in Canadian funds.

- *IRAs and Roth IRAs.* Similar to our RRSPs, these plans are reported in Canada. So long as no contributions are made to a Roth IRA after 2008 while the taxpayer is resident in Canada, income from a Roth IRA will be considered as pension income in Canada. This means that the taxpayer may elect that income earned within the Roth IRA is not taxable as it is earned. If the election is not made or contributions are made while the taxpayer is resident in Canada (after 2008), then the Roth IRA is treated like any other investment and earnings are taxable as foreign investment income. Distributions from a Roth IRA are not taxable. Income from an IRA (not a Roth IRA) is taxable when received if it would be taxable in the U.S. This means withdrawals are taxable except when transferred from one IRA to another.

Claiming the Foreign Tax Credit. When there are withholding taxes on foreign pensions, you can usually offset them with the Foreign Tax Credit, which is calculated on Form T2209 *Federal Foreign Tax Credits* and then ends up on Schedule 1, Line 405. This credit can be confusing even if you use tax software. Here are some tips to help you get it right:

- The calculation must be done for each foreign country so be sure to specify what country the taxes were paid to so that the software can make the calculations and claim the credits.
- A foreign tax credit is only available if Canada has a tax treaty with the foreign jurisdiction to eliminate double taxation. Be sure that the taxes paid are eligible.
- If your federal taxes are not sufficient to absorb the federal credit, a provincial tax credit is also available (calculated on Form T2036 *Provincial or Territorial Foreign Tax Credit*).
- In the case of a foreign tax credit on business income, a credit that cannot be absorbed can be carried forward to the following taxation year. However, non-business foreign tax credits that are not absorbed cannot be carried forward.
- When your Canadian tax rate is low, you may not be able to recover all of the foreign taxes paid using the foreign tax credit. If so, your software should take a deduction for the excess foreign taxes paid.

Sound complicated? It is! Fortunately, your tax software will likely do most of these calculations in the background.

Withdrawing Other Investments. Most taxpayers supplement their pension income with income from investments held in non-registered accounts. Their filing profile is therefore often layered in with an investor's profile and the way that income from investments is realized has important consequences for their overall tax position.

Certain amounts included in investment income and, therefore, in net income do not represent cash income available for spending. The taxable amount of a dividend from a publicly traded corporation is normally 38% greater than the cash amount of the dividend, for example.

In another example, compounding interest income must be reported annually even though cash is not received until maturity. While interest rates have been low recently, those planning retirement for the future when interest rates may be higher will want to take this into account in their retirement income planning now.

Together with the start of superannuation benefits including withdrawals of RRSP deposits, earnings from investments can be quickly eroded, especially when income reaches the thresholds at which the clawbacks of the Age Amount and OAS benefits begin. When net income is too high, the amount that is spent for long-term care (if based on net income levels) will increase too.

Benefits from insurance products—disability and long-term care insurance or life insurance policies—can ensure prosperity is maintained on disability without taxation and, for surviving family members, after death. Income earned in these plans is usually tax deferred and the total benefits received by beneficiaries are generally not taxable.

Software Tips. If a taxpayer will be in a lower-tax bracket during life than at death, it may make more sense to withdraw money now, and if not needed, to make gifts to loved ones during life. This can be easily illustrated using your tax software. Consider withdrawing enough money to "top income up" to the end of the lowest tax bracket.

Example: Joyce, age 80, is a widow. She has $350,000 in her RRIF. Her annual income is $44,000 which she is comfortable living on. She lives in Ontario and has a marginal tax rate of 31.15%. When she dies, her remaining RRIF balance will be added to her income and will be taxed at more than 46%. If she draws $25,000 additional funds from her RRIF she will both stay in the 31.15% tax bracket and avoid the OAS clawback. That money will then be taxed at 31.15% rather than the 46% rate applicable when she dies.

This results in a tax savings of $3,700 for each year that she makes the extra withdrawal. If she does not need to spend the money, she can leave it to her heirs without CRA taking 46% of it.

The Bottom Line | Several opportunities become available to reduce taxes as you retire. Splitting the taxation of a retiring allowance over two or more years, for example, either by arranging for payment over multiple years or using your RRSP to spread out the income. Once you begin receiving your retirement income, plan the layering of private pension and investment income with CPP and OAS to manage taxes. If you have RRSP accumulations, plan your withdrawals so that you pay less tax on the income than if it were taxed as a lump sum when you die.

42

Splitting Pension Income With Your Spouse

Taxpayers who receive pension income that is eligible for the pension income amount may elect to split up to 50% of that income with their spouse or common-law partner. The transferee reports the split income reports it on Line 116. The taxpayer who received the income reports the full amount received on Line 115 and claims a deduction on Line 210 for the elected amount.

 CHECK IT OUT | **How do I elect pension income splitting?** The amount to be split is to be set out annually in an election which will accompany the return of both taxpayers. The election will be made on Form T1032, *Joint Election to Split Pension Income.*

The split pension amount:

- is deemed to be income of the transferee;
- is deductible by the transferor; and
- is treated as if the income were received by the transferee, being eligible for the pension income amount if from an RPP or if the transferee is over age 64.

Both the transferee and the transferor must be residents in Canada at the end of the taxation year in which income is to be split or at the time of death.

Eligible Pension Income

For taxpayers who are under 65, eligible pension income includes:

- payments in respect of a life annuity from a superannuation or pension plan, and
- amounts received from the following *because of the death of the taxpayer's spouse*:
  - RRSP annuity;
  - RRIF payment;
  - DPSP annuity; and
  - amounts accrued under certain life insurance policies and annuities.

For persons over 65, eligible pension income includes:

- payments in respect of a life annuity from a superannuation or pension plan;
- RRSP annuity;
- RRIF payment;
- DPSP annuity;
- the interest portion of annuity payments; and
- amounts accrued under certain life insurance policies and annuities.

Impact of Splitting on Tax Payment. Where pension income that is split was subject to tax withholding at source, the portion of the withholding tax that relates to the split amount is deemed to have been tax withheld from the transferee, not the transferor. What this means is that the withholding tax follows the income. The transferee and transferor are jointly and severally liable, however, for the tax due on the split amount.

Example: Gary and Virginia are a retired couple. Each receives Old Age Security and Gary has RRIF income of $40,000 from which $4,000 in income taxes was withheld. Gary and Virginia can elect to transfer $20,000 of Gary's pension to Virginia by each filing the T1032 form. If the election is not made, Gary would owe $1,055 while Virginia would owe nothing. If they make the election, their total tax bill would decrease by $1,337 and because $2,000 of the income tax withheld would also be transferred to Virginia, each would have a refund of $282.

Splitting eligible pension income involves balancing potentially conflicting outcomes on the tax return, as shown below. Your software will help you optimize these effects?

	Potential Conflicts of Pension Income Splitting	
Transfer from	Higher income spouse to	Lower income spouse
OAS	May reduce clawback	May increase clawback
Age amount	May reduce clawback	May increase clawback
Spousal amount	Will reduce claim	
Age amount transferred	Will reduce claim	
Pension amount	No effect	May increase availability
Federal tax rate	May be reduced	May be increased

Case Study | Optimizing Pension Income Splitting

Colin is a teacher who recently retired at age 62 with superannuation of $35,000. He decided to take CPP early to travel with his wife, Aimee, who is 65 and has never worked out of the home. How can pension income splitting help this couple? For these purposes, we will assume there is no other income or deductions.

Before pension income splitting, Colin's income (including $6,000 CPP) is $41,000. Aimee's only income is her Old Age Security. Aimee is not taxable, but Colin's tax bill is $4,400. By electing to split half of his pension with Aimee, Colin's tax bill is reduced to $2,416, but Aimee's tax bill becomes $1,302. Still, the net savings in taxes payable as a result of the election to split Colin's pension is $682.

Deductions and Credits to Offset Private Pension Income. There are no deductions specific to pension income. However, there are some important tax credits. As you have learned, when you start receiving qualifying periodic pension income, you'll qualify for the $2,000 Pension Income Amount, as explained above. However, before leaving this topic, you need to understand other credits specific to seniors that can help to average down income in retirement.

Transfers from Spouse or Common-law Partner. When the lower-income earning spouse has insufficient income to absorb the following non-refundable tax credits, the balance of the unused amounts may be transferred to the higher income earner, using Schedule 2 (which carries up to Line 326 on Schedule 1):

- Age Amount
- Pension Income Amount
- Disability Amount
- Tuition, Education, and Textbook Amounts

Once again, prepare both spouses' returns in a couple of different ways to ensure the best benefit is achieved using these options.

Supporting Other Infirm Adults. Additional credits are available where a taxpayer supports an adult dependant, other than a spouse. An infirm adult is someone who lives in Canada, age 18 and over, who is mentally or physically disabled and related to the taxpayer by blood, marriage or adoption. A credit for the care of infirm adults may be claimed under one of three different provisions, using Schedule 5.

Line 305 Amount for Eligible Dependant. If the supporting person is single and living with the infirm adult dependant, this credit may be claimed if the infirm dependant is a parent or grandparent and lives with that taxpayer. Formerly known as the Equivalent-to-Spouse Amount, this claim provides for a credit based on an amount of $11,038 in 2013 if the dependant is not infirm; $13,078 if the dependant is infirm. The claim is reduced dollar for dollar by the net income of the eligible dependant and so is phased out completely when the dependant's net income exceeds $11,038 if they are not infirm or $13,078 if they are.

Line 306 Amount for Infirm Adults age 18 or Older. The credit is $6,530 for 2013 and is reduced by the dependant's net income over $6,548 and so is phased out completely when the dependant's net income exceeds $13,078 in 2013.

The net income thresholds for the Eligible Dependant Amount and the Amount for Infirm Dependants usually result in no claim under these provisions for the care of dependant seniors, because often their income level, based on the receipt of OAS (including supplement) and CPP, is too high.

Line 315 Caregiver Amount. This is a non-refundable tax credit of $4,490 in 2013 if the dependant is not infirm and $6,530 if the dependant is infirm. This credit is available to those supporting individuals who care for elderly parents or grandparents or other infirm adults in that supporting person's home. The dependant's net income threshold is higher ($15,334 in 2013), so the Caregiver Amount is often available when the other credits are not. It therefore makes a better claim. The claim is phased out completely when the dependant's net income exceeds $21,864 if the dependant is infirm or $19,824 if the dependant is not.

Example: Anna is a widow who supports her brother Charles in her home. Charles is confined to a wheelchair, is 60 and his only income is a CPP disability pension of $1,100 per month. Although Anna is eligible to claim any of these credits for her brother, his $13,200 income eliminates the Amount for an Eligible Dependant and the Amount for Infirm Adults. Anna can claim the Caregiver Amount of $6,530.

Note: In certain circumstances, a taxpayer may qualify to claim the Amount for Infirm Dependants Age 18 or Older or the Caregiver Amount. Where both are available, the Caregiver Amount must be claimed. Note that the Caregiver Amount requires that care be provided in the claimant's home while the Amount for Infirm Dependants does not. Either of those amounts is reduced by any claim made under the Amount for Eligible Dependant.

Disability Amount. As people age, disabilities begin, as discussed in Chapter 27. It bears repeating here that this lucrative tax credit should claimed if the taxpayer or spouse has:

- a disability that is severe and prolonged, which is expected to last for a continuous period of at least 12 months, starting in the tax year; and is
- markedly restricted basic activities of living.

Marked restrictions include the following conditions:

- Permanent blindness (a CNIB number is usually available),
- Severe cardio-respiratory failure,
- Inability to feed or dress oneself,
- Inability to perceive, remember or think,
- Inability to walk,
- Inability to speak,
- Inability to hear, or
- Inability to contain bowel or bladder functions.

Taxpayers who must receive therapy like kidney dialysis may claim this credit if a doctor certifies that at least 14 hours per week are taken for such therapy.

Form T2201A *Disability Tax Credit Application* must be completed by the applicant and T2201B *Disability Tax Credit Certification by a Qualified Practitioner* must be completed and signed by a medical doctor, optometrist, psychologist, occupational therapist, audiologist or speech-language pathologist and so on. Generally, the CRA requires that these forms be filed in the first year that the credit is claimed.

The Disability Amount may be claimed if there is a claim for Attendant Care Expenses on the return. However, the Disability Amount may not be claimed if the costs of a full-time attendant or care in a nursing home or institution are also claimed as a medical expense unless the amount claimed is less than $10,000 ($20,000 on the terminal return).

Medical Expenses. See Chapter 26 for a list of allowable medical expenses.

 The Bottom Line | Pension income splitting is lucrative. Be sure you do it if you qualify!

43

Your Home Based Business

Today there are millions of small businesses in Canada. They are led by small business owners of every type: retail store owners, consultants, professionals, commission salespersons, farmers, fishermen, and bed and breakfast owners. Thanks largely to improvements in communications technology, all generations can make lifestyle decisions to work from home in a self-employment capacity often after retiring from employment.

Entrepreneurship, in fact, is on an upward trend in Canada. Up to 150,000 new business are expected to emerge in the next ten years[8]. Canada also has the lowest insolvency costs in the G20, and we have recently recruited thousands of new immigrant entrepreneurs as well. Business owners are distinct from other types of taxpayers. They are people who invest their time and money first, to reap the rewards of both profit and equity in their enterprises later. There is lots of risk involved, too.

The Canadian tax system takes this into account. Business owners can write off business losses against other income of the year; they can also split income by hiring family members to work in their enterprises. When they sell their qualifying Canadian Controlled Private Corporations, each shareholder may also qualify for an $800,000 capital gains exemption, starting in 2014; an increase over the current $750,000 amounts.

Many of those successful ventures of the future will begin in the basement of someone's home. To reap the full benefits of the tax preferences available, the small business owner must understand the rules of the tax-filing game. In this chapter we'll discuss the rules from the perspective on an unincorporated home based business.

---

[8] Ernst & Young G20 Entrepreneurship Barometer 2013.

Getting Started. Briefly, here are some of the things you need to know when you start a home-based business:

- **You have a new relationship with CRA.** Your obligations to keep meticulous records, self-report income, make remittances like payroll source deductions, quarterly tax instalments, and GST/HST are new to you. Take the time to understand these obligations when you apply for your required Business Number.
- **Record retention is law.** Because your legal obligation is to self-assess your income, the deductions that will reduce it and then to report net business income on your personal tax return, expect to open your books to CRA's audit scrutiny. Most businesses will be required to match income and expenses and so you'll need to understand the difference between the cash and the accrual method of reporting your income.

 CHECK IT OUT | **How is business income reported on the tax return?** The tax form for reporting business income and expenses is Form T2125 *Statement of Business or Professional Activities*. Check it out in your tax software. You'll note it is a form that contains adjusting entries for personal use of certain expenses; home office use, for example. See Chapter 14 for details.

- **Make your own CPP contributions.** You'll also be required to make your own remittances to the Canada Pension Plan (CPP) when you file your personal tax return, so save up. This is a maximum of $4,712.40 in 2013 – close to $5,000 a year if your net business income is $51,100 or more. This is calculated on Schedule 8.
- **Always document and separate personal-use components of any of your expenditures.** Treat your business like an individual: open a separate business bank and use business charge card accounts. Do not give CRA a reason to go through all your personal accounts.
- **Know when your business is considered to have started.** When did it go from being a sideline or hobby to a viable going concern? The key is… when was there a reasonable expectation of profit or earning income from the business? This is an important conversation to have with a tax professional, because that advisor can also help you understand whether your business should be incorporated and when the optimal time for this should be.
- **Establish your fiscal year end.** This is normally December 31 for most unincorporated small business organizations; however, speak to your tax advisor if you feel there is a bona fide business reason to choose a non-calendar year end.
- **Write a formal business start plan**, including a marketing and cash flow analysis plan, a formal budget and set up the ability to make comparative reports in the future. These documents will all go a long way to winning a tax audit, because you will be

able to show that your business is not a hobby. That's important, because the losses of a legitimate business can be used to offset other income of the year.

- **Keep a daily business journal** to document your networking, contacts with suppliers and others who will help you build and grow your business. This will again help justify a legitimate business start but also help you keep your auto distance travel logs as well. Remember, use Google maps to figure out the distance between your workplace (even if the base of the business is your home office) and your clients, suppliers, post-office, etc. that you visit for business purposes.

- **Classify deductible expenditures properly**, into operational and capital items, to facilitate proper applications and do some long-term tax planning. You will be able to write off the full costs of your operational expenses—those fully used up in running your business, like rent, supplies, wages, printing, freight, etc. However, assets—those items with a useful life of over a year, are subject to depreciation. On your tax return the method of depreciation used is a declining balance method and assets are categorized into classes with specific rates assigned to each. A deduction called *Capital Cost Allowance* (CCA) results. This deduction can be taken at your option. As a result, tax planning can take place to postpone the deduction to offset higher income in future years, or to speed up the application of a loss.

- **Know the value of your tax losses** and how to apply them to other income in the current year and in the carry-over periods. Most businesses can use their losses to offset all other income in the current tax year, other income of the previous three tax years, and other income of the next 20 tax years in the future. Clearly these losses are very valuable in the start-up years and should be utilized. This opportunity is also a reason not to incorporate right away, unless there are liability or other reasons, such as family income splitting with dividend sprinkling. Talk to your tax pro about this.

- **Meet the onus of proof**—annually. The ability to defend any "grey areas" which could be open to interpretation, is a position of power you do not want to give up to a tax auditor, who doesn't know your business or your business plans as well as you do, yet may challenge your business loss deductibility. You can show reasonable expectation of profit better than the auditor can—because you know the future: the potential income earning capacity of your business because you made an up-front investment in assets, business relationships and the making of the products or services you sell. Don't give up your edge by keeping poor records during the year.

- **Review your business organization structure often:** at least every six months in the start-up period. Is the proprietorship the best format, or should you be considering a partnership or corporation? Is there a better way to split income with family members or a better compensation structure for the owner-manager?

- **Remember that barter transactions will affect your income:** when your business trades goods or services for other goods or services, the fair market value of the goods or services you accept is income of your business. If the accepted items are used in your business their value may also be a business expense. Be sure to account for these transactions in your records.

- **Pay family members, according to the rules.** Income splitting is easier when you are self-employed and can reap some very good results in reducing a family's tax load. Consider the Case Study below.

Case Study | Planning to Reduce Taxes With Income Splitting

Steve currently makes $84,000 in his small unincorporated business in BC; he wants to pay his new wife Carin half this amount, as they work together in the business. How much will the family save on taxes if they split income?

Currently Steve pays $20,349 in income taxes (including $4,712 in CPP Contributions). If he pays Carin a salary of $40,000, his net business income will be reduced to $42,193 (The business will need to pay the employer portion of Carin's CPP contributions.

As a result, Steve's tax bill is reduced to $9,422 (including $3,830 in CPP contributions) and Carin's tax bill will be $5,232 (plus CPP contributions of $1,807). Together they pay $18,267 for income taxes and CPP contributions.

That's a savings of *$2,082* each year by splitting the income. As a bonus, Carin will now be eligible for a CPP retirement pension when she reaches age 60, and potentially (depending on eligibility), a CPP disability benefit.

This family should also be looking closely at how to maximize earned income for RRSP/PRPP purposes. This involved producing enough taxable income to reach contribution maximums. There are many benefits. The RRSP or PRPP contribution will reduce net income on the tax return, thereby increasing some tax credits. Future retirement income will be earned on a tax deferred basis. In addition, it's possible to tap RRSP funds for the Lifelong Learning Plan or Home Buyer's Plan. Couples who plan well can even use their tax refunds to fund their Tax-Free Savings Accounts (TFSAs)—another way to be sure all their eggs are not in one basket.

To legitimately write off the costs of hiring family members, certain rules must be followed:

- work must actually be performed by the family member;
- the amount paid must be reasonable for the work, time an effort put into the business by the family member and should be similar to the amount that would be paid a stranger in the same capacity; and
- the amounts must be actually paid and a normal paper trail, including payroll source deductions and T4 Slip issuance, is required.

Claim Expenses of the Business, Properly. Visit with a tax professional to properly set up the accounts for the income and expenses you'll be claiming in your small business. Your business expenditures, assuming you have a reasonable expectation of profit from a viable commercial activity, fall into six types:

1. Current
2. Capital
3. Prepaid
4. Restricted
5. Not allowable
6. Mixed use expenses

Current Expenses. These are used up in the course of earning income from the business. Examples are office supplies, wages, rent and other overhead costs. These costs are usually fully deductible against revenues.

Capital Expenses. These expenditures are for the acquisition of income-producing assets with a useful life of more than one year. This includes cars, buildings, equipment and machinery. These expenses are subject to capital cost allowance rates and classes which allow for a declining balance method of accounting for the cost of wear and tear.

Prepaid Costs. Most businesses must report income and expenses on the accrual method of accounting. In that case, the prepaid expense is prorated and deductible in the year the benefit is received. A good example is insurance, paid in advance for a 12-month period, which may span a fiscal year end. Only those on the cash method of accounting may claim the full costs in the year paid. This is generally only farmers, fishers and very small businesses.

Non-Allowable Expenses. Fines or penalties imposed by any level of government (including foreign governments) are not tax deductible. However, this does not apply to penalty interest imposed under the Excise Act, the Air Travellers Security Charge Act and the GST/HST portions of the *Excise Tax Act*. Also not allowable, the cost of golf club memberships. Be sure to discuss these and other expenses that fall into each category with your tax advisor.

Restricted Expenses. This includes the costs of meals and entertainment (50% deductible), and the costs of attending conventions (only 2 per year). Home workspace expenses are restricted to net income from the business.

The Requirement to Collect and Pay the GST/HST. As a small business owner in Canada you may be required to collect the Goods and Services Tax (GST), which is currently 5% at the federal level and/or the Harmonized Sales Tax (HST), if you make sales of "taxable" goods and services in your business, also known as "supplies" for the purposes of this tax.

The GST/HST is imposed on every taxable supply made in Canada. In addition, supplies which are made outside Canada but enjoyed in Canada will also be subject to tax when they are imported into Canada.

The recipient of the supply is the one who must pay the GST/HST. It is important to identify who the recipient of the supply is because it is generally only the recipient that can recover any GST/HST paid as an "input tax credit".

Although almost everyone pays GST/HST on taxable supplies, there are some exceptions. Certain organizations and groups including some governments and Indians may not have to pay this tax. In some cases, supplies are taxed at a rate of 0% (these are known as zero-rated).

Small suppliers, those with gross revenues under $30,000, need not collect the tax (but may elect to). Specifically, a small supplier is defined as a person whose worldwide taxable supplies are equal to or less than $30,000 in either a calendar quarter or over the last four consecutive calendar quarters. In applying this definition, you are required to add together taxable supplies made by all persons with whom you are associated.

There are many rules around your GST/HST compliance obligations. Be sure to cover these with your tax advisor carefully. Taking a bookkeeping or tax course for proprietorships is a good opportunity for anyone considering a small business venture. (check out knowledgebureau.com for some options).

 The Bottom Line | Owners of a small business can have both: tax efficient income today, and the potential to substantially enhance their net worth by building tax efficient equity for tomorrow. They keep the first dollars they earn and so can invest sooner, building wealth more immediately. Filing an audit-proof tax return is a must. Do speak to a professional advisor to set up on the right foot.

44

When to See a Pro

Taxation has a big effect on the building of personal and family wealth, and when you work hard to keep an eye on earning tax efficient income and saving with tax efficiency, too, you will be blessed with enough financial resources in retirement to check off all the "wants" on your bucket list.

But throughout the all-important retirement period, you must continue to think "tax." One important reasons is because your relationship with CRA has changed. You now may be making quarterly tax remittances on your own behalf for the first time.

In addition, the only way you'll get a raise in the future is if you keep an eagle eye on how to continue to accumulate, grow, and preserve your savings. The key reason for this is that tax erosion is a big risk factor, but one that you have more control over than others like inflation and market fluctuations. Tax efficient retirement income planning is important if you want to fund an adequate retirement—whatever that means for you and the length of time you are expected to live.

This is about layering in different types of income sources over as long a period of time as possible to stay within lower tax brackets. Enhanced by pension income splitting, this planning can save you thousands of dollars—*every year*. Working with a team of financial specialists—tax specialists, retirement planners, insurance advisors, legal advisor—can make a big difference for you and may well be worth the investment, especially if you go from employment to self-employment in retirement.

PART 6

Be Sure

You're almost done filing this year's tax returns. Before you hit the "send" button to NETFILE or close the envelope if you're paper filing, it's important that you take pause: have you claimed all the tax deductions and credits your family is entitled to? Do you have all the back-up documentation to justify both all the income you are required to report as well as the offsetting tax preferences? Did you take advantages of all the tax changes that may apply to you this year? On quick review, here are some of the key changes to double check:

1. **Form T1135 Foreign Income Verification:** File this if you have specified foreign assets and the total cost of all property exceeded $100,000 Canadian. CRA is looking for more details on this form starting in 2013. If you have received a T3 or T5 from a Canadian issuer for foreign property in your investment accounts, exclude these assets.

2. **No or Low-Income Credit Filers:** Canada Child Tax Benefits, GST/HST Credits and Working Income Tax Benefits have been increased. See Appendices that follow.

3. **Employees:** Employer contributions to many group accident and sickness plans becomes a taxable benefit in 2013. The Canada Employment Amount has increased to a credit of $1,117 and if you collected EI during the year, net income of $59,250 will require a repayment of regular benefits for repeat claimants. Those working overseas will receive a lower Overseas Employment Tax Credit as the credit is being phased out.

4. **Pensioners:** OAS benefits increased to $6,579 this year and the OAS clawback begins at a net income of $70,954. The Age Amount has increased to $6,854 and this will be clawed back when net income reaches $34,562. There are changes to the pension income splitting election form and first-time German social security pension recipients will receive a 34% exemption for 2013.

5. **Investors:** There are changes to RDSP rules. RRSP/RPPP maximums have increased to 18% of earned income to a maximum of $23,820.
6. **Small Business:** Pensionable Earnings for CPP have increased to $51,100; there are changes to restricted farm loss rules and new for 2014—the capital gains deduction will increase as will taxation of small business dividends.
7. **All Taxpayers:** Most of the personal tax credits you will qualify for have increased due to indexing (see the Appendices). Form T2201 *Disability Amount Certificate* has also been split into two separate forms: T2201A *Disability Tax Credit Application* and T2201B *Disability Tax Credit Certification by a Qualified Practitioner*. First-time donors are now eligible for an additional 25% credit on cash donations up to $1,000. Parents who adopted in 2013 will be able to claim expenses over a longer period than in prior years. In addition those who are disputing claims for charitable donation tax credits or other tax shelters will find that they have to pay at least 50% of the taxes in dispute even before the dispute is resolved.

Remember, it is always a good idea to print your tax returns for the recordkeeping system described in Chapter 1—your permanent, working copy and your audit defence files. Review these procedures, so that you can better manage subsequent communications from CRA. Finally, be sure, to understand the consequences of non-compliance, the subject of our last chapter.

45

Avoiding Penalties

Exercise Your Rights: It's About What You Keep

Filing a tax return is about what you keep. That's one of the important tax secrets of rich people: by investing their precious resources of time and money to their best tax advantage, they manage risk better, with family net worth that keeps growing no matter what the taxman or the economy throws at them.

Because you understand your tax-filing rights better, you can make better investment decisions. You'll put your savings into the right "buckets" to grow in, and this is extremely smart because you will need to be more tax astute to get ahead in the near future.

If you have been shocked to find a balance due rather than a refund, don't hesitate to file your return to avoid late filing penalties. This is an important first step in keeping more money, even if you can't pay your bill immediately. You may wish to have a pro look over your return (or prior returns) to see if they can find something you missed. But don't fail to file. *Gross negligence penalties* of 50% of taxes owing can be added to your bill. Interest will compound on that on a daily basis. It's very expensive.

Taxpayers who are found to participate in *tax evasion* will face more penalties by being charged with an offense. When a taxpayer is guilty of an offense, a criminal prosecution takes place. While in the case of gross negligence, the *burden of proof* is on the taxpayer; in tax evasion cases, the burden is on CRA to show that there was willful evasion and that there is no reasonable doubt of the crime.

Those convicted of tax evasion face a series of penalties, the most common of which is a fine of not less than 100% and not more than 200% of the tax sought to be evaded or credits sought to be gained. This penalty could also be accompanied by a prison term of not more than five years.

Know the difference between tax avoidance and tax evasion, especially if you are doing your own return by computer. Which is legal? Here's a true-to-life example to make the point about tax evasion, the activity that is a criminal offence:

Case Study | The Underground Economy

A group of pre-retirement tax seminar attendees were asked by their instructor to consider this scenario: an estimation for a basement renovation is in progress. The contractor says, "The fee is 'X' with a receipt, and 'Y' (substantially less) for cash…" Which quote would you take?

Many in the audience thought it was perfectly acceptable to take the Y option, turning a blind eye to their active participation within the underground economy. Few were outraged by the fact that the contractor, assuming he would not report the cash received, would be doing so at the expense of honest suppliers and taxpayers as a whole.

Consider other common scenarios: a babysitter refuses to take on care for a new baby because the working mother wants a receipt… "I give no receipts," she says, and in apparent justification, "It costs my husband too much on his taxes." Or perhaps your domestic cleaning help wants cash too?

Is this *tax evasion*? The answer in all cases is yes. Tax evasion is the act of making false or deceptive statements in a return, certificate, statement or even an answer filed or verbally given to the Canada Revenue Agency, with the intent to willfully evade the payment of your taxes. You'll also be caught if you willfully make deceptive entries or omissions in your books. A person who destroys, alters, mutilates or otherwise willfully disposes of the records or books of account to evade the payment of tax is also asking for prosecution.

Record Retention. You must keep records and books of account for *at least six years after the end of the taxation year to which those records relate.* However, CRA has the right to demand that records be kept longer.

What's a "record?" This includes anything that contains information, whether in writing or in any other form, including electronic forms. If books and records are inadequate the penalties can be steep:

- a fine of not less than $1,000 and not more than $25,000; or
- both a fine and imprisonment for up to 12 months.

You may request permission to destroy records before the six-year period is up. By filing a special form—T137 *Request for Destruction of Records*. But we don't recommend it: such a request invites the taxman to consider verifying those records prior to destruction.

Voluntary Compliance. Missed something after you filed your return? The good news for those who may have uncomfortable consciences, is something called "*voluntary compliance.*" If you initiate an adjustment of your tax returns to report the correct income and deductions or credits for the tax year, you'll avoid the gross negligence and tax evasion penalties. However do not file another tax return.

 The Bottom Line | Tax avoidance—arranging your affairs within the framework of the law to pay the least taxes legally possible—is your right and it's legal. It's only a criminal offence if you evade taxes, mess with the books, or stick your head in the sand and don't file at all.

Appendices

We have come to the end of another tax filing year and my 51st book! Thank you for taking the tax filing journey with all of us. We now present several resources to help you review the results on your tax return and do some planning throughout the year with your advisors.

Appendix 1 Personal Tax Filing Milestones: Check out this calendar of tax events and record them in your personal devices. These dates require your attention. Also, mark in the dates you have received your Notice of Assessment or Reassessment from CRA. These dates preserve important appeal rights for you.

Appendix 2 Carry Forward Information: This is your guide to the figures from this year's tax return that should be carried forward, or in some cases carried back to adjust prior filed returns. These amounts are lucrative as they can help you reach back and recover taxes paid in the past, or reach forward to reduce taxes payable in the future.

Appendix 3 Summary of Tax Credits and Clawbacks: These important figures will help you file better tax returns in the current year and in prior years when adjustments may be necessary.

Knowledge Bureau Report: At Knowledge Bureau we publish a weekly e-newsletter that keeps taxpayers and their advisors abreast of changes due to federal or provincial budgets, economic and policy issues and jurisprudence—what is happening in the courts. It's free and our way of helping you stay on top of it all. Be sure to subscribe at www.knowledgebureau.com.

Knowledge Bureau Certificate Courses: We invite you to participate in free trials of our certificate courses; they are open to laypeople as well as professionals and cover diverse topics from personal and corporate tax preparation to cross border tax, use of trusts in tax and estate planning, tax efficient retirement income planning, death of a taxpayer, and business succession planning. For more information on those courses and the financial books we publish visit knowledgebureau.com

We hope to hear from you. In the meantime, have a wonderful year!

Yours in tax savings,
Evelyn Jacks

Appendix 1. Personal Tax Filing Milestones 2014

January
- **Jan. 2:** Reduce your tax withholdings at source: file your TD1 form to claim tax credits and a T1213 form.
  - Make your TFSA contribution.
- **Jan. 30:** Interest payment on inter-spousal loans.

February
- **End of Month:** You'll receive T4, T5 slips
- Federal Budget (dates vary)

March
- **March 3:** RRSP filing deadline (60 days after year end)
- **March 15** Quarterly Instalment due
- **March 31:** T3 slips due
  - File "Advantage" Tax Returns for TFSA, RRSP due 90 days after year-end.
  - File Form T1-OVP to pay RRSP Excess Contributions Penalty of 1% per month due 90 days after year-end.

April
- **April 15:** U.S. Tax filing date
- **April 30:** Individual tax filing deadline
  - Late elections for 2010 pension income splitting expires

May
- Update will, powers of attorney and health care directives

June
- **June 15:** Quarterly instalment due
  - Tax deadline for self-employed individuals and their spouses
- Closer Connection Exception Statement for Aliens (IRS Form 8840)
- Election to make CPP contributions for 2012. File Form CPT20
- **June 30:** File RC293E TFSA *Return for Excess, Prohibited, Non-qualified or Non-resident Contributions*

July
- Portfolio and cash flow review
- Review RRSP meltdown strategies
- Instalment payment review: Did you have to pay more than $3,000 when you filed your T1 return? If so, you may be required to make quarterly tax instalments starting September 15!
- Form RC312 *Reportable Transaction Information Return* due

August
- Back-to-school expense planning review
- File for WITB prepayment

September
- **September 15:** Quarterly Instalment due
- Book medical appointments, dental appointments, glasses, etc. to claim expenses before December 31.
- Review asset purchase strategies—cars, computers, buildings, equipment, etc. to acquire before year-end to increase Capital Cost Allowance claims.
- Review donations strategies and give before December 31.

October
- **Thanksgiving:** Review family income splitting, cottage valuation, plan inter-spousal loans and asset transfers
- **October 15:** IRS Form 4868 to apply for an extension of filing time

November
- CSB, CPB, investment portfolio review
- Plan charitable giving, medical appointments

December
- **December 15:** quarterly instalment due
  - Tax Loss selling
- **December 31:** Make RESP, RDSP contributions; transfer RRSPs to RRIF if you turned 71; make 2014 TFSA contribution
  - Adjust T1 returns for errors or omissions to prior filed returns (2004 to 2013)
  - Annual instalment for farmers and fishers

Appendix 2. Carry Forward Information

You can adjust returns	Significance
The preceding ten years	• To correct errors and omissions for most federal provisions. • To correct errors and omissions for GST/HST Rebates (Line 457).
The preceding three years	• To apply capital losses to capital gains in those years. • To apply non-capital losses to income of prior years. • To adjust most provincial tax credits.
Over a 24-month period	• Medical expenses can be claimed over this period ending on and including the date of death.
The current and immediately preceding year	• To apply previous net capital losses carried forward against other income in the year of death, after their application to capital gains in current and prior three prior years. • To claim charitable donations in year of death.
The preceding 11 months	• To recover unpaid Child Tax Benefits and GST Credits. Note: late applications may be allowed with sufficient documentation.
The following year	• To use unclaimed medical expenses of the previous year to make a claim for the best 12-month period ending in the tax year.
The next three years	• To make or amend a joint election to split pension income. • To recover overpaid EI premiums in cases where employee did not qualify (e.g. significant or majority owner of a corporation).
The next five years	• To use any charitable donation tax receipts. • To deduct student loan interest.
The next seven years	• To minimum tax carry forwards. • To claim legal fees in excess of RRSP contributions in respect of job termination payments.
The next 10 years	• To apply allowable Business Investment Losses (BIL) against other income. Thereafter, unabsorbed loss becomes a capital loss.
The next 20 years	• To apply unused non-capital losses to other income (previously: seven years for non-capital losses incurred before 2004, 10 years for losses incurred in 2004 and 2005).
Indefinite time	• To use RRSP deduction when there is RRSP room (individual or if no longer age-eligible, to spousal RRSP if spouse is under age 71). • To use capital losses against capital gains up to and including year of death. • To use unclaimed RRSP deductions, up to & including year of death. • To use tuition, education and textbook amounts.

Appendix 3. Refundable and Non-Refundable Tax Credits Summary

The Benefit Year. The GST Credit and Child Tax Benefit are based on a July to June benefit year. Income levels quoted are for net income from the previous taxation year. Rates for the specified time period are indexed based on CPI for prior December.

Split Child Benefits. Note that after *June 2011*, each parent who lives with the child can receive 50% of any GST Credit and Child Tax Benefits. Each parent will want to invest these benefits in the name of the child to build up a great education fund, but also to avoid tax on resulting investment earnings.

GST/HST Credit

	July 2013 to June 2014	July 2012 to June 2013
Adult maximum	$265	$260
Child maximum	$139	$137
Single supplement	$139	$137
Phase-in threshold for the single supplement	$8,608	$8,439
Family net income at which credit begins to phase out	$34,561	$33,884

Canada Child Tax Benefit

	July 2013 to June 2014	July 2012 to June 2013
Base benefit	$1,433	$1,405
Additional benefit for third child	$100	$98
Family net income at which base benefit begins to phase out	$43,561	$42,707
NCB: First child	$2,221	$2,177
NCB: Second child	$1,964	$1,926
NCB: Third child	$1,869	$1,832
Family income at which NCB begins to phase out	$25,356	$24,863
Family net income at which NCB supplement phase-out ends	$43,561	$42,707
CDB Maximum benefit	$2,626	$2,575
Family net income at which CDB begins to phase out	$43,561	$42,707

Working Income Tax Benefit

2013 Rates	Most Provinces		British Columbia		Alberta		Nunavut	
Working Income Tax Benefit	Single Taxpayer	Family (or Single Parent)	Single	Family	Single	Family	Single	Family
Minimum earned income	$3,000	$3,000	$4,750	$4,750	$2,760	$2,760	$6,000	$6,000
Credit rate	25%	25%	21%	21%	20%	20%	5%	10%
Maximum credit	$989	$1,797	$1,230	$1,952	$1,080	$1,620	$620	$1,241
Clawback of income begins at	$11,231	$15,509	$12,301	$16,579	$11,766	$16,044	$21,392	$27,275
Clawback rate	15%	15%	17%	17%	15%	15%	4%	8%
Income for maximum credit	$6,956	$10,188	$10,607	$14,045	$8,160	$10,860	$18,400	$18,410
Credit fully clawed back	$17,824	$27,489	$19,536	$28,061	$18,966	$26,844	$36,892	$42,788

Clawback Zones for 2013

The following table shows clawback zones for personal amounts for 2013.

Credit	2013 Reduction Begins	2013 Credit Eliminated
Old Age Security	$70,954	$114,815
Employment Insurance	$59,250	Varies with EI amount
Age Amount	$34,562	$80,255
Spouse or Common-Law Partner Amount (not infirm)	$0	$11,038
Spouse or Common-Law Partner Amount (infirm)	$0	$13,078
Amount for Eligible Dependants (not infirm)	$0	$11,038
Amount for Eligible Dependants (infirm)	$0	$13,078
Amount for Infirm Dependants	$6,548	$13,078
Caregiver Amount (not infirm)	$15,334	$19,824
Caregiver Amount (infirm)	$15,334	$21,864

Summary of Personal Amounts for 2011 – 2013

Personal Amounts		2011	2012	2013
Basic Personal Amount	Maximum Claim*	$10,527	$10,822	$11,038
Age Amount	Maximum Claim*	$6,537	$6,720	$6,854
	Reduced by net income over*	$32,961	$33,884	$34,562
Spouse or Common-Law Partner Amount	Not infirm*	$10,527	$10,822	$11,038
	Infirm*	$10,527	$12.822	$13,078
Eligible Child under 18	Not infirm*	$2,131	$2,191	$2,234
	Infirm	$2,131	$4,191	$4,274
Amount for Eligible Dependants	Not infirm*	$10,527	$10,822	$11,038
	Infirm*	$10,527	$12,822	$13,078
Amount for Infirm Dependants	Maximum Claim*	$4,282	$6,402	$6,530
	Reduced by net income over*	$6,076	$6,420	$6,548
Pension Income Amt.	Maximum Claim	$2,000	$2,000	$2,000
Adoption Expenses	Maximum Claim	$11,128	$11,440	$11,669
Caregiver Amount	Not infirm	$4,282	$4,402	$4,490
	Infirm	$4,282	$6,402	$6,530
	Reduced by net income over	$14,624	$15,033	$15,334
Disability Amount	Basic Amount	$7,341	$7,546	$7,697
	Supplementary Amount*	$4,282	$4,402	$4,490
	Base Child Care Amount*	$2,508	$2,578	$2,630
Tuition and Education Amounts +Textbook Tax Credit	Minimum Tuition	$100	$100	$100
	Full-time Education Amt. (per month)	$400 +$65	$400 +$65	$400 +$65
	Part-time Education Amt. (per month)	$120 +$20	$120 +$20	$120 +$20
Medical Expenses	3% limitation*	$2,052	$2,109	$2,151
Refundable Medical Expense Credit	Maximum*	$1,089	$1,119	$1,141
	Base Family Income*	$24,108	$24,783	$25,279
	Minimum earned income*	$3,179	$3,268	$3,333
Donation Credit	Low-rate ceiling	$200	$200	$200
First-Time Donations	Rate	0	0	25%
	Maximum Donation	0	0	$1,000
Canada Employment Amount	Maximum*	$1,065	$1,095	$1,117
Children's Fitness Amount	Maximum	$500	$500	$500
Home Buyers' Amount	Maximum	$5,000	$5,000	$5,000
Children's Arts Amount	Maximum	$500	$500	$500

*Indexed.

Appendix 4. Additional Resources

Canadians & The IRS
What YOU Need to Know About Uncle Sam
By Angela Preteau

Did you know that the number of days you spend in the U.S. each year can deem you to be a U.S. resident for tax purposes? This would mean that you would be subject to all the U.S. tax laws and reporting regimes. If you are not careful, you could technically be in the United States as an "illegal alien." You could even be a United States citizen and not realize it, and that has tax consequences.

More and more Canadians are traveling to the United States on vacation, investing in U.S. securities, purchasing U.S. real estate, and even marrying U.S. citizens, and the majority of them are doing so without realizing there can be some potential tax consequences to their actions. Don't get caught—get the tax facts.

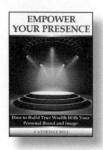

Empower Your Presence
How to Build True Wealth With Your Personal Brand and Image
By Catherine Bell

"Presence" has always held a certain mystique that is empowering and attractive—it can improve relationships, transform situations, and influence success.

Whether starting out in your career, asking for venture capital, meeting potential clients, or advancing into a new social environment—including retirement—you will want to stride forward with confidence and ease. EMPOWER YOUR PRESENCE is about developing that distinctive quality that can create opportunities and propel you to new heights.

This is a must-read book for ALL generations—Gen Y (18 to 33), Gen X (34-48) and Boomers (49+) —who want to invest in their best attributes, passions, and skills and market their unique promise of value as an important part of their ongoing personal success.

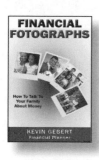

Financial Fotographs
How to Talk to Your Family About Money
By Kevin Gebert

"I wish my parents had talked to me about money." If this resonates with you, you are not alone. Millions of families have a difficult time embracing financial conversations so crucial to the ongoing health of family income and capital. This is especially true in times of transition: changes in health, career or retirement.

If you are raising a young family and challenged with how to teach principles for healthy money management, this book's for you! But if you are in your mid-thirties and wondering how to broach the subject of your role in the financial future of your ailing parents, you'll love this read, too.

Financial Books to Help You Grow and Preserve Your Wealth
At leading bookstores or order online at www.knowledgebureau.com

Index